Every person, from your past, lives as a shadow in your mind.
Good or bad, they all helped you write the story of your life,
and shaped the person you are today.

- Dee Zantamata

Roll back the curtain of memory now and then,

Show me where you brought me from

and where I could have been,

Just remember, I'm a human and humans forget

so remind me, remind me dear Lord.

Unknown

Insanity On The Road To Glory

Insanity On The Road To Glory

Estie Culler Bennington

Published by Alabaster Book Publishing
North Carolina

Copyright 2012 by
Estie Culler Bennington

Published by Alabaster Book Publishing
P.O. Box 401
Kernersville, North Carolina 27285
www.PublisherAlabaster.biz

Book design by
David Shaffer

Cover Design by
Dallas Midgette
www:dmcreativeworks.com
and Sarah Bennington Hogan

First Edition

ISBN 13: 978-0-9840004-1-8

Library of Congress Control Number
2012904218

ACKNOWLEDGMENTS

Richard R. Bennington, my husband, for all his kindness and patience. Every word I wrote in scratchy cursive handwriting, he typed and re-typed it into our computer. He still loves me, in spite of the number of drafts he typed over the years, and by doing so, he learned more about me than he ever wanted to know. Thank you, Richard, for encouraging me, and demanding my best. I love you.

Troy, Paul, and Ralph, my older brothers, who shared with me bits of humor in some sad situations during our young lives. **Martha and James**, my younger brother and sister, who lived this story with me. I love each of you and I am thankful we are family.

Sarah Bennington Hogan, our daughter, for proofreading the manuscript and for her talents and suggestions on the design work. Without her the book (and my life) would be black and white. She adds the color. I love you.

Halli Hogan, our nine-year-old granddaughter, photographer for my picture in the back of the book. It is amazing what she can do with technology and with my heart strings. I love you.

Alice Sink, a friend, author of sixteen books and retired High Point University English Professor, for seeing the value in my manuscript and insisting that I complete this project. Compliments coming from her truly inspired me.

My friends from the Guilford County Clerk of Superior Court's office: **Nancy Walker**, my Editor, a dedicated, good natured friend with a brilliant mind, whose work was invaluable in correcting and improving the manuscript; **Janet Godwin**, who let us borrow her lake house for weekends to critique the manuscript, and offered her insightful attention to detail (such as describing an outdoor john); **Sarah Luther**, a glamorous lady who is herself a born writer; **Teresa Murphy,** who was diligent in her observations and comments and brought homemade oatmeal cookies; **Lynn Stevens**, who was moved to tears when she read portions of the manuscript out loud; and **Gail Vernon**, who is kind hearted and an excellent writer, kept us laughing. All of them had more faith in me than I had in myself. I am thankful you are my friends, and love each of you.

Sara B. Griggs, PhD., my friend, life coach and spiritual mentor, who also read my manuscript. Thank you for loving me unconditionally and without criticism.

Robyn K. Zanard, M.D., and Rev. Billy Rintz, who read the book in process and gave me their blessings.

Linda Albright, a cousin who gave me copies of some of my family pictures.

Two of my Mills Home Friends, **Sandy Penley** and **Harry Walls**, who read the manuscript and offered their input; to **Harry** for inspiring the title, Insanity on the Road to Glory. I will forever be grateful for their friendship and OL.

Dixie and Dave of Alabaster Publishing Co., for guiding me through the book publishing process and for being gentle and overlooking my ignorance.

Dedications

To the honor and the glory of God, my Creator, Provider, and Protector, and in loving memory of my Grandma, Estie Culler, for whom I was named. We were two peas in a pod.

To my happy memories of Ralph Henry Culler, an older brother who had an opportunity to read a draft of this book before his death and encouraged me to finish the project. He taught me to never be ashamed of the scars that life has left on us because healed scars mean the hurt is over, the wound is closed, and we endured the pain.

Estie Culler Bennington and her older brother,Ralph Culler, visiting "The Lord's Mission", Culler Road near Pilot Mountain, NC, 1990

*He does not provide for his relatives,
and especially for his immediate family, he has denied
the faith and is worse than the unbeliever.*
I Timothy 5:8 NIV

Prologue
Mama's In Pain

Shirley did not know her good-looking husband, Abraham, was a religious nut, lazy and crazy. Both eighteen years old and high school drop outs, they were married by a Justice of the Peace, across the state line in Dillon, South Carolina.

They made a good looking couple, Abe, short for a guy and Shirley, right tall for a girl. They stood about the same height with Shirley having the edge by a couple of inches.

Everything about their appearances was opposite. He had a head full of light blond curls and his eyes were blue. Shirley had long, dark brown hair which was straight-as-a-stick and her dark brown eyes were enormous. The attraction was magnetic.

Abraham was unemployed and Shirley was soon pregnant. They made their home in the relatively new Clara Cox Housing Projects, apartments for low income families, on Russell Street in High Point, North Carolina.

High Point is in the center of the state, half-way between the Blue Ridge Mountains and the Atlantic Ocean beaches. The city was named High Point because it was located on the highest point of the railroad tracks, stretching from Charlotte to Goldsboro. Shirley wanted to live in this industrial town because of the job opportunities. High Point has taken pride in its reputation of being an international leader in the manufacturing and marketing of home and office furnishings and has been recognized as the "Furniture Capital of the World." She was confident they would find good paying jobs at Marsh Cabinets, Tomlinson Furniture, Amos Hosiery, Slane Hosiery, or one of the other mills or plants located within a stones throw of the housing projects. Abe settled on High Point because of the numerous and well-established Protestant churches. Green Street Baptist, First Methodist, Calvary Methodist and First Baptist lined the downtown streets and were within walking distance of the housing projects.

Abraham Culler never looked for a job. He didn't even pretend to. He spent all his time reading and memorizing his Bible, while sitting in their only upholstered chair. The fabric on the old chair was so worn and dirty, it was impossible to determine its original color. When Abe did leave the apartment, it was not unusual to find him preaching on the corner of High Street and Main Street across from the train depot.

In the 40's and 50's, it was not uncommon for young men, including Billy Graham and Oral Roberts, to have "the holy calling from God to spread the word of Jesus Christ." Shirley desperately needed Abe to get a job, to work and help take care of his family, but she certainly could not and would not dare argue or even question Abe's "holy calling." After all, it was "from God," therefore, Abe had no choice in the matter. He could not work because "God's Holy Calling" required him to read and study his Holy Bible and preach the gospel of Jesus Christ. Shirley was disappointed, but she kept her feelings to herself.

**My Daddy -The Loco Street
Preacher**

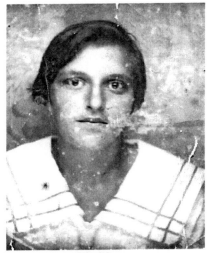

My Mama

Abe's behavior was often eccentric and peculiar – plumb odd. He did bizarre and erratic things. In fact, when it came down to it, he not only acted strange, he was strange. Yep, Abraham Culler was unpredictable and weird. No one understood Abe. He was what people think of as "way out in left field," and "off base" in his thinking.

Abe functioned with limited reasoning ability and lacked good common sense. One thing was for sure, Abe's sanity was questionable. If Abe was examined and evaluated by medical professionals, he would, in all probability be labeled with any number of mental disorders. Everyone who knew him, (though none would say so – not out loud) was all in agreement, with one hundred percent degree of certainty, that Abraham Culler was a "Certifiable Religious Nut."

In every attribute, character trait, and emotion, Abe was extreme. He was extreme at both ends of the spectrum. He was soft spoken at times, and at other times he could shout to the high heavens. He was as calm as a cucumber and he was very nervous, shaking like a leaf on a quaking aspen tree. His actions could show good judgment like wearing a warm coat on a cold day or poor judgment like wearing the same warm coat on a simmering

August day. His behavior and actions could be normal, and then he would act like a complete idiot. Constantly at war with his own demons, he often strutted around, pacing back and forth with his fists balled up and close to his head and mouth (like the boxer warming up in the ring. he had been before he met Shirley and before he received his "Holy Calling from God"). He threw punches into the air, taking quick, snappy shots at his opponents, those demons only he could see.

As the years passed, Shirley stayed pregnant and Abe stayed in the old chair, reading his Holy Bible, writing notes in the margins and underlining verses with a red pencil. He remained unemployed. Three sons were born within four years of their elopement to South Carolina. Abe, a God-fearing, hard-shell Baptist, knew God was abundantly pouring out His blessings on their holy matrimony. A man of tremendous faith, knowing he and God could do all things; Abraham single-handedly delivered each of his sons. And within moments of their first cries, he baptized them in the name of the Father, the Son, and the Holy Ghost, by complete immersion in a galvanized dishpan of dirty, bloody water.

To further show his love for God and his desire for his family to be set apart for service to God, he named his sons Matthew Shadrach, Mark Meshach, and Luke Obednego. The names of the authors of the first three books of the New Testament are Matthew, Mark, and Luke and they were followers and disciples of Jesus Christ. The boys' middle names, Shadrach, Meshach, and Obednego, were the names of three men in the Old Testament, who were thrown into a fiery furnace. An angel was with them, and miraculously they were not burned and their hair wasn't even singed. Shirley thought it was a wonderful story of God's protection, but that didn't necessarily mean they were good names for her sons. She wondered how in the world her boys would ever learn to spell their middle names, when she had difficulty pronouncing them. The only comment Shirley ever uttered about Abe's choice of names was, "Well, thank God for the New Testament."

After each delivery and baptism, Abe always placed his newborn son in Shirley's damp and weak arms. He examined with pride (counting all ten fingers and toes) the gift from God, his beautiful new baby boy. He sang to the top of his lungs,

Praise God from whom all blessings flow,
praise Him all creatures here below,
praise Him above ye Heavenly Host,

7

praise Father, Son and Holy Ghost.
Well, a hollering and jumping preacher may have been his "holy calling." Singing was not.

After the birth of Luke, to Abe's shame and disappointment, Shirley miscarried. Abe flung a flinging fit, which included throwing every plate drying in the red plastic dish drainer on the kitchen counter. Each plate flew across the kitchen and crashed on the hard floor or shattered against the wall. Shirley was grateful she was out of the direct line of fire. Shirley accepted and quietly suffered through Abe's angry tirades.

Shirley's second miscarriage pushed Abe over the deep-end. He was mortified, wounded deeply, and positive God was withholding His blessings -- more healthy children. In all certainty, Abe knew God was punishing Shirley for her backsliding, sinful life style.

Out of necessity, Shirley became a sock folder at Amos Hosiery Mill. The mill, which operated three shifts, was directly across Russell Street in front of Clara Cox Housing Projects. She happily accepted the job to have money to feed her growing boys; and she was grateful to be hired to work first shift, so she could spend time with them after school.

Abe ranted and raved, pushed and shoved, whined and complained about his wife working. He would pull his favorite trump card, and do what he did best, which was to quote Scripture verses, one after another, hardly taking a breath, shoving and stabbing his finger in her face and shouting: "Wives must submit themselves to their husbands," "the husband is the head of the household," and "wives obey your husband, for this is the will of the Lord."

Anytime Shirley was out of Abe's sight (which was only when she was working at the hosiery mill), his irrational mind and illogical thinking would conjure up visions of her in sinful sexual scenarios. In these escapades, real and happening right in front of his closed eyes, Shirley was not a mere participant. She was a willing uninhibited instigator. Enthusiastically, Shirley pursued an intensely active lead, like a "Hoochie-Koochie" girl, and without any shame or restraint. Because of his own perverted thinking and imagination, the imagined sight and sounds of Shirley's pleasure drove Abe insane with jealousy. He kept Shirley on a short leash, pulled tight and choking her. He controlled her every move. In his mind he believed she was "whoring around with every Tom, Dick, and Harry in town."

Abraham pounded at Shirley's head. Verbally and physically, he would hammer away. Verbally, he repeatedly accused her falsely, and called her every degrading name he could think of. "You're nothing but a slut. You low down hussy. You terrible tramp! You wicked whore! What will it take for me to drive it through that stupid skull of yours? You sinner! Repent! Repent, and sin no more. Your soul is doomed to everlasting damnation. You will burn in a lake of hell fire. God has cut off His blessings! He will not give any more children to our holy matrimony, while you are making a fool of me; doing who knows what, with who knows who! You are a disgrace to God, a disgrace to me, and a disgrace to our family. Jezebel!" Abe shouted. "You will be thrown down, trampled upon and stomped on! Dogs will eat you alive. Jezebel, you are a cursed woman! Jezebel! Jezebel!"

Abe's sharp and pointed tongue jabbed and pierced deep holes in Shirley's soft and tender heart. The razor edges of his tongue sliced away at her soul, the very core of her being. Abe's tongue lashings whipped her bruised emotions, ripped her fragile self-confidence into thin shreds, and gouged out what little self-respect Shirley possessed.

When Shirley thought his shouting had subsided, his powerful voice roared long and loud once again; it was more like the sound of a wild animal, a ferocious bull, not at all human.

"You are a fornicating slut. Bow down on your knees and repent. Beg God to forgive your sin-sick soul. Drop to your knees now!" he bellowed. Shirley only knew how to be Shirley. She had always thought more highly of others than herself. She was submissive and obedient to her husband. She possessed a sweet humble spirit, and she was gentle and kind. Shirley had learned a few lessons the hard way. She knew it was not wise to respond to Abe's verbal attacks, which assaulted her decency, and her integrity. She ignored his abusive, degrading name calling, and his bold-face lies. Regardless of Abe's opinion to the contrary, Shirley was nobody's dummy. Rather than stand up against Abe and his physical strength, she willingly obeyed and quietly knelt. To Shirley her choices were limited; she would rather kneel on her own accord and initiative than be knocked to the floor by Abe – the wild bull.

"Repent! Be washed clean in the blood of Jesus. The precious blood of the Lamb can cleanse the filthy stains from your evil heart. You must repent and turn away from your sins," Abe ordered. He paced back and forth, aroused by his anger and his righteous indignation. (The wild bull, with fluent strong movements becomes stiff, jerky, and spastic – still a bulky bull; yet, moving like a cocky bantam rooster.)

With her knees on the hard floor beside their unmade bed, Shirley bent at the waist and sank her sad face in the sheets on the old mattress; the very same mattress where their three sons had been conceived, the very same mattress where her boys were born. At conception, and/or at birth, either way, the lives of her precious babies began, on this mattress. Now Shirley's mind, not for the first time, wondered if there was a God above or if there was a God anywhere. If so, how could God allow these beatings? And, if these beatings were necessary, why on earth, of all the places on earth did it have to happen in this almost sacred spot, this mattress, the home of love and hate, the home of beauty and now ugliness, and the home of much goodness, and now a home full of evil?

Shirley's tears of sadness, which Abe misinterpreted as tears of guilt and shame, fell on this very same mattress. Her head was bowed and her heart was crushed in agony because of her failure to please Abe with more healthy children. Her tears soaked the sagging mattress.

"Repent sinner, repent," Abe shouted. He lifted both of his arms high, and each hand was balled tight into a strong fist, his sledge hammers, prepared to pound.

And he pounded her with all his might. To better position himself, he straddled her with one foot on each side of her bent legs, his knees rammed into her lower back. He alternated his fists and pounded her head over and over, again and again. As each fist hammered her head, he shouted at her: "Sinner! Slut!" He pounded, right fist, then left fist. "Whore!" His fists hammered her head. "You Jezebel. You terrible tramp!" Abe swung each of his fists and Shirley sank her head deeper into the mattress. His right fist, then his left fist, clobbered her head. "You horrible low down hussy!" Abe pounded and pounded. The swift and strong movements of Abe's arms rising up and then swinging down repeatedly were in rhythm with his shouts of obscene names. "Bitch!" Abe's fists hit her head with all the strength he could muster.

His mind exhausted, the name calling stopped. His arms, two fisted hammers, continued to beat in rhythm with the cadence in his mind. Right fist, then left fist, each blow hammered her head harder and grew in strength and force.

Over the years, no matter how angry and violent Abe became, Shirley continued to work. She had no choice. Even with all of

Estie's Mama, Daddy and Three older Brothers

The Loco Street Preacher's Bible

his righteous condescending whoop-de-la, Abe never offered to work and let her stay home. He was too lazy, and he was too crazy.

God's so-called punishment on Shirley lifted slightly on December 24, 1946.

Blond headed, close in age, eight year old Matt Culler and his younger brothers, Mark, age six and Luke, age five, were also close in size, not a half inch difference in their heights. They shared the same hand-me-down clothes and shoes from the Salvation Army. They were also close friends, good buddies. They fought each other like brothers do, but if anyone else picked on one of the Culler boys; they were "crusin' for a brusin'" because they would have to take on all three brothers. They were equally smart and well behaved. They each feared their Daddy, with good cause.

Under the white enamel kitchen table, the brothers were sitting on the floor, with their legs criss-crossed, Indian-style. Intentionally, they had been trying not to hear their Mama's screams and cries for hours on end. The door to the bedroom was opened a crack and they could hear their Mama crying. "Please, Abe, get a doctor. This time it hurts so much worse. My God! Oh, Oh, Oh, God! Please!" she begged.

"You don't need a doctor. Trust Jesus. Jesus Christ is THE Great Physician," their Daddy answered.

"Well, then go get Jesus, how about it?" she snapped. Her anger and frustration at Abe had reached an all time high, as did her level of pain. "Oh! Oh! Please get help. Get a doctor! Help me! Oh God, help me!"

"Come unto Me, all you who labor and are heavy laden, and I will give you rest," he quoted the Bible verse from memory.

Wordless groans and wailing moans, begging and pleading and the shrill ear-splitting screams were enough to scare Matt, Mark, and Luke half to death and then some. It was obvious their Mama had not received the relief or help she so desperately cried for. The boys' tears silently rolled from their large brown, puppy dog eyes and streaked down their dirty faces, as they bit their even dirtier fingernails.

"Abe! Damn it! For God's sake, will you, for once, shut up and get a doctor? Get somebody. Get help," their Mama insisted.

"My help cometh from the Lord. He is THE Great Physician!" Abe exclaimed loudly.

"Abraham Culler! Now, listen to me! It doesn't have to be THE Great Physician. Jesus must be too busy right now. We've called on

Him for hours! Oh God! Oh God! It's killing me! I can't take it any more! Please! Please, somebody help!" shrieked their Mama. Her face was covered with red splotches; her stringy hair was dripping with sweat.

"I can do all things through Christ, who strengthens me," Abe shouted and shook his old brown Bible in her face. "Shirley, it's all written in God's Holy Word. He will give you strength. Why don't you trust His promises?" Abe preached at her, as if she had nothing in the world better to do than to give her undivided attention to him. Never mind the fact their baby was entering the world at that very second.

"Mama, Mama," Luke whimpered. "God, please don't let anything happen to Mama," he cried.

"Mama's going to be fine," Matt whispered and gave Luke a quick reassuring hug. In their hearts, they believed in God and they believed God would help their Mama. "Mark, keep Luke here and keep his mouth shut," Matt said. Matt crawled out from under the table.

Mark grabbed Matt's leg and clamped down on it, a snapping turtle hanging on for dear life. "Don't leave me here! Where are you going?" he whispered.

"Mama is in pain. Daddy must be trying to kill her. I'm gonna' look and see what's going on in there. Now, turn loose of my leg." Matt tried to sound brave but his voice squeaked.

"Okay, hurry back. Watch out and don't let Daddy see you." Mark slowly relaxed his iron clad grip and released Matt's leg.

Matt quietly crawled on his hands and knees, staying low to the floor. When he reached the bedroom door, he peeped around the edge of the door frame. He saw his Daddy stooped on his knees beside his Mama's bed. Matt's mouth dropped open in surprise. Actually, more than surprise, he was flabbergasted. Spellbound. He did not believe what he saw with his own eyes; a bloody little baby was squirming on the floor. He crammed his balled up fist into his wide open mouth to silence the screams that were exploding within him. He did not budge. He watched, not blinking an eye, mesmerized at the sight of his Daddy lifting the slippery, mucus covered baby off the floor. His Daddy stood and held the little bitty baby (who looked more like a soaked rat – pink and slippery – than a newborn baby) up toward the ceiling. "I baptize you in the name of the Father, the Son, and the Holy Ghost," he said in a loud preachy voice.

Regaining his senses, Matt jumped to his feet, accidentally bumped the bedroom door and it slammed against the wall. The banging noise startled his Daddy, who glared angrily at him with mean blue eyes. Matt was pale and he kept one hand mashed in his mouth. His Daddy laid the newly baptized baby on Mama's breast.

Matt rushed back and slid under the table with his brothers. Thankfully, their Mama's tormenting screams and cries had ceased. They lay perfectly still on the floor for a long time. Finally, "Is Mama dead?" Mark asked, and then he held his breath, afraid to hear the answer.

"No, of course not," Matt said, trying to reassure himself as much as his little brothers. "Mama will be alright, she just had her baby," Matt stated with authority. "So, let's pray for her." Matt and his younger brothers huddled close to each other, folded their hands, and closed their eyes. "Dear God, please help Mama. Don't let her hurt anymore and please don't let her die. Keep us warm and the new baby, too! In Jesus name, Amen," Matt prayed.

Each of the boys, without speaking another word, and keeping their own thoughts private, soon fell asleep under the kitchen table, on the cold concrete floor. During the night,

Matt woke up and tiptoed around in the cold dark apartment in search of quilts or blankets. He found an old, green, wool army blanket and covered his brothers and himself. Tomorrow is Christmas day, he thought and went back to sleep.

"Wake up! Wake up! It's Christmas Day! Come here! Come here and see what the good Lord has given us!" Abraham loudly yelled. The boys crawled out from underneath the safe haven of the table, stood and stretched their stiff bodies. Their sleep had been uneasy. They stumbled into the bedroom, rubbing the sleep out of the corners of their eyes. Each grinned sheepishly at their Mama. She was awake, but still lying in bed. A baby with dark brown hair was nestled in the crook of her arm. "Merry Christmas," she mumbled in a hoarse voice so soft and weak, they could barely hear her. "Come meet your baby sister. Come close and get an eyeful," she said.

Their Daddy was seated on the side of the bed. The boys shuffled shyly toward their mother, but stopped quickly because their Daddy stood abruptly. "It's Christmas, and like that first Christmas so long ago, when Jesus was born, we too have been visited by angels, who left us your sister, as a gift from

God. Her name is Pearl Rose. Her first name is Pearl, because she is a precious gem in the sight of God. Her middle name, Rose, is a sweet, perfumed flower, red, beautiful and delicate. Never forget this baby, Pearl Rose, is a Christmas gift from God," he expounded.

Shirley motioned and smiled to encourage her sons to come closer. "Take a good look at your darling baby sister, and while you're at it, give me a kiss. How about it? Merry Christmas. I love you all so much," she whispered. The boys, one by one, smiled and giggled at their baby sister, and kissed their Mama on the cheek.

Again, their Daddy abruptly interrupted the sweetness of the moment. "Stand tall and recite the Christmas story from the Gospel of Saint Luke. Little Luke, you lead this year," Abe demanded.

Luke and his brothers were confident in their ability to quote these particular Bible verses. It had been drilled in their heads every Christmas since their births. During the past month or so, their Daddy made them practice, saying the verses over and over without a single mistake. If one of the boys hesitated, or said the wrong word, or forgot a word, their Daddy would just as soon slap him in the mouth as look at him. Sometimes the blow was so forceful, it would land the boy on the floor; at other times he would get a busted lip. With each knock upside the head, the boys' hearts were bruised and the very spirit of their beings were squashed and shattered to smithereens.

The boys stood; Luke, so sure of himself, started and Matt and Mark joined in,

"And there were in the same country, shepherds abiding in their fields, keeping watch over their flocks by night. And, lo, the Angel of the Lord came upon them, and the glory of the Lord shone round about them; and they were sore afraid. And the Angel said unto them, 'Fear not: for, behold, I bring you good tidings of great joy, which shall be to all people. For unto you is born this day in the City of David, a Savior, which is Christ the Lord. And this shall be a sign unto you; Ye shall find the babe wrapped in swaddling clothes, lying in a manger.' And suddenly there was with the angel a multitude of the heavenly host praising God, and saying, 'Glory to God in the highest, and on earth peace, good will toward men.' Luke, chapter 2, verses 8 through 14."

It was Christmas Day at Preacher Culler's house, same as any other day, except for the newborn baby girl, Pearl Rose.

Pearl Rose was weak, feverish and had a

swollen knot on the top of her head. Despite their Mother's pleas, their Daddy would not hear of obtaining any medical treatment for Pearl Rose. "She is in God's care. Jesus requested little children to come unto him. God can move mountains, and if it is God's will, He can remove the bump right off Pearl Rose's head," he said.

Pearl Rose lived cozy and warm for nine months, protected in the safety of her mother's belly. She lived only a week in the cold, damp apartment in the housing projects.

Pearl Rose died December 31, 1946. She was placed in the cold frozen ground in Oakwood Cemetery in High Point, North Carolina. There is a marker on her grave, it reads:

Pearl Rose Culler
December 24, 1946 – December 31, 1946
"Asleep in Jesus"

Her grandmother, Abraham's mother, wrote a poem to Abraham and Shirley, in memory of their baby girl, Pearl Rose.

In an humble home in High Point, N. C.
lived Daddy, Mother, and their little boys three.
They were happy & joyous as Christmas drew

**My three older brothers at our home in the
housing projects, High Point, North Carolina**

Written for Troy & Gladys Culler by his Mother
in memory of their baby girl, Pearl Rose Culler,
Born December 24, 1946 - Died December 30, 1946

In an humble home in High Point, N. C.,
Lived Daddy, Mother, and their little boys three.
They were happy & joyous as Christmas drew near,
With gifts & remembrances from friends they
            held dear.
On Christmas Eve God gave them a little baby girl
            so sweet,
No gift was so welcome, their joy was complete.
Five pounds was her weight, her hair was dark
            brown,
She most talked with her eyes, as she watched
            them around.
They talked and played with her just six short days,
Then God, for some reason, came and took her away.
And while they are sad and cannot understand,
They know she is happy in a far better land.
They some day, can go to her in that home on High,
And be reunited with loved ones in the sweet by & by.
So look to the Lord Jesus, who alone can give us
            relief,
And loves us so dearly, "He is touched by our
            grief".

**Poem written to Daddy and Mama by his Mother,
Grandma Culler, in memory of Pearl Rose Culler. Born
December 24, 1946 - died December 30, 1946**

near, with gifts & remembrances from friends they held dear.
On Christmas Eve God gave them a little baby girl so sweet, no gift was so welcome, their joy was complete.
Five pounds was her weight, her hair was dark brown, she most talked with her eyes, as she watched them around.
They talked and played with her just six short days, then God, for some reason, came and took her away.
And while they are sad and cannot understand, they know she is happy in a far better land.
They some day, can go to her in that home on High, and be reunited with loved ones in the sweet by & by.
So look to the Lord Jesus, who alone can give us relief, and loves us so dearly, "He is touched by our grief."

Three more babies would be born into Preacher Culler's family. However, since the death of Pearl Rose, Shirley made it known that a doctor would deliver any more children she had. Regardless of what Abe did or said, there was no changing Shirley's mind about it. He could whoop and holler, quote and misquote the Bible, and generally raise all kinds of holy hell, but Shirley paid him no mind. She remained calm, because she had learned from other employees at the mill about a wonderful doctor in town, Dr. Joseph Slate. He would make house calls to deliver the babies of mothers living in the projects. The news of Dr. Slate brought tears of joy to her eyes and hope to her heart. "Dr. Slate is compassionate, gentle and kind. He will also let you pay him what you can afford to pay, when you can afford it," explained Lois, a friend who folded socks at the mill with Shirley.

So only months later, when Shirley again found herself more than a little pregnant, she called upon the services of Dr. Slate. Intellectually, she was certain she could endure the physical pain of child birth; however, in her heart, with one hundred percent certainty, she was sure she could not bear the greater suffering and agony of the death of another child. Dr. Slate had only one requirement: no husbands were allowed in the room at the time of the delivery. Thank heavens! Abraham would not be in the room!

After the fast and easy delivery, Dr. Slate swaddled the baby girl snuggly in a clean white sheet and gently slid her into her mother's outstretched arms. "Shirley, what do you want to name your baby daughter?" he asked.

"Should I ask Abe his choice of names?" she asked.

"Only if you want to," he said.

"Well, in that case, I name her Estie after her Grandmother, Abe's mother. That dear lady has always been so kind to me. And her middle name is Irene, same as my middle name. Yep, Estie Irene. How does that sound?" Shirley asked.

"Perfect," Dr. Slate answered. "So Shirley Irene, you and Estie Irene rest easy in God's loving care, now and always," he said.

"We will," Shirley whispered.

Dr. Slate observed mother and daughter briefly, mindful yet again as he always had been of the mysteries and miracles of childbirth. He tiptoed from the room and silently closed the door behind him.

Shirley held Estie close to her heart. Happily, she hugged her and lightly kissed the top of Estie's smooth bald head. In that instant, Shirley's heart clinched and cried for her baby girl, who, less than a year before left her with an empty heart and empty arms. Before gaping in wonderment at Estie's baby pink face, Shirley gazed upward. "Oh, Pearl Rose, I wish you were here with us. I've missed you every day. It would have been marvelous if you and Estie could have grown up together, and played and laughed together, known each other, and been best friends. I love you so much, Pearl Rose, and I always will."

Again, Shirley kissed Estie's head. She adjusted her arms to enable her to gaze into

Estie's face. "Estie, I love you, but I am so afraid. I am scared half to death. I fear losing you. Please don't leave me like your sister, Pearl Rose, did. Please, please stay with me. I love you and Jesus loves you too. Jesus, please don't take Estie. Please leave this precious baby with me," Shirley softly sobbed. Her warm tears splashed on Estie's head.

There was the slightest tap on the bedroom door and it opened. Dr. Slate stepped back into the room and stood beside Shirley and Estie. "Sorry to be a bother. Sorry to intrude. But, well, I want to have a prayer with you," Dr. Slate said. He tenderly placed his hands on the heads of both mother and daughter. "God, our Father and Creator, may Shirley and Estie Irene rest easy in Your loving care. Wrap them tight and keep them safe in Your strong arms now and always. Amen." Opening his eyes, Dr. Slate peered into Shirley's frightened, huge brown eyes, which were swimming in tears. Dr. Slate's eyes were searching Shirley's for the stability, dependability, and peace, he knew she possessed. "And, Shirley Irene, you can be assured Estie Irene is in excellent health and she'll not be needed in heaven for years to come. Don't be afraid. Love her. You see, love wipes away all fear. Love and fear cannot co-exist simultaneously in one heart. There's not enough space for both. As you love Estie your fear will diminish," Dr. Slate said. Shirley smiled and rubbed tears from her eyes.

"Thank you," she sniffled.

Dr. Slate stepped closer. "Shirley, no more tears today. Estie's wet head indicates she has been baptized, sprinkled really well in her Mother's tears," Dr. Slate joked.

"Okay, thank you. Thank you for your prayer. I will forever remember that Pearl Rose is in heaven and Estie Irene and I are both in God's loving care, here on earth. We will rest easy in that assurance. You can count on it," Shirley said. Her eyes were dry and a smile formed on her lips.

"I'll count on it. Take care and get some rest," he said.

"I will. Thank you for teaching me about love, and how love gets rid of fear. I appreciate your kind words of encouragement," Shirley said. Her eyes appeared confident and steady.

"Oh, hush now and get some rest," Dr. Slate said. He turned and left the room.

For it was You who formed my inward parts
You knit me together in my mother's womb.
Psalms 139:13 NIV

Welcome to my world. I am Estie Irene

Daddy Holding me at three months old in front of the housing project apartment where I was born.

Estie as an infant

Estie

Culler. Just call me, Estie.

So far, the best experience of my life is growing hair. I am born bald. Peach fuzz rapidly appears on my bald head; then blond hair sprouts and takes off growing. My brother, Luke, likes to brush my fine blond hair and tries to make it curl on top. He loves to stick out his tongue, cross his eyes, make goofy sounds, and blow air bubbles on my belly. Luke loves to make me laugh. Laughing is the most fun in my life – Luke making me laugh.

Teething, now that's a horse of a different color. My gums, uppers and lowers, swollen, sore and constantly drooling slobber, irritates the daylights out of me. Strange – how growing hair is painless. It doesn't hurt anywhere. Yet, growing teeth causes pain to the gums. And, for some unknown reason, it causes doo-doo to happen more often. It irritates me! I'm miserable! Nothing's worse than a diaper rash, a bright red burning bottom covered with bumpy blisters. Growing teeth is literally a pain in the butt. I'm not sure whether to scream my head off or scratch my bottom off. I don't know how to scratch, but I can scream. And I do!

I am walking and have been able to walk for months. Luke and my other brothers, Mark and Matt, enjoy helping me learn to walk, and more importantly to laugh, when I fall down. They lift me up to my feet and hold me steady, until I am back in balance and ready to try again. With time, I learn to run into their open arms, which makes them laugh and me giggle. Brothers are a good thing.

Growing hair and teeth is 'bout all I know of life so far; except I also know, Mama is there to latch onto when I am hungry. Mama or one of my brothers changes my diaper when it is dirty; however, Mama wants me to be potty trained soon. Sooner rather than later, because another baby is on the way.

My Mama, with Dr. Slate's professional assistance, delivers another baby girl. Dr. Slate's expertise boosts Mama's confidence in him and in herself, making the experience smooth and easy.

In the living room, as Dr. Slate is preparing to leave with his medical bag in one hand, he looks toward Daddy and announces, "Congratulations, Mary Ruth is a beautiful healthy baby girl." Before Daddy can express his usual negative thoughts and opinions, Dr. Slate turns his attention to us kids on the floor and ignores Daddy. He sets his satchel down. He folds his lanky body, squats on his haunches and his bony knees stick up to the tip of his pointed chin. Matt and Mark are on the floor arm wrestling, and Luke is playing "This little piggy went to the market" with my bare toes. Dr. Slate playfully pats the top of Luke's head of straight blond hair and with his long arms, he hugs me affectionately.

"Guess what?" Dr. Slate asks me. "You've got a little sister, Mary Ruth, to play with now. She's as cute as you are." I smile, shyly hiding my head behind Luke's back. Dr. Slate stands with bag in hand and takes long strides toward the front door and glances back at the boys, "Don't you fellows make tomboys out of your girly sisters, now you hear?"

"Just a cotton pickin' minute!" Daddy bolts from his seat, dropping his tattered old brown Bible from his lap. "Who gave you the right to name my daughter, Mary Ruth?" Hot under the collar, his face red, his offensive voice cranks up a couple notches louder. "Where exactly did the name, Mary Ruth, come from?" Daddy asks in disgust.

"Well, Preacher Culler, I am surprised. Surely, you know Mary, the mother of Jesus. She is all over the place in the New Testament. And, Ruth, well don't you know, in the Old Testament there is an entire book named for her?" With a satisfied smile, he bends his agile body and scoops up the old Bible from the floor and lightly tosses it back to Abe.

"I know. I know." Abe sputters. "Of course, I know Mary the mother of Jesus, I know Mary Magdalene, and I know all the other Marys. And furthermore, Ruth was Naomi's daughter-in-law." His voice is vicious and he is talking so fast, spit flies and he appears to be foaming at the mouth, as he jabs his pointer finger at the good doctor's chest. "What I want to know is, who said you could call my daughter, Mary Ruth, or anything else, for that matter?" Daddy asks.

"Shirley, her mother, named her. And, she honored your previous wishes; first name from the New Testament, and middle name from the Old Testament. I assured her that you would be pleased with the names she chose. The paper work has been completed and is here," he says patting his jacket pocket. "And it will be recorded in the Register of Deeds office at the courthouse today." As he heads for the door, Dr. Slate smiles again at us kids, "It's sunny outside. Why don't you kids come on out and play? Your mother needs to rest a little before you see her and Mary Ruth."

In less than two years, Dr. Slate is back at our apartment in the projects to deliver what is the last of Daddy's children. Daddy knows better than to put up much of a fuss, so he keeps his place in the living room, with his mouth shut, and his eyes riveting on the Word of God in the old Bible on his lap.

If things get easier with practice, after six kids Mama is a Pro. Yet, she gives credit to Dr. Slate for the smooth and near painless birth of her seventh child, a son. She names him John Joseph. "Abe already has a Matthew, Mark, and Luke. Now with our new baby boy named John, he'll have a complete set of the four gospels," Mama says with a grin, and the doctor can't help but chuckle. "And Abe can think the name Joseph is for the Old Testament character who had the coat of many colors, or for Joseph, the earthly father of Jesus. Whichever, he can have his pick. But, Dr. Joseph Slate, I want you to know this baby is named in honor of you. You are as kind, and as gentle, as any of those Bible folks. I thank you for your help and I will always be grateful to you," Mama says with all sincerity.

Dr. Slate's face glows with warmth and his eyes mist with humility. He pats Mama on the hand, and he manages to reply, "Thank you so much and I am indeed honored. Now you get some rest. Take care of yourself and take care of that handsome baby boy, John Joseph."

My eyes fail from weeping; I am in torment within,
my heart is poured out on the ground...
Lamentations 2:11 NIV

Chapter 1
The Smell of Fear

My Daddy is bound to be the devil he preaches about. Oh no. No. He can't. He can't. He can't do that! I realize Daddy's downright, God–awful, rotten intentions. "No. No. Don't. Please. Please. No. Don't you dare!" I scream. The door to the outside john is wide open and Daddy has an evil smirk on his face. His eyes bulge, as he stands over the hole in the wooden seat.

Daddy moves Mama and all six of us kids from the housing projects in High Point,

North Carolina to the foot of Pilot Mountain into a dilapidated, tar-papered shack which he dedicates to the honor and glory of God and names it the "Lord's Mission."

During a freezing spell a pregnant stray dog seeks refuge under the "Lord's Mission." "Mama Dog" gives birth to five teeny-weeny puppies. A few days after the puppies are born, Daddy hands me an old bushel basket and tells me to put the puppies in it. I lovingly and ever so gently lift each puppy away from "Mama Dog," slide them from under the "Lord's Mission," rub their heads and tickle their bellies. With pride, I choose a name that suits each puppy's appearance and personality. I whisper to each fuzzy puppy, and call them by name: "Blackie," "Spot," "Pepsi," "Pepper," and "Freckles." I place them in the basket. They snuggle close together as I carefully carry the basket to my Daddy. He yanks up each one of my adorable little puppies by the nape of the neck and cold-heartedly drops it into the stinking shit. I scream, cry, slap my Daddy's legs, and beg him, "Please, please don't! Please save them. Please, please don't do it. You can't! You must save them. They are my puppies. Please stop."

"Estie, I'm not keeping these mangy puppies, so shut up or you will be next!" Daddy shouts.

Daddy's cruelty to the puppies sickens me with the smell of fear and I choke on the foul taste of hate in my throat. It is repulsive – thick green slime twists around in the pit of my belly and crawls up my throat. I throw up, hoping to rid myself of such utter grossness and brutality. I want to claw my eyes out. Oh, how much better to be blind in both eyes than to have witnessed the unthinkable brutality. I fall flat on my stomach, lie face down in the dirt beside the john, kick my feet and beat the frozen ground with both my fists, and cry my broken heart out. I wish Daddy would eat shit and die.

At four years old, I have a paying job "puttin' in 'bacca." I am a tobacco "hander." As a "hander", I stand on a two foot high tree stump which has been made as smooth and flat as a table top. I reach into a wooden bin and remove a handful of picked tobacco leaves and hand them to the "tier." The "tier" wraps twine around the stalk end of the leaves and ties them to a rough wooden stick. Then, the sticks, heavy with tobacco, are hung in the tobacco barn to dry by the heat of a wood burning fire.

Puttin' in tobacco is hard, back-breaking

work, yet I have the time of my life! Me, being considered old enough to work with my older brothers, Matt, Mark, and Luke, tickles me pink. I feel all grown up and want to do my best. I take pride in doing my job right – fast, but also neat. Our pay is free rent and everyone receives a dollar a day which we all give to Mama. Our whole family works in the tobacco field, but of course not Daddy, he's a preacher, nor my little brother, John Joseph, 'cause he is only a baby. My little sister, Mary, is also too young to work, but she hangs around with us in the field and barn. She sits on the dirt floor of the barn and plays in the loose dirt, letting it sift through her fingers.

My hands, black and gummy from tobacco residue, and my Daddy killing my puppies, are some of my first memories.

Pilot Mountain is one of a kind! It is unique with a solid rock knob in the center of the top. The locals call it the "big pinnacle." At the foot of the mountain, a good ways down the red dirt road is a paved driveway on the right side leading to Daddy's Uncle Dock's home. A new green Ford pick-up truck and a green John Deere tractor are usually parked next to his white, two story farmhouse. The farmhouse has a wrap around front porch, a green front door, green window shutters and is surrounded by thick green grass. The porch furniture is white wicker and the chairs have green and white plaid seat cushions. There is a green glider, a porch swing, and a round table covered with a green ivy-patterned tablecloth. The red, white, and blue American flag always waves from a pole attached to the porch post.

On the far end of the red dirt road is where my Daddy's Aunt Martha, and her husband, Uncle Lebert, live. Their unpainted house has a charming tiny front porch. It is not necessary to have steps because the porch is only one step above the ground. On the porch are a couple of straight back, straw bottom chairs, two old rockers with mixed match quilted cushions, a fly swatter or two, and church fans scattered here and there. The front yard matches the red dirt road. In fact, there is no way to know where the side of the road stops and the yard begins. It is all the same, a few rocks and red dirt. A rope swing, with a wooden board for a seat, hangs from one of the thick branches of a tall maple tree.

Red wax begonias with polished-looking, green and dark burgundy leaves bloom in orange clay flower pots, of different sizes. Red blossoms of petunias dangle from green ropy vines in other pots. These flower

pots line most of the edges along the front
porch, saving only spots of room, here and
there, for stepping off the porch. I sit in the
empty spots, swing my legs, drag my bare feet
through the red dirt, and pinch the dead heads
off the petunias. Chickens run freely all over
the place in the yard, on the porch, and they
occasionally flop their wings and fly to a low
tree branch and roost a while. A round well,
with a tin roof, is in the back of the house. The
well has a hand crank used to wind and unwind
a rope with a water pail tied to the end of it for
retrieving water.

On the back porch the wall of the house
is full of anything and everything you can ever
need, hanging on long nails. There are blue
pots used for canning fruits and vegetables,
pots for chicken feed, and pots for the pig's
slop. Maxwell House coffee cans and Crisco
lard cans have two holes poked in them with a
wire tied between the holes to form a handle.
These cans are for blackberry and cherry pickin'.
There's a milk can, a mop bucket and a mop
hanging on a nail, stringy-end up on the wall.
There are buckets for carrying ashes from the
fireplace and the wood burning stove, a bucket
of clothespins and a couple of extra dippers
for drinking water from the well. I don't know
if the wall holds up all these necessities, or if,

the necessities hold up the wall.

Our house is an abandoned tenant house, actually a shack, belonging to the Culler heirs. A mile or so up the road is Uncle Dock's house, and about a mile down the road is Aunt Martha's.

The front porch on the shabby shack is rotting planks lying snug to the ground. There are two front doors. One door leads to our tiny inadequate home; and Daddy nails a crude homemade sign over the other door, declaring it to be the entrance to "The Lord's Mission."

Our house has one bedroom with two full beds, and the living room has a faded old couch with the stuffing and springs poking through the thin fabric. With several broken window panes stuffed with cardboard, the place is downright freezing in the winter. The only heat in the house is from a wood burning cook stove in the kitchen. A few steps outside in the back yard is the "johnny house." The close proximity of the john to the kitchen causes an offensive stench to linger profusely around the dirty house.

When the tobacco crop is "tied up" and "put in" the warm barn, and the sweet scent of drying tobacco permeates the autumn mountain air, overnight God erases the green off the leaves and paints them different shades of brilliant oranges, bright yellows, and radiant reds. The warm mid-day sun produces highly saturated vivid colors. Pilot Mountain is always a splendid sight. However, at the peak of North Carolina's autumn season, its grand imposing beauty is magnificent.

Excitement buzzes. Routines at the "Lord's Mission" change. Mama enrolls my brothers in Pinnacle School and she finds employment at a shirt factory in Mt. Airy, a few miles north of Pilot Mountain. The foreman offers Mama a ride to work. She must first hike two miles or so up the red dirt road to the black top paved intersection, and be waiting promptly at five o'clock in the mornings. She agrees to the conditions of his offer. If Mama says she will do it, you can count on it! She is always there – always on time.

Mama wakes before daybreak, pokes the cooling embers in the stove, adds more wood and blows on the embers until they blaze up into flames. She fries her hoecake and stirs up hot water gravy. Before leaving home for work, she makes sure Matt, Mark, and Luke are out of the one bed they sleep in.

At the factory she does production work; therefore her pay is based on the number of shirts she folds. She folds a half dozen shirts while her co-workers are still thinking about it. She is a dedicated, hard working employee, and she is rewarded with pay raises for her speed and efficiency.

Mama recognizes, to her disappointment, Daddy is not only lazy and crazy; he is also eaten up with jealousy. No matter how hard Mama works, Daddy is positive she is "running around on him with her boss." All the boss ever does is provide her transportation, which is not out of his way. Daddy goes on rampages and orders her to stop her adulterous ways! He will not allow such shenanigans! Daddy's delusions and false accusations are incentives to spur Mama to work hard every day. Daddy piddles away the day, lollygagging around the house with his nose in the Bible.

I am stranded at home to care for John Joseph, who we call "JJ," and Mary.

Matt, Mark, and Luke teach themselves to set rabbit traps, steal watermelons, take eggs from under hens, to occasionally ring the neck of someone else's chicken and to pick wild blackberries and cherries. If none of their "groceries" are available, Mama fries hoecake. Sometimes Aunt Martha shares with us her garden fresh vegetables or green beans and tomatoes she has canned from her garden, and jars of jelly she preserves from wild blackberries.

The day before Christmas, a country ham, a bushel bag of Florida oranges, and a brown paper sack of hard red and white peppermint candy sticks are doled out to employees at the shirt factory. The plant closes early because of the holiday. With so much to carry, the foreman offers to drive Mama the couple miles or so to our house. This brings more ridiculously false accusations from Daddy. "You think I believe you were working? Well I don't! You musta' given him something he really enjoys," he hounds her – a snarling, mad dog growling and barking viciously at a helpless, innocent, treed raccoon.

Daddy berates and nags Mama, while she is peeling 'taters. Mama resolves to remain happy and refuses to allow Daddy's anger, jealousy, and bitterness to dampen her cheerful spirit. She chooses to stay calm and in control, and she is determined she will not permit him to get under her skin by his insults and rudeness. She softly hums "Away in a Manger," and focuses her thoughts on Jesus' humble birth. Mama is thankful for the abundance of pinto beans, mashed 'taters, and corn bread. She is thrilled to pieces with the enormous ham and she realizes there will be leftovers for several days after Christmas. Then she will cook up a pot of ham bone soup. She delights in fixin' the delicious meal, her only Christmas gift to her family. Mama receives immeasurable joy at the sight of her growing children, chomping at the bit to gobble down her good ole scrumptious country cooking.

She gives each of us a hug and a sweet smile. "Merry Christmas. I love you. Now, dig in and eat up," she says.

"What the Sam Hill! Not one bite! Don't any of you take one single bite! Not until you recite the Christmas Story." Daddy shouts, bringing the festive mood to a halt.

Matt, Mark, Luke, and even I, stand straight and obey his command, trying not to show our disappointment. Without hesitation, we say in unison:

"And there were in the same country, shepherds abiding in the fields, keeping watch over their flocks by night. And, lo, the Angel of the Lord came upon them, and the glory of the Lord shown round about them, and they were sore afraid. And the Angel said unto them, 'Fear not; for behold I bring you good tidings of great joy, which shall be to all people. For unto you is born this day in the city of David, a Savior, which is Christ the Lord.'"

We are all proud of ourselves; Luke in particular, since it is written in the Gospel of Luke, his namesake.

Not until after Daddy piles his plate with mounds of piping hot food, do we. Mama smiles happily. It is Christmas Day at the "Lord's Mission," same as any other day, except for eight full bellies, and the spicy flavor of peppermint candy turning cartwheels on our taste buds.

I baptize you with water,
but He will baptize you with the Holy Spirit.
Mark 1:8 NIV

Chapter 2
My First Guarded Secret

"Estie, take off your clothes," Daddy orders.

"What for?" I ask. I am surprised by this command. No one else has been made to remove their clothes.

"Because I said so."

"Why?" I ask.

He reaches for me, pulls me closer to him with one hand, and backhands me across the mouth with his other hand. "Now take off your clothes."

I rub my lips; I taste blood. My lip is busted.

The dogwood trees begin to bloom, some pink and others white, and a breeze mildly stirs the crisp fresh air. It's a bright sunshiny day in March, early spring. It is a perfect day to play outside. I teach Mary to skip and to hop on one foot. We have fun. Mama is at work and my older brothers are at school.

Daddy, totes JJ on his strong shoulders, and tells Mary and me to follow him. Mary and I skip along behind him, down the rutty dirt road away from the "Lord's Mission" in the opposite direction of Pilot Mountain. We stop at Grassy Creek, a little stream of muddy water.

Daddy instructs Mary and me to sit down on the smooth river rocks located on the creek bank. He swings JJ from his shoulders and places him on the bank between us. Then he plops himself on the bank also. Mary and I pay little attention to him. We kick off our shoes, dangle our legs and splash our feet in the water.

Our clumsy Daddy struggles out of his old brogans and dirty socks, and neatly rolls up his pants' legs exposing the kinky hair on his calves. He wobbles into the cold water, and carries his Bible in one hand. He flips open his Bible and the pages fall where they may, which is apparently to the exact book and verses he aims to read. He tells the story of John the Baptist baptizing Jesus. The words flow smoothly off his tongue. He knows them by heart; he doesn't even glance at his open Bible.

He wades back to the bank, manages to fetch JJ and to leave his old Bible with his brogans on the bank. He carries JJ out into the knee-deep water. He squats and pushes JJ's head under the water and says, "I baptize you in the name of the Father, the Son and the Holy Ghost." JJ coughs and gags when his head of blond curly hair comes up out of the water. His little body shivers as Daddy places him on the creek bank beside me. He then leads Mary into the water and proceeds with the same ritual with her. I wrap my arms around JJ. Mary returns to my side, wet and cold.

"Estie, I said take off your clothes," Daddy demands.

Scared, I fight back my tears. I unsnap the shoulder straps on my overalls and step out of them, pull my shirt off over my head and stand there, like a dumb bell.

"Take off your 'step-ins,'" he says.

Stunned, I shudder, trembling more from fear than from the cool air. I step out of my panties and drop them on top of my clothes on the creek bank. In a stupor, I stand there stark-naked, captured by the stare of his bizarre eyes. I squeeze my eyes tight and whisper, "Dear Jesus, now would be a good time for you to come again. Please split through the blue sky and rapture me into heaven. Amen." I slowly open my eyes. I'm sure I'll stand on streets of pure gold; but I stand ankle deep in muddy water. My prayers are unanswered.

Daddy tugs me deeper into the cold water, and I resist every step of the way. I plant my feet in the mud and it oozes between my toes. This tug of war causes me to stumble.

"Estie, stand up straight," he says. "There is evil and sin in this world, the sin of Adam and Eve has been passed down through the centuries. God chose me and anointed me as his servant to defeat evil. God uses me in mighty ways, therefore John Edgar Hoover, the head of the FBI, plans to rape you, my oldest daughter, before you are twenty-one years old. Beware! Watch out for him! He will sneak up on you, like the devil, and wrap his slimy self around you, and choke the life out of you. So, I wash and cleanse you, your whole body with the love of the Father, the blood of the Son, and power of the Holy Ghost to purify you from all evil." He cups and dips his hands in the cold water, scoops it up and lets it sprinkle on my head. He slowly rubs his wet hands on my face, shoulders, chest and arms. He again cups his hands and dips them in the water. His wet hands find a resting place, one on my butt and the other one ...uh, on, uh ... my front side. His hands linger and press there too long. He rubs his hands down my legs and my "cleansing bath" continues.

"Estie, by the power of the blood of Jesus Christ, I rebuke the devil and John Edgar Hoover, from taking possession of you and your body. You are now sanctified and I baptize you in the name of the Father, the Son and the Holy Ghost. Amen. Now, Estie, hurry and put your clothes back on," he says.

I waste no time dillydallying. I hustle back into my clothes.

This rotten experience horrifies me. I am at a loss as to what on earth Daddy is talking about; I'll never forget his actions on this God awful day. My thoughts, jumbled as a shuffled deck of playing cards, are conflicted.

I am lost in thought, unaware of sights and sounds in the world around me; my numb feet slowly carry the rest of me along the dirt road. Silent, I am quiet as a dead horse fly.

Why would a Mr. Hoover (whoever he is) want to "rake" me (whatever that is) and choke the life out of me? How will my mind ever comprehend this information? It doesn't.

I feel guilty, ashamed, embarrassed, and dirty deep down inside. How could a "cleansing bath" feel so dirty? I wonder what I did wrong to cause Daddy to act so odd toward me. His words and actions scare me. I must be a freak, a monster, and a disgrace to God. The whole hullabaloo must be my fault. I am not about to tell anyone what has happened at Grassy Creek. My first guarded secret, pushed way back and hidden in the crevices of my brain – to remember no more. However, try as I may, I never forget.

"It's not fair. Your clothes are dry. Mine are soaking wet and I'm cold. I want my clothes to be dry too," Mary whines, drawing me from my bewildered thoughts, as we mosey back up the road to the "Lord's Mission."

"Believe me Mary, you oughta' be glad your clothes are wet," I say.

My hand touches my lip and it is sore. With my mind preoccupied with overwhelming emotional pain, I have forgotten the physical pain of my busted lip. Small potatoes, all things considered. My mind is confused – muddy as Grassy Creek. Needless to say, Daddy rubbing my body with his vile hands dripping with cold, muddy water, rubs me the wrong way.

My thoughts are popping. I can't complete one unpleasant thought before another rotten thought pops around in my brain, taking over the first thought, only to be blown out by another. Pop…, pop…, pop…, racing thoughts; popping faster. Pop…, pop…, pop…, gaining speed. All the puzzling thoughts…, pop…, pop…, pop, run rampantly, burst violently, explode and grow larger and larger. Is there enough space in my bucket head or will they all pop out?

Daddy betrays any inkling of trust I may have had in him. Just the thought of Daddy gives me the heebie jeebies. He is evil up one side and down the other, the scum of the earth and I hate him! I acknowledge my world for what it is: dark, heavy, cloudy and gloomy, even though the sun shines brightly and there is not a cloud in the sky. I recognize my Daddy for what he is – an insane evil pervert with memorized Bible verses spewing from his wicked lips – a poisonous, sneaky rattlesnake slithering through the daisies.

May integrity and uprightness protect me, because my hope is in you.
Psalms 26:21 NIV

Chapter 3
Sunny Side of the Shack

While Mama works and my brothers attend school, Daddy never stokes the fire to keep the flames burning. Often it feels warmer outside the house than inside. I find a dirty, old, long overcoat in the crawl space under the "Lord's Mission." It is caked with so many layers of red clay dirt and dried orange sand that it is impossible to tell its original color. Mary, JJ, and I spend most of the days sitting on the cold ground on the sunny side of the shack. We snuggle close under the coat of unknown color.

Mary and I play "rock, scissors, paper."

Happiness is my older brothers! They are glad to see Mary, JJ and me, when they come home; they lift Mary and me up, swing us in the air and toss us from one to the other. The three of them run fast around the outside of the house and carry the three of us, straddling their lean shoulders. We hang on to their heads for our dear lives and they grab a tight grip onto our feet, which are dangling over their chests. "Getty-up, horsy" and "Ride'em Cowboy," we shout. They do some serious foot racing, with a finish line drawn in the dirt. They switch off their loads by swapping us around on their different shoulders. The competition is stiff; their fast speed is almost equal. Each claims to be the winner. It is fun; yet scary as all get out. They teach us to play "kick the can," "ring around the roses," "hide and seek," and "London Bridge is falling down." We fill our afternoons with fun and games, tickling, wrestling, and a whole lot of laughing – a real hunk-a-dory time.

Mama slowly drags herself home, dog tired and all worn out. She is a Miracle Worker, same as Jesus, regardless of her overwhelming tiredness. The Bible tells of two occasions where Jesus feeds a multitude of people with a couple of fish and loaves of bread. On the other hand, Mama, with nothing at all, no fish, no bread, miraculously feeds the eight of us a multitude of times. Sometimes we have beans and at other times we have 'taters. It is a special occasion for us to have both 'taters and beans at the same meal. Whatever we have, it is, sure as shootin' better than raw fish. We always have a plenty and we don't go to bed hungry. Yeah, I rank Mama's care and compassion right up there with Jesus's.

After supper, Luke reads to Mary and me from an old <u>Dick and Jane</u> school book. Without realizing it, Luke teaches me to read and I love it! Somewhere in my head, a string attached to a light bulb, is pulled and the light clicks on. I can see clearly, not only new words; but I also discover a new world. Dick, Jane, and their silly baby sister, Sally, along with the good dog Spot and Puff, their funny cat, introduce me to a way of life I know nothing about. From the pictures, I observe that Mother is pretty, and her lips are glossy, shiny and red. She washes dishes in a white kitchen sink that has hot, running water; she doesn't leave home to work in a factory. She stays home and takes care of her children. Their Father wears a clean suit to work and looks happy. Imagine that! A Daddy who works!

Our Daddy is no longer in the "street preacher" business since we've moved out here to the country. He comes up with a simple solution to fulfill his "Holy Calling" to proclaim the Word of God and the Gospel of Jesus Christ to all the "lost and dying souls" in the world. Since he cannot stroll the streets of town, choose a busy corner, open his Bible and preach to passersby, he preaches six nights during the week and twice on Sundays *at* all the "hypocrites and sinners" in the "Lord's Mission." Only problem is, there are no "lost and dying souls" or "hypocrites and sinners" anywhere around. However, I am anxious to see what they look like when they do show up. Mama and us kids are the only souls who gather regularly and reverently for his services.

Matthew, Mark, and Luke build a horse-drawn chariot for Mary and me to ride on. They pretend to be the horses pulling the chariot. The chariot is a flat wooden board (spacious enough for Mary and me) with two thick, sticky, burlap colored ropes attached with several knots. On this spring day, JJ sits with his legs crossed, in the middle of the board, happy as a king on his chariot. Mary and I, two mighty strong horses, haul King JJ on his chariot, giving him the ride of his life. JJ laughs, his mouth wet and wide open, with only a few baby teeth and lots of red swollen gums with white buds ready to burst and release more teeth. He is so cute, you have to love him and we all do.

Matt, Mark and Luke are marching in front of us, leading the parade. With their own rhythm they clap their hands, snap their fingers, and stomp their feet and sing loud with strong voices:

"He'll be coming round the mountain when he comes,
He'll be coming round the mountain when he comes,
He'll be coming round the mountain
He'll be coming round the mountain
He'll be coming round the mountain when he comes.
He'll be riding two wild horses when he comes
He'll be riding two wild horses when he comes
He'll be riding two wild horses
He'll be riding two wild horses
He'll be riding two wild horses when he comes...."

Wham! The screen door slams loudly and Daddy bounces out of the "Lord's Mission" side of the dilapidated shack. Daddy, in one quick motion, leaps from the low front porch and springs high in the air. He holds a brown paper sack in his hands, like a quarterback running a football, and lands on both feet in the red dirt yard. He turns back to the porch and sets his paper sack on the edge of it.

"Okay, all of you." Daddy shouts. He scurries across the yard to the front of our parade. "Let's get a move on, yee haw! Put a move on it. Come on now!" He slows down, stepping in between Mary and me. "Come on and sit down," he shouts and slaps his hands to the sides of his legs. "Move it!" He moves in circles around us, herding us in, like a border collie, rounding up sheep. "Okay, all of you sit down. Sit down here on the ground," Daddy says. He motions for us to sit down around him in the red dirt near a wild cherry tree. And, of course, we do.

"Listen to me and learn great wisdom," he says. "I am going to explain to you the purpose of the old wild cherry tree you see budding and beginning to bloom with pale pink blossoms here on the edge of the yard near the dirt road. God knows all things, and He sees the whole picture – past, present, and future. That old wild cherry tree has not always been here. But God in His infinite wisdom knew that on this day, at this very second, I would be here with the determination to promote God's kingdom here on earth. And, He knew I would, on this day, need a tree. God knew I would place a loud speaker in the cherry tree that's growing in this spot." Overtaken with gratitude, Daddy jumps up to his feet, "Praise

His wonderful name! Hallelujah! Thanks be to God!" he shouts. He lifts his arms high over his head. "Hallelujah! Thank you Jesus for this wild cherry tree," he says. In awe and adoration, he gazes up to heaven as if he is waiting for God's reply. We wait in silence with our eyes glued to the blue sky. Daddy looks around at us and his mouth drops open in surprise. It appears he has forgotten we are even there. "Why are ya'll sitting there like knots on a log?" he asks.

We are silent, and wonder if Daddy has lost it. Doesn't he remember that he has ordered us to sit down on the ground?

"Okay, Matthew, skedaddle to the front porch and get that sack with a loudspeaker in it. I need your help hanging it in the cherry tree," Daddy says.

"I will," Matt says. He hops to his feet, slowly swaggers to the porch, scoops up the brown paper sack and saunters, cool and carefree, back to us. He remains standing, opens the sack, and pulls out a loudspeaker, with black electrical cords all tangled up in clusters of tight knots. "This speaker is the kind politicians put on tops of cars and drive through town begging for votes in the county elections. While I unravel the knots," Matt says calmly staring directly at Daddy, "let me tell you a thing or two. You may think God put the tree here for you and your loudspeaker, but, man alive, have I got news for you. This wild cherry tree has lots of purposes and your loudspeaker ranks at rock bottom, in comparison. The real reason, God caused the wild cherry tree to grow in this very spot, is to produce fruit. If God knew you would be here, then He certainly knew Mama would be here too, and He knew good and well, even way back then, she would bake some mighty good cherry pies," Matt says.

The rest of us hold our breath; we are afraid Matt is asking for trouble by mouthing back to Daddy. After seconds of silence, Luke and Mark begin to chuckle. Daddy surprises us and himself too. He laughs out loud and surprises me with sounds I've never heard from him. I'm not sure what there is to laugh about; I'm scared Daddy will jump on Matt with all fours. I laugh also, but only a squeaky sound slips through my lips.

Matt helps Daddy, and the rest of us kids watch in bewilderment, curious to know what's going on. Daddy fiddles and fumbles with the wires. Matt twirls an index finger, draws small circles in the air close to the temple of his head, and points his finger at Daddy. He silently and secretly mouths one word, "loco."

Daddy, with Matt's help, finally manages

to rig up the old loudspeaker. They hook it to a high branch of the wild cherry tree.

Later, I ask Matt, "What does 'loco' mean?"

"It means crazy in the head," he answers.

"Oh," I mumble, because I'm not sure what to say.

"Why?" he asks.

"Just wondering, that's all," I say.

"Well, now you know. Like I said, it means crazy in the head. Do you understand?" He asks.

"Yeah, it means Daddy is really 'loco'. It means Daddy is crazy in the head. Really, really 'loco,'" I say.

"You got it exactly right," Matt says. With the pointer finger on our right hands, we both draw circles in the air at the side of our heads.

"Daddy is loco," we say in unison and giggle.

Fathers, provoke not your children to anger...
Colossians 3:21 KJV

Chapter 4
Three Blind Mice

"All have sinned, and come short of the glory of God. If a man claims he has no sin, he is a liar. The Bible says, 'All have sinned.' It means exactly what it says, 'All.' Every last one of you are sinners bound for hell. If you confess your sins, God is faithful and just, and will forgive you and cleanse you from all unrighteousness. But, no, you rebellious, stiff necked children, you think your ways are better than God's ways. I warn you, call on the name of the Lord Jesus Christ and be saved. Glory! Glor-i-a! Or God will punish you and cast you away in a lake of hell fire. Hallelujah!" Daddy shouts.

His thunderous voice blares through the loudspeaker. He brings forth his God-fearing sermons for the whole world to hear; however, only our family, sitting smack dab in front of him, hear him. His bellowing shouts are loud enough, in fact, too loud! There is no reason to have a loudspeaker hanging in the wild cherry tree. So, the way I see it, Matt is right. The cherry tree is in our yard, not because Daddy ever needs a loudspeaker in it, but so Mama can make cherry pies. Yeah, Matt is right. Daddy is "loco."

Sweat drips from the tip of his wide nose and rolls off his round chin, when he shouts. The "Lord's Mission" has no heat, and the spring mountain weather is still chilly, but my Daddy is shouting up a sweat.

When Daddy commands us to listen, listen we do! Not out of love or respect, but out of fear – not only the fear of Daddy but also the fear of God and His wrath.

At times, Daddy calls on my older brothers to quote memorized Bible verses or to name, in order, the titles of all sixty-six books of the Bible. They stand, shoulders straight, feet together. They clear their throats, reel off with speed and accuracy the words they have memorized.

It is in one of these services, Daddy

instructs Mary and me to sing a song. We don't know what to sing, and he doesn't tell us what to sing. So we put our heads together and decide to sing a cute little tune our brothers sing to us often after school. Standing in Daddy's holy sanctuary, and in the presence of the Holy God, I open my mouth and, as sweetly as I know how, sing "Three blind mice, three blind mice, see how they run." I flash Mary a smile encouraging her to sing along with me, and she does. "See how they run, they all run after the farmer's wife, who cuts off their tails with a carving knife…" We sing our very best; yet, Matt, Mark and Luke silently stifle sniggers with their hands covering their mouths. Their giddy giggles grow into loud laughter. Good laughter – the kind that produces strange snorting sounds from their noses and causes tears to well up in their eyes. They double over at their waists and burst into deep rolls of belly laughter.

What's so funny? Why are my brothers laughing at me? Uh, oh, Daddy doesn't think it is one bit cute! And he let's me and everyone else know he disapproves. He winds up his arm, a ball bat. He is warming up, hankering to knock the ball out of the park. He hauls off and slugs the ball with all his might. The ball, which happens to be my little head, pops into the air and reels round and round, whirling wildly. It's a high fly – a grand slam! It drops hard to the floor on the other side of the room. My spinning head is dizzy. I am stunned and cannot comprehend all I see.

Daddy is all fired up! His face is beet red. He marches back and forth, his knees step high and his elbows swing stiffly. His movements are precise, stiff and jerky. "Children, obey your father," he snarls through clinched teeth; and simultaneously he awkwardly kicks a straw bottom chair. His foot pokes all the way through the chair's straw seat. He becomes jumbled up in the chair, stumbles and falls. Now there are two of us sprawled out on the floor; but, he quickly jumps to his feet and throws the chair out of his way. In the commotion, JJ shrieks loud and shrill.

Land sakes alive, all hell breaks loose! Daddy quickly and unexpectedly snatches JJ, who is nursing, away from Mama, causing her slobbery wet titty to fly free. In a tizzy, he stuffs JJ into the crook of his left arm and with his right hand he grabs Mama's nipple and squeezes her round, swollen, titty. He grips it tight and yanks it hard, causing it to stretch out long and narrow – like a slingshot. When he cannot stretch it out any further, he abruptly loosens his hand and releases Mama. "You're nothing but a low down whore," he roars. The savage beast shows no mercy, only contempt and scorn, as he spits on the floor.

Daddy swiftly throws off JJ's blanket, strips away his t-shirt and diaper and lays him on his back, on top of the altar. The make shift altar is three old rough and splintering wood apple boxes turned upside down and placed close together in a row. Pink, with splotches of red, JJ's itsy-bitsy naked body squirms and his scrawny arms flail and skinny legs kick; like a drowning rat struggling to keep his head above water.

"Children, obey your father!" Daddy explodes. He unbuckles his long leather belt and slings it high over his head and, with one fell swoop, whips little JJ with the buckle end of it. "Children, obey your father for it is the will of the Lord. Abraham offered his son, Isaac, on the altar to be slain!" he shouts. Daddy, hysterical, out of control and out of his everlasting mind, gives no thought of the consequences that may follow his actions. I have been knocked to the floor and may die over here all by myself, and JJ is fixin' to be slaughtered on the altar. Is he going to kill us all? "God, please help," I pray without speaking a word.

Daddy bends over at his waist with both

hands on his knees and gasp for breath. Mama seizes this opportune time to throw herself over JJ. She protects him as a shield. Eyes bulging, Daddy angrily directs his assaulting belt on her back.

Fifteen year old Matt, a sleek, muscular panther, springs up and pounces on Daddy, an unsuspecting prey. Luke, Mark, and Mary, run to Mama to protect her, or for Mama to protect them. Either way, they huddle close together, crouch around the apple box altar. They hug, cry, moan and groan....soft, heart-wrenching sobs.

With all the gumption Matt can muster, he deals the first blow with his fist and socks Daddy hard in his temple. Give and take, blow for blow, a knock-down, drag-out fist fight erupts. Matt shoves Daddy out the front door. He lands flat on his butt in the red dirt yard. Matt flies, a roaring jet, ignited by fumes of pent up hatred and propelled by raging flames of hostility. He crashes on top of Daddy, his targeted landing strip. Matt wraps his hands, and fastens them securely, around Daddy's neck and squeezes tight, a lion gripping the jugular vein. His grip is tight enough to cut off Daddy's oxygen supply and interrupt his breathing.

Matt taps into a deep reservoir of

power he has never drawn upon before, and it is producing immeasurable strength. With his bare hands he is capable of wiping out Daddy; and bring an end to his cruelty, brutality and barbaric actions. Matt glares at Daddy's face and is drawn immediately to his protruding, bloodshot eyes – paralyzed with terror and fear. The same terror and fear he and the rest of his family have suffered at the hands of his Daddy for umpteen years. Matt slowly and deliberately unlocks his hands. Daddy sputters, gags and finally breathes.

Matt, calm and firm, not batting an eye, stares deeply into Daddy's eyes. "You will never lay your filthy hands on my Mama or any of us again, you sorry, low down, sack of horse shit. Now, get the hell on out of here and don't look back. Don't even think about it. Show your face around any of us, ever, and you will end up in little pieces in that shit house out back where you belong! No, even that's too good for the likes of you," he says clearly and confidently.

The powerful jet rises, spits in the dirt, shifts gears and glides slowly and smoothly back into the house.

Matt scoops me up in his arms, hugs me and gently carries me to Mama, where she and my brothers and sister still hunker together around the apple box altar. "He's gone and will never hurt any of us again," Matt speaks with quiet assurance.

With enormous brown eyes, Mama looks up at her oldest son. Tears float in the pots of her eyes and spill over the rims. She reaches Matt's skinned-up and shaking hands and tugs him to the floor with us. "Thank you, son. I am so proud of you, Matthew," she whispers.

We hold tight to one another, arms entwined. We courageously stop the flow of our salty tears and wipe our noses on the backs of our hands, on sleeves and shirt tails. We breathe slowly and deeply, to still the trembling of our nervous bodies, to quiet the hurling hurricanes in our stormy, shook up minds, and to calm the fast, erratic beating of our hearts.

We cling to our Mama, strong, solid, and steady. Mama is our anchor. Eventually, peace falls like a warm soft blanket over the "Lord's Mission."

This is the first time any of Daddy's children stand up to him, and after seventeen years, it is the last time our entire family lives together under one roof.

My oldest brother, Matt, lies about his age at the United States Army recruiting office so he can join. Then he struts down the street to the Clerk of Court's office in the Courthouse and lies about his age again so he can sign a Petition to commit Daddy to a mental hospital. He swears, under oath, that his Daddy is a danger to himself and others. He requests the court to order Abraham Culler be committed to the state hospital to be evaluated and treated for mental illness. The Order is signed. Daddy is taken into custody by the Sheriff and transported to Broughton State Mental Hospital in Morganton, North Carolina.

Though your father and mother abandoned you
the Lord will take care of you.
Psalms 27:10 NIV

Chapter 5
Circles of Puffed Smoke – No Goodbye Kiss

It is late at night, dark as can be. Mama is in the front seat of a beat up old black Ford, being friendly and flirty with the guy who is driving. "Where are we going?" I ask.

Mama is startled at the sound of my voice, like she had forgotten we were in the back seat or maybe she thought we were asleep. "Ya'll kids are gonna' spend the night with your Grandma. I'll be back to get you tomorrow," she says. We kids, Mary, JJ and I, are sitting in the back seat in our new pajamas which were given to us by the man driving the car. He has the car window on the driver's side rolled down a little. I study him as he lights up and chain smokes cigarettes. Every time he inhales a puff, the ashes on the end of the cigarette glow brighter, then fades when he exhales. He exhales and blows puffs of circular smoke, one circle after another, and sometimes one circle goes through the center of the larger, first circle. He makes cigarette smoking look like it is fun.

He parks in the driveway beside Grandma's house. "Wait in the car, and I'll knock on the door and wake up your Grandma," Mama says as she shuts the car door.

She goes into the house and the man stays in the car with the motor running. He listens to the music on the car radio and continues smoking. I like the music and listen to the words of the songs. The light on the radio dial glows orange like the tip of his burning cigarette. He doesn't talk to us, which suits me fine. He is in his own little world, content to smoke and snap his fingers to the beat of "Sixteen Tons." He drums his long fingers on the steering wheel and sings along with the radio, "This Old House Ain't Got No Shingles."

After a few songs, Mama is back at the car. "It's okay for ya'll to spend the night with your Grandma. So, you girls come on," she says. She lifts JJ off the back seat and out of the car. Mary and I slide out also and Mama closes the car door behind me. The man in the car does not tell us goodbye. Mary and I hold hands while we follow Mama to Grandma's open front door. Mama lays JJ, who is sound asleep, on Grandma's pinkish fabric couch. When I look around I see Mama's back, as she steps out of the front door. She is gone. She didn't tell any of us goodbye, good night, or kiss my foot. No hugs, no kisses – nothin'.

Grandma hurries into the living room with her arms full of quilts, blankets and sheets; she wears her nightgown, blue cotton housecoat, and blue bedroom slippers. I help her make a pallet on the floor for us to sleep on. "Be back, Estie. I'll get pillows for you," Grandma says. She smiles and leaves the room. I admire a beautiful lamp with two pale yellow glass globes; one large globe stacked on top of a smaller globe and sets on an end table beside the couch. Each globe has a gorgeous yellow rose on it. Grandma returns with pillows and playfully tosses one to me and drops the other two on the pallet. She hugs Mary, who is more asleep than awake, and Mary smiles and crawls between the sheets and slides way down under the covers. Grandma plants a kiss on top of my head and hugs me. "Goodnight, Estie. I love you three darlings," she says softly.

"I love you too, Grandma. Goodnight." My whole body, with the exception of my eyes, disappears under the covers. Quietly, I observe my Grandma in the glow of the soft yellow rose globes. Magically she produces two fresh, white, cotton diapers. She double folds them and expertly changes JJ. She holds JJ in her arms and sits down in the corner rocker, which is covered with the brown fur of some sort of animal. Above the rocker, I notice the family photograph of Grandma, Grandpa and their thirteen children. Beside the photo is the Purple Heart Award given to their son, Egbert, who appears in the photo in his Army uniform.

Grandma removes her eyeglasses and places them on the end table. I concentrate on Grandma's wrinkled yet, peaceful face. JJ is asleep in Grandma's arms, and soon she dozes too.

"Grandma?" I call in a quiet voice.

"Yes, Estie, what is it?" Grandma whispers. She reaches for her glasses on the table.

"Will you please lay JJ on the pallet with us? He sleeps on the floor with us most of the time anyway."

"Sure." Grandma stands and lays my little brother on her rocker. She kneels, lifts

JJ in her arms, and scoots on her knees to our pallet. She hugs him to her chest and then slips him into the cozy covers between Mary and me. "Good night, John Joseph," Grandma says. She manages to stand up and to steady herself with the assistance of her rocking chair. Grandma reaches the lamp and turns off a switch and only the light bulb in the top globe clicks off and the globe remains lit in the bottom.

"Good night. Sleep tight." Grandma says.

"Don't let the boogers bite," I say.

Grandma chuckles at my remarks. "Estie, it's don't let the bugs bite – not, don't let the boogers bite. Oh, dear, your brothers taught you to say things the way boys talk. But you, my lady, don't say 'boogers.'" She smiles and leaves the room.

Before I drift off to sleep, I think about the cigarette smoking man and my Mama. I feel sad because Mama did not hug or kiss us goodnight. When Mama comes tomorrow, I bet she'll tell us she is sorry for skedaddling without so much as a hug.

I hope Mama doesn't come back to get us early in the morning, because I am crazy about Grandma. Surely, we can spend the day with her, and maybe I can help her make her chocolate cake.

The white sheet covering us smells of sunshine and fresh cut grass. I feel like a Princess, even on a pallet, on Grandma's living room floor.

Blessed are the merciful, for they will be shown mercy.
Blessed are the pure in heart, for they will see God
Matt. 5: 7, 8 NIV

Chapter 6
A Whole Lot of Hissin' and Pissin' Going On

My Grandma's house, like Grandma herself, is attractive and clean. It is located on the corner of Old Winston Road and Spring Garden Street, in Greensboro, North Carolina. It is outside the city limits, but soon to be annexed into the city and a new Sky King Shopping Center is to be built across the street. Grandpa sometimes walks Mary and me across Old Winston Road, a road heavily traveled by transfer trucks and tankers, to an old country store and filling station. He buys us a soda pop, which is a special treat and doesn't happen often. We have difficulty deciding between Orange Nehi and Grape Nehi. So, I get one flavor, Mary gets the other and we swap the bottles back and forth between us, taking gulps and then try to see who can burp the longest or the loudest. And, after each loud burp, we laugh, burp again and laugh some more. What fun! "Girls, you better not ever let your Grandma hear you burping that way. She would be so disappointed," Grandpa says, smiling all the while.

Compared to the "Lord's Mission," it's a gigantic house, with three floors, which consist of a basement, main floor and upstairs We spend lots of time on the huge wide front porch, in the swing that's been painted green several times too many, or in one of the six wooden rocking chairs, some painted green, others painted white. Shrubs, beautiful old hydrangeas, which we call snowball bushes, bloom with round white blossoms and grow high and spread wide in the rich, dark dirt around the battleship gray porch floor.

Behind the house is Grandpa's barn. It has never been painted and has a dirt floor. So the area is a little bit country, with the city trying to butt right on in.

In the dark basement of Grandma's house hangs a single bare light bulb from a thick black electrical cord in the center of the unfinished ceiling. One side of the concrete wall is lined with shelves, floor to ceiling, neatly stacked with glass canning jars full of homegrown vegetables, pickles, fruit, and homemade jellies and jam, in pint, quart and half gallon sizes. On the backside of the room is a variety of Grandpa's carpentry hand tools. An army surplus cot, which is lumpy, bumpy and gotta' be uncomfortable, is in the front corner. A sheet and blanket are folded neatly and lay on a pillow on the cot.

On the main floor is the living room, Grandma's and Grandpa's bedroom, the dining room (which is not used for eating meals) and the spacious kitchen with black and white twelve inch linoleum tile squares on the floor. The kitchen has had an enormous amount of foot traffic causing some of the black squares to appear gray and worn thin. Some of the edges peel up and tear off – a real accident waiting to happen. I try to count the number of black squares and the number of white squares many times, without success. Trying to do so is impossible without going cross-eyed. In the kitchen's breakfast nook, where we have three hot meals a day, is a round, single pedestal table and chairs made of dark wood. As much as I like the round table and black and white squares, there is nothing I like better than "Tom's" clear, glass cookie jar. This is filled with Oreo cookies and vanilla, chocolate and strawberry sugar wafer cookies and sits way back in the corner of the kitchen counter. The thing is — none of us kids can stretch far enough to reach it. The name Tom is written in red; however, I never know who "Tom" is.

Grandma's house is always warm as toast. Between the dining room and living room is a wide floor furnace covered with a metal grate through which the hot air blows. If I am careless, it can burn the dickens out of my bare feet. In the hall is a wooden hall tree with flowers carved in the corners, connected by curly-ques. Decorative metal hooks are across the top and down both sides, with a mirror in the middle and a bench at the bottom with a hinged top which lifts for storage space. The hooks are burdened down with jackets, coats, aprons and bib overalls.

The stairs in the hallway are wide and lead up to the top floor. There are two good size bedrooms and a bathroom upstairs. One of the bedrooms belongs to an unmarried Uncle David, and the other one belongs to a twelve year old male cousin, Roland, whose parents are dead. Roland is six years older than me and rides the school bus to Lindley Park

Junior High School. For all my comings and goings at Grandma's, I never step a toe into either one of their rooms, which they keep locked, with their very own skeleton keys at all times, regardless if they are in or out of their rooms.

The bathroom has a white claw footed bathtub, with hot and cold running water. Hanging over the edge of the tub, a tiny wire tray holds a used cake of Ivory soap. A white medicine cabinet covered with a mirrored door is securely anchored to the white wall above a four legged white sink.

A black seat on a white commode stays in the up position more than the down. Clean towels have been dried in the sun on the clothesline and drape over two silver towel racks. Four different colors of tooth brushes hang on silver hooks beside the medicine cabinet. All four, red, green, blue and yellow belong to someone. None belong to me.

Outside, on the west side of Grandma's house opposite from Spring Garden Street, are steep gray steps with a white handrail and banisters, leading up to a door. This is the private entrance to an apartment with a living room and kitchen combined into a single, large room. The one bedroom is complete with its private bathroom. Grandma's youngest child,

Aunt Nancy, her husband, Dwight, and their two young sons, Bobby, a cute toddler, only a few months younger than JJ, and Billy, her three month old baby, live in the apartment.

One Saturday morning, Aunt Nancy agrees to let me visit with her in her upstairs apartment, and watch her black and white, fuzzy television, if I will play with Bobby and help her keep an eye on him. Billy is in the bedroom asleep in a white wicker bassinette.

One of her friends, a good head taller, and a slight bit slimmer than Aunt Nancy, brushes her own silky long and wavy, black hair. Her friend chats with me and continues to brush her hair. "Well, hey there, aren't you a cute little whipper snapper? Wow Wee! Your hair is so eye catching – so blond and straight. In fact, I would give my eye-teeth for your blond hair!" she exclaims happily. She runs her brush through my hair.

I don't know what my blond head has to do with her eyes or her teeth, but I say, "Thank you, but I will be glad to keep my blond head and you can keep your eyes and your teeth." I stand awkwardly before her smiling green eyes; I feel shy. I am not a shy sorta' girl; but, the bouncier and bubblier she becomes, the more bashful I feel. In most situations, it is not my nature to withdraw, to turn all timid and tightlipped; however, I lack in social experiences, especially when all the positive attention is focused on me.

"Hi, my name is Puddin' Tame. Ask me again and I'll tell you the same," she chuckles. "What's your name?" she asks

Puzzled, my eyes screw up and I scratch my head. "Huh?" I ask.

"I am just cuttin' up. My name is Gail. Tell me your name."

"My name is Estie."

"Oh, I've heard about you. You are the little girl who has Mrs. Essie's name – Nancy's Mama's name. Ain't that right? Mrs. Essie, is she your Mama too?" She leaves me no time to answer, she answers her own question. "I bet so. Well my goodness! Let me tell you what's the truth! Mrs. Essie is the most sophisticated Southern Lady I have ever had the pleasure of meeting. She is polite and courteous to everyone," Gail says.

"Yes, she's my Mama," without any hesitation, I lie; but, not loud. I keep it quiet, and hope Aunt Nancy doesn't hear me and catch me in a lie. Well, maybe it's not a lie. Who knows? All depends on your definition of a Mama, I rationalize. Umm, let me think, a Mama loves and cares for a child. Yep, that's it. And, in this case, I am no liar. She's my Mama.

Now, I feel a little bit bolder, not as bashful.

"My name is Estie. You say it wrong like most people do. It is like the two letters 'S' and 'T,'" I say, drawing the letters in the air with my finger. "Sometimes people get it wrong, but most times, kids call me 'Essie,' making fun of my name. You know, a lot of kids laugh and call me 'Messy Essie,' or when they are mean as a snake, they make hissin' sounds through their clenched teeth. Like this." I hiss through my front teeth, closing my jaws and barely parting my lips. "Hissss," as I wiggle my arm. "Hissss," I hiss some more. A snake, my hand and arm, is slowly squiggling in the shape of the letter "S." "Then the kids laugh and say 'Listen, listen, Essie's a pissin', listen, listen, Essie's a pissin'. They think they are so smart, but they are simply stupid. 'Cause I love my name, and am darn tootin' glad it's 'Estie.'"

"Oh my goodness, gracious in the morning time," Gail says and begins to laugh. Soon she is cackling like a flock of geese. With both elbows bent and her hands tucked in the depths of her armpits, the goose flops her wings, up and down hawking. I think she is giggling. No, that's not a giggle. She is squawking, a silly goose flying loose. She sticks her hairbrush in the hip pocket of her red pedal pushers. She takes my hands into both of hers, and skips in a circle.

She slows down and tries to compose herself. "You are a whipper snapper, not just a cute whipper snapper, but also a funny whipper snapper," Gail says, still chuckling to herself. "Okay, I get the message. You are Estie, not Essie. Sorry, 'bout that. My mistake. Okay. Tell you what. Why don't I call you 'Sugar Booger?'"

Now, Aunt Nancy stands in the living room, and pulls her bedroom door closed behind her. With so much playful entertainment from Gail, I have forgotten about Aunt Nancy. "What on earth's going on? I step away long enough to change Billy's damp diaper, and to use the bathroom myself and it sounds like ya'll went nuts. What's all this racket about?" Aunt Nancy asks.

"You don't want to know what on earth's going on," Gail says.

"And why, exactly, do I not want to know what on earth's going on? What ya'll been up to?" asks Aunt Nancy.

"Well, it's not funny anymore. So forget it." Gail glances toward me. "Estie. Did you hear me? I pronounced your name correctly. Estie," she gives me a goofy smile. "Anyway, if you really wanna' know, Nancy. Let me put it to you this way. Well, Estie and I are having a pissy good time! Oh, me! Oh, my!" Gail exaggerates and pretends to slap herself in the mouth. "Did I say, we are having a pissy good time?" She slaps her mouth again. "I intended to say, we are having a pissy, oops, I mean hissy good time," she says, laughing.

Before Aunt Nancy can comment, I surprise them both; I clench my teeth and, "hissss." I slither my snaky hand and arm, "hissss."

"Okay, already. Don't start that again. You may scare little Bobby or wake the baby," Aunt Nancy says, and she sounds perturbed.

Gail snatches her brush from her pocket and again begins to brush her own hair.

"Okay, already!" Aunt Nancy snaps and raises her voice a tad. "You can stop primping any time now. Gail, you promised to set my hair with this Toni Home Permanent." She holds a packaged box in her hands.

Gail lifts the Toni box from Aunt Nancy's hand, and reads the instructions as she sets the chemicals and curling rods on the kitchen counter.

"Aunt Nancy, I am sorry. I can see you two are talking, but you promised I could watch television. I want to see "Howdy Doody" and I am sure Bobby would like to see it too," I say.

"Well sit there on the floor with him

and I will turn it on," she says. She mashes the button and fiddles with the rabbit ears. I sit down beside Bobby and stare at the television while a white line flickers across the screen. I wait patiently for the television to warm up.

Aunt Nancy sits on a kitchen chair in front of the sink. Gail stands behind her. On the floor, I roll a soft rubber ball to Bobby and watch the television screen which is snowy, blurry, and fuzzy. For all the good it is doing, it might as well be turned off.

Gail, I think is the funniest person in the world, even funnier than Clarabell, the clown.

Laughing with Gail reminds me of Luke and the times he made me laugh with goofy faces and outlandish weird sounds. I miss him and the way he paid attention to me. He enjoyed laughing and making me laugh so much. It was important to him. Luke's purpose for being was solely to make me laugh every chance he got, and he successfully accomplished his purpose.

When Luke taught me the skill of skipping, out on the sometimes mushy muddy, sometimes dried caked and other times dusty, loose dirt road (whatever the condition, it was always red) I often fell on my face. And before I cried out in pain, or even noticed my scraped, bloody shin, Luke was pulling me back up to my feet. "You're alright. You're a big girl," he said. Then, "Looky, Estie. Look at my face. Do you know I am a monkey? Looky. Looky." I looked at Luke and I saw the face of a monkey. His bottom lip was rolled down and inside out, while his tongue was curled up and over his top lip. Both of his eyes were fixed to the tip of his nose, and he pulled at his ears with both hands. Then he took my hand. "Come, Estie. Let's skip away to the moon." I didn't budge. So he hunched over and humped his shoulders, spread his feet apart, bent his knees and squatted slightly. He let go of my hand. He stayed in his stooped baboon position and he bounced up and down, with the ease of a springy slinky; and he scratched his body with both hands. With squatty baby steps, he turned in circles in front of me. His mouth was closed, but I heard muffled, grunting sounds from his fat monkey lips. The holes of his nose were flared wide.

Luke was a living, breathing, jumping, scratching baboon. With his next turn, he faced away from me and his squatty backside toward me. I smiled. I think what a silly brother I have. Then the monkey scratched his butt. My mouth flew open wide and I laughed and laughed. Luke was not only entertaining;

he was plumb hilarious, even more so when he wanted to cheer me up. However, I am aware of more than the laughter; I see Luke's determination. He meant for me to laugh and he stopped short of nothing until he heard me laugh.

I remember Luke took my hand, "Okay, little sister, let's go. You are a good skipper," he said and there we went, my shin stinging and feet skipping.

"Skip, skip, skip to my lou. Skip, skip, skip to my lou.
Skip, skip, skip to my lou. Skip to my lou, my sister."

"Hey, Sugar Booger, what ya' a skippin' and a singin' 'bout over there? Let me in on it and I'll sing too," Gail says. She smiles at me; her lips spread across her face and her green eyes dance and sparkle. Gail's voice brings me back to the here and now.

"What's that awful smell? Shoowee! It stinks." I look at Bobby and check him over good. "It's not Bobby and it's not me. What is it?" I ask. I pinch my nose between my thumb and finger. "Shoowee!"

Gail thinks my comments are funny and Aunt Nancy does not. Gail giggles. Aunt

Nancy is holding a thin yellow and white striped towel close to her eyes with one hand and her other hand holds the rest of the wadded up towel tightly to her nose.

"I told you to hurry and get this stinky stuff off my hair. Now, I'm begging. Please, please, please, get this sewage off my hair! Pleeeease," she whines.

"Stop your whining and bellyaching. I told you before and this is the last time I'm gonna' tell you. The perm solution stinks and there's nothing either of us can do about the odor. Now, grow up and shut up! You're not a baby and I don't want to hear you fussin' any more. You hear me?" Gail asks. From the sound of her voice, I can tell Gail has just about had it.

"Well, for the love of God in heaven, and all the poor children on this earth, will you please tell me how much longer this stinking, rotten shit has to be dripping in my face?" Aunt Nancy yells. Now, from the sound of her voice, it is obvious Aunt Nancy ain't gonna' last much longer with shit on her head.

"Nancy, don't you ask me that again. I am sick and tired of hearing you complain. Whine, fuss, or complain and I'm out the door," Gail says.

"You wouldn't dare!" Aunt Nancy

cries. Her short blond hair is wrapped around curling rods, and soaked in the foul smelling permanent solution.

"If you don't believe me, just try it," Gail warns. "Yeah, try it, and watch me! You'll see!"

This is exciting. I watch them. No telling what's gonna' happen between these two. Gail musta' made a believer out of Aunt Nancy, because she is quiet and asks no more questions. In fact, she doesn't utter a word. She hides her face in the folds of the towel. When I think things are quiet, and rather boring, I hear water running from the faucet.

"Hey, Sugar Booger, listen to the water. Listen, sounds like it is hissing. Listen. Listen. Hear the hissin'. Someone must be pissin'," she says and we both crack up laughing.

"You remind me of my brother, Luke," I say.

"Well, that's a horrible thing to say to me. I'm a girl," Gail pouts.

"Oh, you know what I mean!" I say.

"Well, for your information, Sugar Booger, I am a girl with long wavy hair. No brother of yours can look like me, and I don't need to put stinky sewage on my hair. See my waves," Gail says. She flaunts her long wavy hair as she spins like a ballerina.

"No, of course not. You're really fun. I didn't say you remind me of my brother because I think you look like a boy. No, not at all. My brother, Luke, always makes me laugh. Gail, you make me laugh too," I explain.

"Oh I see, that is a sweet thing to say to me, Sugar Booger," Gail smiles again with her lips, eyes and entire happy face.

"Okay, already," Aunt Nancy snaps. "The water is running. Hop to it and get this stinking sh… uh, stinky, uh, you know what, off my hair right now," she demands. She whips the wet towel from her face and holds onto a corner of it, she spins it fast in circles a few times and then quickly she slaps the loose end of it on the countertop, causing a loud pop. The pop startles me and it causes Bobby to scream and then cry. "I sure hope you're happy now, look what you caused!" Aunt Nancy shouts. "You've made Bobby cry."

"You, popping that towel, and no one else scared your Bobby and that's why he is crying. And, as I've said……" Gail yanks her pocketbook off the kitchen table, and once again her happy smile lands on my face. She looks me in my eyes – eyeball to eyeball, oval gems, flashy and green (like the jewels on Grandma's shiny emerald ear bobs) to round buttons, slick and brown (like the ones on

Grandpa's heavy winter Sunday coat).

"So long, Sugar Booger and thanks for the fun. I am sure your brother, Luke, misses you too. He's a lucky guy to have you for a sister. Everyone oughta' be glad to have you as family, Sugar Booger," Gail says.

"You better not let my Mama hear you calling her that. She doesn't allow talk like that in her house," Aunt Nancy warns.

Gail turns to face Aunt Nancy and calmly says, "I'm outta' here." She opens the door and quietly closes it behind her.

Shock and surprise registers on Aunt Nancy's face, and more than likely on mine also. I play "peek-a-boo" with Bobby, and he finally stops crying.

"Well, some friend she is! She ups and goes, leaving this nasty stinking shit on my hair. Essie, you may as well leave too," she says.

"You know my name is Estie, not Essie," I say.

"I can call you anything I want to. Besides, my Mama's name is Estie, and, as far as I'm concerned, she is the one and only Estie. I don't care a flying flip who you are. You're not good enough to have my Mama's name. So leave now, Essie," Aunt Nancy says. Mad as a hornet, she sounds as if she is about to cry.

"Suits me, and I'm outta' here too. You

can mispronounce my name or poke fun at it, like most children do. It's alright with me. I'm kinda' used to it. Like you said, Aunt Nancy, 'I don't care a flying flip' what name you call me. I am Estie and Estie is outta' here."

I slam the door behind me and run down the steps two at a time. At the bottom step, I turn and run behind the crepe myrtle tree and sit in the sand. I wonder which Grandma would dislike the most: Gail calling me a "Sugar Booger" or her own daughter calling that stinking stuff "shit."

She speaks with wisdom and faithful instruction
is on her tongue.
She watches over the affairs of her household
and does not eat the bread of idleness.
Women do noble things, but you surpass them all.
Proverbs 31:26-27, 29 NIV

Chapter 7
Butter Bean Up My Nose

I love my Grandma! Her name is Estie Culler, same as mine. She smells and looks squeaky clean with the fragrance of Prell shampoo, Ivory soap, and Juicy Fruit chewing gum. She files her fingernails in an oval curve and shines them with clear polish. Little, white half moons rise at the base of each nail. Grandma twines her long, white hair into a single braid which hangs down the middle of her slim back, and extends way beyond her waist. She coils the braid into a neat, round bun using a few bobby pins to secure the bun at the nape of her neck. She then slides a decorative, tortoise shell comb on each side of the bun to hold it in place. My Grandma is beautiful and smart. Her eyes are Carolina blue, and hold tremendous wisdom. Her expressions are pleasant, happy and confident. She smiles and sings a lot.

Grandma dresses as proper every day as she does on Sunday, with a crisp, clean dress, stockings and matching pumps – some lace up, some slip on. She begins the day with a necklace, her watch and a pair of clip-on ear bobs, which pinch and are soon removed and placed on the window sill above the double white kitchen sink. She dabs on a smidgen of light pink lipstick and uses compact powder on her face. Around the house, she wears one of her clean, ironed and starched homemade aprons tied around her waist. She appears dressed up to me, because my Mama wore work clothes: denim pants and shirt or a plain cotton dress, no make-up and no jewelry.

On Saturdays, Grandma works all day as she does every other day. In addition to all her regular chores, she bakes from scratch a yellow cake with chocolate icing and allows JJ, Mary and me to scrape the mixing bowl clean

and lick the wooden spoon. Scrumptious!
Grandma washes clothes while the cake bakes.
I help her hang the clothes on the line to dry,
by handing her clothespins from a hand woven
straw basket. I help her snap and string green
beans and shell peas and butter beans.

While the laundry dries, Grandma and
I take the city bus to the A & P grocery store.
The bus, which happens to make its last stop
in front of Grandma's house, is full and we sit
close to the back near where the colored ladies
sit. I wave at the colored ladies sitting behind
us and they wink or shyly wave back to me.
They sparkle from their white Colgate teeth
right down to their spit shined shoes.

"Grandma, why do the colored people
sit in the back seat?" I ask.

Before Grandma can answer the
question, a grumpy old lady with a sourpuss
face and a mustache on her upper lip, sitting
across the aisle from me replies, "Do you not
know?" she asks. "It's because they are dirty."

"No, they are not," Grandma says, in a
firm voice.

"Sure they are. See how black they are.
They are so dirty the black won't wash off.
They will not come clean," she insists.

"They are spic-and-span, clean as a
whistle," Grandma says. "Estie, pay her no

mind."

The sourpuss shrugs her shoulders, fiddles with her pocketbook and sticks her nose up in the air, "Well, I never," she says.

"Estie Irene," I know to listen up when Grandma calls me by my first and middle names, because what she is about to say is important; it's a life's lesson she wants me to remember or a principle she wants me to live by.

"Estie, outward appearance means diddly squat, zilch, absolutely and positively nothing. Beauty is all in the heart. Yes, Estie Irene, God looks into the heart. What's in the heart is all that matters. You keep your heart clean and pure; it brings a smile to God's face and that is the important thing – not the color of your skin. Estie Irene, you have brown eyes and mine are blue. Both brown and blue are good. Neither one is better or worse. All people, God's children, are the same, regardless of skin color. All are good. All are equal. Always remember that," Grandma says.

"Yes, Ma-am, I'll remember," I reply.

"And the fact is changes are coming. Yes, changes are coming. Soon everyone will sit anywhere they want on the bus. Real soon," Grandma says.

At the next stop, one of the spic-and-span ladies walks by me on her way to the door.

"Hey, my Grandma says you and me can sit together real soon," I say.

She smiles. "I sho' hope that be's da truth," she whispers. "Law, yes, I do, Sweet Jesus, I sho' do, I sho' do," she says as she steps off the bus.

We exit the bus at the A & P grocery store. After buying a few groceries, Tide laundry detergent, two cans of sliced peaches, a loaf of white Merita bread, a dozen eggs, a can of Carnation milk and a pound of butter, Grandma collects her S & H Green Stamps. We then walk next door to the Guilford Dairy Ice Cream Bar. This is the same Guilford Dairy Company which has delivery trucks driven by men dressed in brown uniforms. They deliver fresh milk in clear glass bottles with round cardboard lids to Grandma's front porch.

We enter the dairy bar. Metal bar stools with red plastic covered seats are lined up at a white Formica counter. Small, wrought iron, red topped tables with matching wrought iron chairs are scattered around the room. Grandma and I sit at one of these tables; she orders herself a scoop of vanilla ice cream and a Coke float for me.

On Saturday evening after Grandma washes her hair, she sits on her low vanity chair which she places close to the floor furnace. With brush and mirror in her hands, her heap of long, white, wet hair loosely hangs over one shoulder clear down to her waist. "Estie, you want to brush the tangles out of my hair?" she asks.

"Oh, yes, sure I do," I answer. She hands me her hairbrush.

Grandma looks at my reflection in her hand held mirror. "Estie, take that worried look off your face. Everything will be okay. I'm sure your Mama is coming back real soon and you always have a home with me, as long as you need it. Remember, we are two peas in a pod." Grandma does her best to reassure me and I smile at her in the mirror. I love my Grandma; however, I am sure she doesn't know if or when Mama will ever return.

The sleep-over at Grandma's house lasts too many nights, and it's more nights than Grandma can handle. Her health declines, but she doesn't complain.

When my aunts, first one and then another, come by to visit Grandma, I hear them discuss different scenarios concerning where JJ, Mary and I can live. They talk about sending us to live at the Methodist Children's Home in Winston-Salem or the Baptist

Orphanage in Thomasville, whichever is the first to have available space. Grandma has our names added to the waiting lists.

I hide beside the refrigerator and I listen to Grandma and Aunt Nancy talk softly at the kitchen table. The softer people talk around Grandma's house, the harder I listen.

Grandma says, "Abraham will never agree to Estie, Mary, and John Joseph being adopted."

"Maybe he would let them be adopted by Preacher Cumbo and his wife, Vera, if they would take all three of the kids," Aunt Nancy says.

With my hand in my pocket, I find a hulled butter bean. I roll it over and over between my thumb and my fingers. I strain hard to hear every word and the things they are saying make me feel nervous and scared.

"Well, it would also help if Preacher Cumbo and Vera would agree not to change their names. They have already said they would like to adopt Mary and John Joseph. They really don't want to adopt Estie because she is older and remembers more. They said if they decide to adopt Estie, they would want to change her name to Esther, so it would be a biblical name like Mary and John Joseph. I don't think Abraham would like that and I wouldn't either.

Estie is my namesake."

My goodness, I don't know how it happens, but the butter bean is stuck up my nose. I slide down the wall and sit on the floor to better position myself to dig the butter bean out of my nose. I am afraid it will be there forever and it might start stinking or it might start sprouting. I panic; no one will ever want to have anything to do with me.

Sitting beside the refrigerator reminds me of Luke and a song he taught me:

Lulu had a tugboat, Tugboat had a bell
Lulu went to Heaven, Tugboat went to hel-lo
Operator give me number nine, If you disconnect me
I will kick you right behind the refrigerator, There was
a piece of glass
Lula fell upon it and cut her little, ask me no more
questions;
I'll tell you no more lies. This is what Lula said, just
before she died

"I would be glad for one of the kids to stay with Dwight and me, if I didn't already have two younguns of my own. Maybe Teresa and Curt could keep Mary since their daughter, Dreama, is about the same age," Aunt Nancy says.

"I'll check with Ronnie and Geraldine

to see if JJ can stay with them until something else can be worked out," Grandma says.

I am breathing fast – short, shallow breaths through my mouth because there is a bean sprout growing out of my nose. My rapid breathing turns into crying, coughing and gagging, which causes Grandma and Aunt Nancy to stop their conversation. I hear their chairs slide on the floor as they rush to check out the commotion.

"Estie, honey, what's wrong?" Grandma asks.

"I have butter beans growing out of my nose," I say, crying.

Grandma kneels on the floor beside me. "There are no butter beans growing out of your nose. Take your finger out of your nose. That is what is making it hard for you to breathe," she says as she hands me a delicate handkerchief from her apron pocket. I blow my nose into her handkerchief and the bean shoots out of my nose. Grandma wraps her arms around me and holds me tight against her chest.

"Grandma, I want to live with you. I don't want to go anywhere else."

"Estie, don't worry your little noggin. You will always be with me. I'm not letting you go anywhere. We are two peas in a pod."

I show Grandma the slimy butter bean in her handkerchief.

"My goodness, you do have beans growing in your nose…" We both burst out laughing.

*For to one is given, by the Spirit the word of
wisdom….To another the working of miracles….
I Corinthians 12:8, 10 KJV*

Chapter 8
Hair of Angels and Snow in a Can

I toss icicles – long strands of shiny silver foil
– in a happy-go-lucky, haphazardly way on the
cedar tree, which Grandpa has set up in the
corner of the living room. Grandma smiles
and sometimes laughs, as she places the icicles
in an orderly manner. We string the tree with
colorful Christmas lights, and strands of candle
shape bubble lights. We use little homemade
wire hooks to hang decorative plastic balls and
ornaments of all colors on the branches of
the tree. Grandma carries in a chair from the
kitchen. I stand on it; stretch to the highest

branch I can reach and hang a crystal clear glass star.

The tree is gorgeous and surely to goodness, nothing else can be added to enhance its beauty. Then, Grandma lifts a plastic bag out of a larger Woolworth's paper sack. "Estie, you'll have to sit on the couch and watch me now. This," she pulls out a wad of whitish, pinkish stuff, which appears to be as soft as cotton, "is angel hair," she says.

"The angel hair is beautiful, Grandma," I say, and reach my hands right in there with hers.

"No. Estie, go sit on the couch and keep your hands away because this will cut your fingers all to shreds, if you let it."

"Well, Grandma, I won't let it! I won't let it cut me! Why would it cut my fingers, but not yours?" I ask.

"I am careful Estie, I will not let it cut mine," Grandma says. She plugs in the lights and then gently but quickly spreads the angel hair on the green cedar and over the bright color lights.

"I promise I won't let it cut my fingers either. Anyway, I don't believe angel hair can cut. It's so soft. It's not the devil's pointed tongue or sharp pitchfork tail. It's angel hair!"

Grandma's hands, full of angel hair,

stops the wavy movements. She smiles at me and tries real hard not to laugh. She can't control herself and burst out loud laughing. Not sure what's so funny, I giggle also.

"Estie, honey, where did you ever hear tell of the devil's pointed tongue – or his pitchfork tail – for that matter?" She can barely talk because she laughs so hard. She wipes the tears of laughter forming in the corner of her eyes. She notices my confusion, and hugs me. "Oh, dear, honey, I'm not laughing at you. But, do you think this stuff is angels' hair? You really believe its hair that's been cut off an angel's head?" she asks.

"That is exactly what you said Grandma. You called it angel hair. What am I supposed to think?" I ask. She doesn't answer, only laughs a little more. "Well, any old way, I know angel hair can't cut my fingers," I say.

"Estie, this, uh, well, uh, the angel hair ……" she begins, but she still giggles and she tries to stop by biting her upper lip.

"Grandma, where in the world did you ever get angel hair anyway? And if you tell me it came from Woolworth's Five and Ten Cents Store, I'll know you are only kiddin' me," I say.

"Well, Estie, guess what? It did come from the dime store and it's only called angel hair. It is not really the hair of angels. Estie, its spun glass – thin and fine – and it is as sharp as the devil's tongue and tail. It's not angel hair or any other kind of hair. It's spun glass and believe me, it can cut you," Grandma explains. I am still more than a little confused. She keeps laughing, but her laughter is softer and she continues to spread the spun glass (why didn't she call it that in the first place?) over the tree. The bright glow of the lights and the soft glow of the bubble lights are elegant underneath the swirly waves of the stuff from Woolworths.

Our tree is gorgeous! I realize it is the first decorated Christmas tree that I remember ever seeing. "Grandma, this is the only Christmas tree I've ever seen! Nothing in the world could be more beautiful! Thank you! Thank you for letting me help you decorate it. It's been so much fun."

"Well, Estie, being with you is always fun. The tree has to be the prettiest you've ever seen, since it's the only one you've seen. But, I am sure you will see more Christmas trees, larger and more beautiful than this. You're young and I hope you and I can decorate many more Christmas trees together. Besides you're my helper. I just couldn't do it without you. Now, I have something else for you to try your hand at," Grandma says. She hands me a can. "How would you like to spray snow on the glass of the front door?" she asks.

"Yes, sure, but how does it work?" I ask.

"Push the button on top and point it toward the glass and snow will spray out of the nozzle," she says.

On the front porch, I spray snow on the glass of the double French doors. Amazing! My Grandma is a magician. Lights that bubble, angel hair and now snow packed in a spray can! It's magical! I am proud of myself for spraying snow all by myself. I stand on a chair to reach the top corners.

I finish, go back inside with an empty can and find Grandma in the dining room. She has a box on the table which has little figurines; each individually wrapped in a piece of old newspaper. "Estie, would you like to place these on the buffet? It is a nativity scene set," she explains.

Now, I truly marvel and exclaim, "You think of everything, Grandma!"

"I would never forget to display these. It's the whole reason we have Christmas – to celebrate Jesus' birthday. We would never leave baby Jesus out of Christmas. It wouldn't be Christmas without the Christ child," she says.

She points to the long, dark wood buffet. "This is the best place in the house to display the nativity. I think you can handle this job, while I clean up and store these boxes away."

"Okay." Even though each figurine is made of plastic and cannot possibly break, I carefully place the donkey and cows together, outside the cardboard stable, which I put in the center of the buffet. I place three wise men, each carries a gift, beside three camels. I arrange two shepherds, both hold a long staff, and all the sheep rest at their feet, on the other side of the stable. I place the plastic baby Jesus in the front center; he's on real straw and wrapped in a silky purple cloth. I group Mary and Joseph close on either side of the baby Jesus. I stand back and look at the scene. I move a sheep slightly closer to a shepherd and I move Mary closer to Jesus. Now that's exactly right.

"Grandma, look! What do you think? Does it look okay or should I change it around anymore?" I ask.

Studying the nativity scene with her wise eyes, Grandma says one word, "perfect." She hangs her arm around my shoulder. "Perfect," she says again.

"Grandma, I have a question," I say.

"Sure, honey, ask."

"Well, my sister is Mary and my baby brother, JJ, is John Joseph. They each have the names of Jesus' mama and daddy, Mary and Joseph. I wonder why you and I didn't get a name from the Bible too. Do you wonder why Estie is not in the Bible?" I ask.

"No, I've never wondered why, but I don't have a brother named Joseph or a sister named Mary. I only have one brother and his name is Hoyt and that's not a biblical name either," Grandma says.

"You only have one brother, my goodness. I have four. Be glad Hoyt's not a biblical name. At least it's not 'Shad rack, Me shack or Obedigo,'" I say and laugh at myself because I can't pronounce their names correctly. "I like their first names; they are from the Bible too – Matthew, Mark, Luke and John."

"I have six sisters and none of their names are from the Bible. Let's see. I'm the oldest, Estie, then there's Zora, Neva, Addie, Carrie, Grace and Louvinia," she says.

"Their names may not be in the Bible but they are odd names. Can you say them again?" I ask.

"Yes, Zora, Neva, Addie, Hoyt, Carrie, Grace and Louvinia," she repeats the names.

"Grandma, Grace is a name in the Bible," I say.

"Well, the word 'grace' is in the Bible but it's no one's name, and anyway, how do you know so much about the Bible?"

"Daddy reads the Bible all the time and he 'preaches' it to us non-stop."

"Do you mean to say that your Daddy 'teaches' it to you?"

"No ma-am, he preaches it to us and Grace is the woman who saves us from all our sins."

"Grace is no woman," Grandma says.

"The Bible says, 'for it is by Grace we are saved and she washes us and cleans us from all unrighteous stuff," I say.

"God's grace washes and cleans us and God's grace is well, uh, well, it's grace – what we don't deserve, but God gives it to us anyway. It may be confusing to you and to me, somewhat, but nevertheless grace is amazing. And whatever it is – it is no woman!" Grandma says kinda' frustrated. "Anyway…"

"Well, my goodness. I'm sorry you only have one brother, but I ain't gonna' give you any of mine; even though I can't pronounce their middle names – Shad rack, Me shack, and Obedigo, and of course John Joseph. That's an easy one to say, but I like to call him JJ. And, I'm glad we call Matthew, Mark and Luke by their first names," I say.

"Yes," Grandma smiles. "I guess it is a little odd to have so many Bible names in one family. Your Daddy's name, Abraham, is in the Bible too. Naming him Abraham was my idea. It's a good strong name. Maybe that's why he wanted you children to have biblical names."

"Why isn't 'Estie' a name from the Bible?" I ask.

"You're not to worry about 'Estie' not being in the Bible, because it doesn't matter. What matters is one day both of us 'Esties' will be in Heaven with Jesus, the Christ child. You are special! You have my name. I am so proud of you, Estie. Don't forget wherever we are, we are both 'Estie,' and we will always be connected by our names." She picks up a string of gold ribbon lying among the decoration boxes. She holds one end of the ribbon to her chest and the other end to mine. "We have a gold ribbon tying our hearts together," Grandma says. She smiles sweetly into my eyes and then squeezes me with a warm hug. "I have thirty-one grandchildren and I love every one of them; however, honey, you are my only 'Estie,'" she says. I feel the gold ribbon tying our hearts together tightly.

I am special. I am loved.

Grandma is all a twitter! Her house is jam packed with all her children, exceptin' my Daddy, and like my Mama, his whereabouts are unknown to me. I really don't think about it enough to care one way or the other.

I have more uncles, aunts and cousins than I ever dreamed possible. They scurry around the living room and dining room, bumping into each other – like dumb sheep. They try to make their way to the kitchen, where Grandma serves delicious food to eat. They appear to be caught up in a game of "follow the leader," without the leader. They herd into Grandma's house from far and near. Miami, Florida, where Uncle Warren and Aunt Janet live is the farthest away and Uncle David, who still makes Grandma's house his very own, comes down from his upstairs bedroom.

I perch myself on a foot stool beside the Christmas tree, and I scoot it even closer to the tree. At some time or another, I see everyone, as they stream by the tree, look at it and place gifts of all sizes and shapes and wrapped in paper of Christmas colors – red, green, white and gold. They inspect the gifts and search for their own name, but they don't notice me. I smile up at each one of them. I hear a few compliments, "Mama decorated a pretty tree this year, ahhh, it's beautiful!" Some say nothing at all.

"It is not a pretty tree, only a regular old cedar tree. I helped Grandma. She and I decorated it and now the regular cedar tree is our beautiful Christmas tree," I mumble and no one hears me. They stroll by, drop their gifts, hug someone behind them and move on by, without a glance in my direction.

"Don't touch that stuff on the tree. It's being out-lawed because it's dangerous," an older boy whispers to a younger girl as he grabs her hand. "It's angel hair and it will prick your fingers and cut your hands," he says.

"It will only cut your hand if you 'let it.' Me and Grandma didn't 'let it' cut our fingers or hands," I say.

The older boy scowls at me for a second and then points his nose toward the top of the tree. "If you helped Grandma with this tree, that explains the crooked star hanging there. It's not nearly close enough to the top of the tree," he says sarcastically.

"Mama's trees are always beautiful. Even when I was a little girl, I would watch her turn an ordinary tree into a marvelous thing of beauty," a gorgeous lady with curly, black hair says to a handsome man, who puts presents under the tree. I notice he has tight arm muscles.

"I didn't have to just watch, I hung ornaments and icicles. I am Estie. I am Grandma's helper. We are two peas in a pod,"

I say, and they pay me no mind. "Yeah, we are two peas in a pod and a gold ribbon ties our hearts together!" Trying to talk to them did no good; they are gone without so much as a smile, not even a nod.

God sets the lonely in families…
Psalms 68:6 NIV

Chapter 9
All Alone in a Crowded House

My uncles and aunts shop at the Sears and Roebuck Store and purchase Grandma an automatic washing machine. A couple of uncles lay new linoleum on the kitchen floor. Off with the old black and white squares that I have hopped on, jumped on and tried to count a zillion times. They replace it with a roll of linoleum which has all different colors of specks – like paint drops on the floor. Uncle Warren hangs new wallpaper in the dining room.

On Christmas Eve, my uncles and aunts exchange gifts with their Pollyannas; this reveals the person's name they had secretly drawn from a hat last Christmas. Supposedly they have kept the name a secret since then, but I doubt any of them, especially the aunts, who talk a lot, have ever kept anything a secret. They open their gifts and act surprised. They swap gifts of warm clothing, electric mixers, electric razors and electric blankets. Aunt Nancy receives the oddest present, an electric hair dryer with a plastic pink bonnet to cover her wet hair and blow it dry.

My cousins, some of whom I am only beginning to learn their names, open one present each: Shelley, a pair of roller skates with a key; Olivia, a pogo stick; Dreama, a huge stuffed pink poodle with a lavender bow tied around its' neck. For the boys, there are footballs, baseball bats, ball gloves and model cars, puzzles, and a couple of chemistry sets. Wrapping paper, packing paper and curly ribbon are scattered about the living room, dining room and kitchen; lots of commotion, happy banter and laughter going on at Grandma's house.

JJ finds me on the floor and puts his head on my lap to muffle his crying. That's when I realize JJ, Mary, and I did not receive one single gift from anyone. I comfort JJ and rub my hands through his damp hair. Before

I become too upset because everyone neglects us, here comes Grandma to the rescue. She quickly hands JJ and me a gift and whispers "Merry Christmas." She seeks out Mary and gives her a gift too. JJ wipes his eyes and opens his gift, a "jack in the box." It frightens him and he cries even more than not having a gift at all. I wind up "jack" and show JJ how "jack" pops out of the box and plays music; pacifying him, hoping to make him stop crying. Mary and I receive a coloring book each and a box of new crayons. There are twenty-four color crayons and none of them are broken. "You and Mary will have to share with each other," Grandma says. I didn't ask how we could share crayons, or anything else, with each other since Mary lives with Uncle Tom and Aunt Jean. Maybe this means Mary and JJ, who lives with Uncle Jack and Aunt Sarah, are coming back to Grandma's house. I hope so, because I miss them.

In Grandma's crowded living room, full of family, I am alone. I feel so lonely and out of place. Mary, JJ and I have each other, but no one has us. Where are Matt, Mark and Luke? Does anyone give them a Christmas gift? I remember our last Christmas, how Mama had enjoyed cooking a delicious meal for us. We, my parents, brothers, Mary and I, had each other then; we belonged to one another, which means more to me than anything, even pogo sticks and pink poodles.

Everyone gathers to fill their plates and to eat in the kitchen and in the dining room; the kids sit on the stair steps in the hallway, or anywhere they can find a seat. I lose my appetite. I wander out the front door, knowing no one will miss me. Slowly I walk around back of the house and open the large door on Grandpa's barn.

I have been in the barn a couple of times before. Grandpa showed me where he stored the raw peanuts from his garden. He keeps some in an old black metal foot locker. I open the locker and help myself to a handful. I sit on the loose dirt floor, and shell a few raw peanuts and hold them in my hand. I think of my Mama and my brothers. I even allow myself a minute to think of my Daddy. What makes him so loco? His entire family loves each other, laughs a lot. They pick, joke, and have fun. None of them are lazy nor idle away time memorizing the Bible constantly. They all work hard and love their children.

I struggle with the mixed thoughts and feelings I have toward my Mama and my Daddy. I want to see Mama and especially my brothers so badly. When I ask Grandma where my Mama is, Grandma tells me the truth. "I don't know where your Mama is or when she will come back around, but your Mama will be back. Mark my word on it. I'm sure she misses you too. I don't know when, but I am sure she'll be back," Grandma says.

Matt has been to visit Mary, JJ and me at Grandma's house and he tells us he has to report to Fort Bragg Army Base in Fayetteville, NC to learn how to be a good soldier. With his huge brown eyes, he reminds me of Johnny Cash except now he has a buzz haircut and an Army uniform. I am so proud of him and love him enormously.

Matt and Grandma whisper between themselves and I strain to hear, and I do snatch bits and pieces of their conversation. I can hear and can understand some of the words and those words baffle me and jab me square in the center of my heart. "Mama has gone and I don't know where she is… Mark and Luke are in Jackson Training School (which sounds like a good place to me, like a college, or boarding school)…. Daddy, dangerous to himself and others, is in the hospital." Matt and Grandma share their news with each other. I am bewildered and confused by what it all means. I fear not knowing the details, yet, I'm not sure if I want to know.

When Mama abandoned JJ, Mary, and me at Grandma's, she also left Matt, Mark and Luke with nobody; sixteen, fourteen and thirteen years old to fend for themselves. That is plainly what they do, by shoplifting, truancy, vandalism, vagrancy, and automobile theft. I defend them and justify their actions. Shoplifting – they are hungry, in need of food, a basic necessity of life. Truancy, well, who wants to go to school, if there is no one to make you? Besides, who feels up to attending school after sleeping in unlocked cars, (which makes them vagrants)? Cops get after them. They have no where to go – what can they do? Steal a car and get the hell out of Dodge? These are the self survival crimes that land Mark and Luke in Juvenile Court and then in the custody of the Jackson Training School and Detention Center near Concord, North Carolina.

Alone in the barn, no one comes looking for me, which only reinforces my loneliness. I strain my brain and squeeze my eyes tight to visualize Matt, Mark and Luke; to recall their faces, and to hear the chatter of their voices and their spontaneous laughter. And there before my eyes they appear. "Come on Estie. Stand up straight," Mark says.

"We need you to help us. It's Christmas!"

Matt says, and they all giggle.

Luke grabs my hand and pulls me to my feet. "Estie, let's recite the Christmas story. You know the one in Luke, my book." Luke smiles at me.

Tears stream down my face as my brothers and I recite, ever so softly, the story of the birth of Jesus from the Gospel of Luke.

And there were in the same country shepherds abiding in the field, keeping watch over their flocks by night. And, lo, the angel of the Lord came upon them, and the glory of the Lord shown round about them; and they were sore afraid. And the angel said unto them, 'Fear not; for, behold, I bring you good tidings of great joy, which shall be to all people. For unto you is born this day in the city of David a Savior, which is Christ the Lord. And this shall be a sign unto you; Ye shall find the babe wrapped in swaddling clothes, lying in a manger.' And suddenly there was with the angel a multitude of the heavenly host praising God, and saying, 'Glory to God in the highest, and on earth peace, good will toward men,'
we quote.

Wouldn't Daddy be proud as a peacock? His children quote the Christmas story from the Bible, and he doesn't coach or force us.

I smile and swipe the backs of my

hands on my face and wipe my eyes with the palms to remove my tears. The peanuts aren't in my hand anymore. Luke must have them in his. When I open my eyes, I stand alone. I saw my brothers' faces, heard their voices and their giggles. Now they are gone. I am alone again, and so sad.

But, what a miraculous Christmas gift! One I treasure.

I slip out of Grandpa's barn, closing the door quietly behind me. Glancing up to latch the door, my eyes are drawn to the dark sky; three shooting stars glimmer and shimmer across the heavens. I catch my breath. "I love you too," I whisper to all three of them.

A good name is more desirable than great riches.
Proverbs 22:1 NIV

Chapter 10
A Little White Lie and It Breaks Two Hearts

At Grandma's house, we often attend Manley Avenue Baptist Church, which is only a hop, skip and jump down Spring Garden Street to the right on (you guessed it) Manley Avenue. It is a small, white, cinder block church. It has an outdoor bathroom, and even though it is church property, it's still a john and stinks like one. I wonder why Grandma has a clean white bathroom and this church has a nasty outdoor john. Toilet paper is available, not Sears and Roebuck catalogs, for wiping things up. The roll of toilet paper hangs on a nail poked into the wall. Beside the stinky john is a recently built picnic shelter for church dinners. Now why they chose to build a picnic shelter before having clean restrooms is a mystery to me. Priorities out of order, I'd say.

The church always smells of musty mildew and Lysol spray. The Sunday School classrooms are located in the underground basement that begins to flood with the prediction of a sprinkle of rain. The classrooms have white paint on the cinder block walls which is peeling and has turned green and black with mildew and mold. There are pink and blue children's chairs with legs stained from standing in water. The rooms have felt boards on which the teachers place cut out, felt Bible characters to illustrate Bible stories.

I anticipate attending Vacation Bible School every evening for a whole week at the church. I hope I can make a friend who can jump rope fast and won't hassle me about my name. Often kids poke fun of my name, "Estie." I cringe and wish for a name like Mary. Yeah, my sister's name is popular. Lucky girl. There are lots of girls named Mary...Mary Sue, Mary Lou, Mary Ann. Then there is odd ball, "Messy Essie."

The first evening of Vacation Bible School, mothers register their cute daughters, with acceptable names. The girls wear crinolines under their starched plaid dresses with white collars. Some of the girls have their hair in pig tails and others in pony tails; and regardless of which tail their hair is combed in, it is shiny and clean. I wait alone at the end of the line, no crinoline, no plaid dress and my blond hair is short and gapped up. Messy Estie, an odd ball.

The stern lady at the registration table notices me. "Do you want to come to Vacation Bible School, too?" She asks.

"Yes, Ma-am," I answer, nervously.

"Are your parents here?"

"No, but they want me to enroll."

"Okay, what is your name?"

That is the first question to be answered on her form. I look at her. It is the moment of decision. I hesitate briefly – "Linda, Linda Culler," I say with a straight face, not batting an eye. So just like that, I enroll in Vacation Bible School using an alias. I'll have fun all week being a "Linda."

Parents, families and friends are invited to come to the church for a commencement program on Friday evening where there is a display of the crafts the students have made. There are Popsicle stick baskets, plastic lanyards, and potholders woven with loops in all different colors. The commencement program is to recognize the kids who memorize Bible verses; I am proudly one of the few. We sing songs, "This Little Light of Mine," "Deep and Wide," and "Roll Away," with the appropriate hand motions.

The kids sit toward the front of the church and the adults are behind us. The last item on the program, before fellowship with grape Kool-Aid and Oreo cookies, is to present each child with an official certificate of completion of Vacation Bible School signed by Mrs. Sylvia Tolbert, the Director of Vacation Bible School and their class teacher. Mrs. Tolbert, slim and very proper, makes some remarks about how glad she is to have so many children attend Vacation Bible School this year. She requests that the children make their way up to the podium to accept their certificate (and a handshake from the preacher, Rev. Tanner). She calls the name of each child in alphabetical order and it doesn't take long to announce "Linda Culler," and when she does, I slide down on the bench, lowering my head. Oh, no, what will I do? My Grandma sits right back there. She is all smiles because she is proud of me, "Estie Culler" her namesake.

"Linda Culler," the name is called again, louder this time, and a girl, lucky enough to be named Mary Lou, nudges me with her elbow.

"Get going, she's calling you," she whispers. The church falls silent. The kids stare at me, and my teacher, Mrs. Brinkley, glares at me, with a puzzled expression and motions encouragingly for me to come to the front of the church as the others have done.

I love my Grandma and she loves me. She is Estie and I am Estie. She is always so happy and giddy because I have her name. I couldn't move if I wanted to. I'm stuck to the seat in my shame for changing my name. My Grandma's feelings mean so much to me. I would not want to hurt or disappoint her for anything in the entire world. If I accept the certificate of Linda Culler, she will be furious with me for changing my name and she will not like it one iota that I lied; and that I lied in church, in front of God and everybody. Mrs. Tolbert looks directly at me and says, "That's okay; you may pick up your certificate later."

Whew. Maybe since I didn't get up when Linda Culler's name was called, Grandma didn't have any idea Mrs. Tolbert is calling me. Oh, to be so lucky! I am disappointed in myself for the hurt this will be to Grandma. When the program is complete, I feel Grandma's delicate but firm arm circle me. She is right smack dab beside me, tenderly drawing me tight to her. "It's okay, Estie, I didn't always like my name either, but please don't ever change your name again, okay?" She gently turns my nervous body to face her and I see hurt in her eyes. "You are Estie – my Estie, and I love you. Please be proud of your name. It is you and it is me. Remember there is a gold ribbon attaching my heart and your heart."

We depart from the church without the Kool-Aid and cookies, and without Linda Culler's certificate, slowly stroll, hand in hand, back to her house. At the sight of her white house, Grandma softly squeezes my hand. "You know Estie, we are two peas in a pod. Yes we are, just two peas in a pod."

Watch out for false prophets.
They come to you in sheep's clothing,
but inwardly they are ferocious wolves.

Matthew 7:15 NIV

Chapter 11
A Sunday Afternoon Walk

"Psst, Psst!" Startled, I look up and right there in plain view is my Daddy. He hovers over us, one hand on his hip, and his old Bible stuck under his other armpit. "Estie. Estie," Daddy calls. Surprised, my mouth gapes open. Goodnight in the morning time! Daddy appears out of nowhere. He is supposed to be in a mental hospital because his brain doesn't operate right. What is he doing here? His white shirt is clean and he has on blue and white striped, seer sucker pants. His face is clean shaven and Brylcreem plasters his thinning curls down to his head. His hair has enough oil on it to grease the wheels of a locomotive.

It is a clear, blue sky, day – not a single cloud. JJ and Mary visit at Grandma's. We play outside in the cool sand pile under my favorite tree, a large crepe myrtle with pink blossoms. The color and fluffy cone shape of the blossoms look like pink cotton candy. The tree has soft bark which I peel off easily and see and smell the shiny white wood. I drag a toy metal shovel (so old that most of the red paint has been rubbed off) through the sand and make roads with intersections. For scenery beside my roads, I place particles of the pink blossoms in the sand for shrubbery, use twigs for stop signs, jack rocks for railroad crossings, and red hotels and green houses from an old monopoly game, for my town. Mary and I play make believe, and build a little town with streets that wind around the trunk of the crepe myrtle tree. JJ walks and runs, and the little stinker knocks down our creations and bulldozes his way through our little town.

"Hey, Estie, bring Mary and John, we're going for a walk," my Daddy calls to me. "Hurry, come along now," he says. I feel frightened. I hesitate, stall and try to decide how to handle the situation. Should I leave Mary and JJ, run into the house and tell Grandma that Daddy is here and not in the hospital anymore? She may know that already. So I decide not to leave Mary and JJ for one second. He's sick in his head, and can't help it, but he's still a despicable monster; not to be trusted. I am afraid of him, and nervous. His presence causes my hands to shake. I stand up and my knees tremble.

I take JJ's sandy hands and he leaps to me. I brush sand off his pants and realize his pants are damp. "I need to change JJ's clothes," I say.

"It doesn't matter. He'll be okay, let's walk and then we can take care of his clothes." I am hesitant, but we go with our Daddy. He picks JJ up and carries him in his arms. "Mary, you hold Estie's hand." We walk down Spring Garden Street, by neat white houses, with freshly mowed yards. Red geraniums and pink begonias in clay flower pots sit on the edge of front porches. We have been down this road before, to attend Manley Avenue Baptist Church; but, when we approach the intersection of Manley Avenue to turn toward the church, we don't turn. We follow Daddy and walk further down the road into unknown territory, as the sun sinks and darkness surrounds us.

We are near a busy highway. I hear

transfer trucks roar by in the distance. I feel hungry and exhausted. I spot a Howard Johnson's orange and blue neon sign. Daddy flees into the woods in the opposite direction of Howard Johnson's with JJ in tow. Mary and I trail behind. The aroma of French fries and burgers drifts from the restaurant. Daddy plods on, deeper and deeper into the thick woods. I can not see the highway or the Howard Johnson's sign. Tall trees surround us.

Daddy finally stops and puts JJ down. He orders Mary and me to sit down beside JJ on the damp ground covered with soft, green moss and long leaf pine needles. "This moss is soft and we'll sleep here for the night. If we get cold, we'll cover ourselves with these pine needles," he explains.

Stuttering I ask, "In the woods? You mean, we'll sleep in the woods?"

"Yes, now Estie, don't ask so many questions, lay down here and keep John and Mary with you."

"But where are you going?" I ask.

"Don't keep asking questions. I am going to hustle back to the restaurant across the road over there and see what I can round up for us to eat. Don't ya'll move. Remember, God is with you and will protect you; I'll be back in a snap. Go to sleep. I will bring you

136

something good to eat," he promises.

I am too tired and sleepy to complain.

Daddy drops to his knees, lowers his head and lifts both arms with hands open to the dark heavens. He prays out loud, "Almighty God, I beseech your protection on these your children. Amen." This prayer has the fewest words I have ever heard him pray. If that is all he has to say to God, why does he kneel to the ground on his bended knees? Can't God hear him while he stands up? He heaves himself up to his feet, speaks not a word and he disappears into the dark.

Mary and JJ are soon asleep. JJ sleeps between Mary and me so he cannot wander off. I don't think they make a squeak.

I hear all kinds of weird noises in the stillness of the night. With every creak and crack, I hold my breath. Daddy had thrown my puppies in the "john." He would, no doubt, leave us here in the dark woods forever. However, that might be safer than being with him. I make up my mind to sneak over to the Howard Johnson's restaurant and beg someone to telephone my Grandma. I am glad I have memorized her number, BR7-051. It is dark, pitch black, and I can't abandon Mary and JJ. "Mary, are you asleep?" I whisper.

"Uh huh."

"I love you."

"Love you too."

I face JJ and Mary and press my ear tight to the ground. I hear the heartbeat of the earth. Every thump and thud alarms me to the realization of the existing dangers we are in. I didn't know people sleep on the ground in the dark woods. This must be how Indians and pilgrims lived before they had teepees and log cabins.

What's that spooky screech coming from behind me? I quietly twist and turn my body over the other way and stare into total darkness; I squint my eyes and survey the eerie black. After a while, I flip back over to reach and touch Mary and JJ – still there and still breathing. I toss and turn, strain my ears, and my nerves. I listen and wait. What do I anticipate? The boogie man, a slimy snake, a sneaky spider or some scary beast…a ferocious bear, and then as it changes from pitch-blackness of night, to gray morning light, I see a bear. I hold my breath, squeeze my eyes shut, pray earnestly, beg God to protect us and not let the bear see us. In the dawn of gray mist, the stout bear in reality is my Daddy. I am relieved, but not too much. He is a beast of a different sort. I want to telephone Grandma and tell her we spent the night in the woods without a morsel to eat and no blanket to cover us.

Daddy brings two pieces of cold dry toast, sliced in neat triangles and wrapped in a white paper napkin. "Here share this with them," he says and tosses the toast to me. "Come on, get up and pee here in the woods. We gotta' skedaddle!" he says.

After the odd experience of sleeping that night in the scary woods, Daddy, as if all is normal, has us follow him out of the woods and back across the road to the Howard Johnson's. He directs us up some back steps of the two story motel, and guides us around to the front, and then down the front steps. Strange. It appears to anyone who watches (as if the night has eyes) that we are a happy family checking out of a comfortable motel room.

The motor idles in the tractor of a transfer truck with the words "Great Southern Motor Lines" painted on it in red letters. The driver is a neat, small man in navy blue work pants and a gray shirt with a patch on the pocket which identifies him as "Clarence." He stands beside the driver's side door. He doesn't talk a lot, but he smiles with a twinkle in his green eyes that sparkle through wire rimmed glasses. His thick red hair is parted more in the middle than to one side. He looks more like a college professor than a truck driver. This spry little man jumps up, quick as a snap, to the driver's seat. He reaches the pedals and sees over the steering wheel without a lick of trouble! To my amazement he does it all like a pro. It is Daddy who has problems hoisting up us kids and difficulty maneuvering himself into the seat. Our first ride in a transfer truck couldn't have been better. Mr. Clarence shows Mary, JJ, and me the sleeping quarters in the truck, above and behind the seat. All three of us shimmy right on up there and get ourselves comfy. We are snug as a wool glove, nestled close to each other.

I tend to get motion sickness and my stomach goes tipsy turvy, especially if I look out the window of a moving vehicle. So, to close the sleeper compartment and to prevent me from seeing all the trees and poles fly by, I slide a thin black cloth curtain that is sewn over a wire, across the sleeper's entrance. In the warmth and darkness of Mr. Clarence's sleeper, I sleep like a baby lamb in the arms of Jesus all the way to Norfolk, Virginia.

As if it is by God's divine providence, Bill's Truck Stop is lit up with neon lights that advertises food and drinks on one side of the road and on the other side is a huge pitched tent. A hand-painted sign hanging between two posts reads: Old Timey Revival, Nightly – Singing and Preaching, Prepare to meet God. Everyone Welcome, 7:00 PM.

"First of all, I want to thank my Savior, the Lord Jesus Christ, for saving my lost soul on July 1st, 1930, at a tent revival in Jamestown, North Carolina, when I was a strapping thirteen year old. There was a great depression going on in America. Brothers and sisters, there was nothing depressed about me! Jesus came into my heart and set my soul on fire! Praise the Lord! He has never left me. I was a sinner bound for hell. Jesus reached down in the mud and the mire and lifted me up! I've been washed in the blood of the lamb. Jesus planted my feet on the solid rock," Daddy preaches.

There are some "Hallelujahs" and "Amen's" in the crowd.

When Daddy preaches his voice changes. He shouts, that's a given, but that in itself isn't the most noticeable difference. It has something to do with a grunt sound. He speaks so fast; he breathes with difficulty. He isn't the only preacher using this evangelical technique. Evidently, it is the mark of a Spirit-filled preacher to grunt and catch his breath simultaneously. The radio preachers are experts at it. It appears to me to be a stalling technique used while they think of something else to shout. The silence is filled with shouts of "Gloria," "Hallelujah," and "Amen."

Daddy continues, "Praise His holy name! Glory be to God! This rock is Jesus! Glo-r-ia! The storms of life may come and the wind may blow, but He plants my feet on the solid rock. Should I stumble, or should I fall, the blessed hand of Jesus always picks me up and sets my feet on the straight and narrow path. Glo-r-ia! You must be planted on the solid rock of Jesus Christ, who died, was buried, arose, and ascended into heaven. And listen to me, Glo-r-ia! Jesus Christ is coming again! In the hour that you thinketh not, He will make His glorious appearing. In a moment, in the twinkling of an eye." Daddy slaps the palm of his hand down hard on the pulpit, causing a startling loud pop from the microphone. "He will split open the eastern skies! Praise His name! The time is nigh, the stage has been set and everything is in place. In 1948 the Jews began to rebuild their nation. Listen to me. The time is at hand, the King of kings and the Lord of lords will split through the clouds of the eastern sky! Hallelujah! Hallelujah! Praise the Lord! Praise His Holy Name!" Daddy preaches loud. He skips across the stage and the congregation is on their feet, shouting and praising the Lord.

He kneels to the altar, where there is a drinking glass, a dipper and a five gallon galvanized bucket full of water. Daddy fills the dipper with water and pours the water into the clear glass, and he places the dipper back in the bucket. He stands and drinks the water down in a few long continuous swallows.

"Excuse me," he says. "Let me catch my breath. I am so excited about Jesus Christ's second coming; it takes my breath away. I know I will rise up off my feet and meet Jesus in the air! Hallelujah! You too can join us in the sky. You must confess your sins. Name them, one by one. All have sinned and come short of the glory of God. Believe in the name of Jesus Christ, and thou shalt be saved. Prepare to meet God. Walk the straight and narrow path. If you don't, Jesus said, 'wide is the gate and many go therein.' You go down the path that leads straight to hell and you will burn in everlasting fire. Glo-r-ia! And there will be weeping and gnashing of teeth."

By now Daddy's white shirt is drenched with sweat. It's hot outside the tent, but beneath the tent full of sweaty bodies, the temperature jumps up at least ten degrees. Daddy is wound up good! Each person is hotter than a peck of chili peppers. The tent is hotter than a furnace burning full blast. The heat is unbearable for the men in the crowd who have on shirts buttoned all the way up to their necks under their bib overalls. They have circles of sweat (growing larger) under their armpits and onto their shirts. The overdressed ladies, in long dark skirts and long sleeved blouses, wave fans in front of their sweaty faces. The thick cardboard paper fans, stapled on a stick, courtesy of Rice Funeral Home, have a colored headshot of Jesus, with a full beard, long wavy light brown hair and blue eyes.

"Brothers and Sisters, I praise God I am bound for Heaven. I'll walk on streets of pure gold! And that opportunity is yours too, because of this book." He raises his Bible high over his head and quotes, "'Whosoever believeth on Jesus shall be saved'…Glo-r-ia… Amen. I am here to bear witness that this is true," he says.

Mary and I sit on the front row in folding wooden chairs; our feet dangle and swing back and forth. JJ plays in the sawdust on the ground.

"My wife abandoned me. She left me and these three precious children, who sit on the front row. If it were not for my Savior, the Lord Jesus Christ, I don't know what I would have done or how we would have survived.

Glo-r-ia! But He is my good shepherd. He leads me in green pastures beside still waters and He prepares a table before me. I am here to tell you that the Lord, He doth provide. Glo-r-ia! Just this afternoon, God used a Christian truck driver to provide me, and my three babies, a hot meal right over there across the street at Bill's Truck Stop."

"Praise the Lord," the spirited crowd shouts.

"He is always there, when you trust Him and, it is written in Romans 8:28, 'all things work together for the good of those who love the Lord,'" he says.

A lady, in a brown dress and no make-up, sits on a chair behind us, leans forward and with her flabby arms, she hugs Mary and me. "God bless your little hearts," she whispers.

I sweetly smile at her and then pretend to listen to Daddy.

"And now, Jesus calls me," he says, as he takes out his old Bible. "Turn with me," he flips open his Bible, "to the Gospel of Saint Mark, chapter 16, and verse 15, where Christ was giving the great commission to the eleven remaining disciples: 'Go, ye into all the world and preach the gospel to every creature.' Jesus laid a burden on my heart, and He calls me to California to load Bibles on ships and to smuggle them into Communist China. I cannot tell you the name of the secret organization because of the dangers and risks involved," he says. Without warning, he begins to cry.

I have never in my life seen Daddy cry, or appear anywhere close to tears. This is a surprise. I discovered then and there that Daddy is a phony. He fools these Christian people with his fake tears. The preacher in charge of the revival, Brother Jarrett, has thick black hair combed in a duck-tail and he sports a slick light blue suit and white loafers. Apparently he doesn't know the sheep from the wolves. He stands up, throws his arms around my Daddy and the two of them cry, boohoo – a couple of overgrown babies who need their diapers changed.

Preacher Jarrett pulls away from Daddy's arms and says, "Brother Randy, you and your boy, Johnny, get the buckets. I feel the Holy Spirit in this place and He is leading me to extend to each of you the opportunity to give. Oh, what a blessing it is to give! Open your hearts and wallets! Give a love offering to Brother Culler and his precious children. Glory be to God."

When songs are sung, prayers prayed, the buckets are overflowing with cash, and the local flock has left the tent, Brother Jarrett gives Daddy a fistful of bills. He divides the rest of the money between Brother Randy and himself..

Apparently my Daddy doesn't know the sheep from the wolves either.

For I was hungry and you gave me something to eat.
I was thirsty and you gave me something to drink.
I was a stranger and you invited me in, I needed
clothes and you clothed me...
Whatever you did for the least of these
You did for me.
Matthew 25:35-36, 40 NIV

Chapter 12
Mrs. Sarah is Glamorous

Daddy rings the doorbell on the charming white house with black shutters. No one answers. He sits down on the front steps and we do too.

"This is where my brother, David, and his wife, Helen, live. David is in the United States Navy and this is a military house. We will live with your Uncle David for awhile.

We'll see the largest Navy base and ships in the world."

Beautiful maple trees, with leaves, which are beginning to turn yellow and gold, line both sides of the narrow street. Their abundant branches and full limbs intertwine forming a canopy of leaves rendering the neighborhood cool, shady and dark, even in the bright light of day. Too much shade prevents grass from growing in the yards and the ground is soft brown dirt. After a while, Mary and I play in the dirt and walk on the exposed tree roots.

Finally, Uncle David drives his two tone green Ford to the curb in front of his house. He hops out of the car, not surprised to see us, and waves his arm and motions for Daddy to come over to his car. Uncle David and Daddy stand about the same height and have the same build, but Uncle David has dark brown hair and eyes. I watch as they talk by the car. I am curious because I don't remember ever seeing Uncle David. Daddy calls us to the Ford. He points to each of us, says our name as he introduces us to our Uncle David. "Kids, this is your Uncle David. His wife, Helen, is in the hospital and has recently had a baby boy named Charlie. We won't be staying. They are too busy with the new baby and visitors are not allowed to live in the Navy houses," Daddy says.

Uncle David drives us to the downtown bus station and hands Daddy money to buy us one-way tickets to Grandma's house in Greensboro, NC. We bound out of the car and Uncle David waves bye to us. Before he drives away, Uncle David calls out of the driver's open car window, "Estie," he yells. I turn toward his slowly moving car with my hand to my forehead shielding my eyes from the bright glare of the afternoon sun. Uncle David smiles and our brown eyes meet. "Estie," he says again. "My Mama sure does think the world of you. You are her pride and joy. She loves you and will be happy when you and your brother and sister are back at her house." Uncle David waves again, we both smile and he drives out of the parking lot. I like Uncle David even if we didn't set one foot inside his house.

Daddy puts a coin in a jukebox and selects a Hank Williams song, "Your Cheatin' Heart." We eat grilled cheese sandwiches in the café of the bus station. We plan to catch a Greyhound bus and travel back to my Grandma's and I am happy. I can't wait to hug her; to bathe in her white bathtub with Ivory soap; to eat some of her delicious meatloaf and sweet potatoes from Grandpa's garden; to sleep in a bed with not one but two clean white sheets – one under me and one covering me, and to sink my head in a soft feather pillow covered in a white pillow case.

Daddy does not buy bus tickets. We sleep in an empty boxcar in a railroad yard that night.

How we meet Mrs. Sarah Luther is beyond me, but I sure am happy we do. She owns a brick house and she lives alone. Her husband has either died or is in the Navy stationed at sea. Either way, he is not there and we are.

Her house is also on a street lined with maple trees. Autumn is in the air and orange and yellow marigolds, and chrysanthemums of all colors, gold, rust, red and purple, are blooming. Carved pumpkins, jack-o-lanterns, add a splash of bright orange to the steps and front porches. Two jack-o-lanterns smile brightly, one on each side of the entrance way to Mrs. Sarah's front porch. Their triangle eyes and crooked teeth glow from the light of the candles burning inside each pumpkin. I am fascinated and spellbound at the very idea of a pumpkin with a face. We can't figure out how a candle could be inside a pumpkin. Mrs. Sarah shows us how the thick stem on the top of the pumpkin has been cut and can be removed from the pumpkin's head. Wow! What else have we missed in life!

There are sidewalks around the blocks in Mrs. Sarah's neighborhood where kids ride bikes, skate, play hopscotch and jump rope. The living room in her house is decorated with table lamps, fancy vases, and black and white photographs in silver frames. It is lovely. The home has an apartment in the full basement. For the first time since leaving Grandma's, we sleep in a bed. Mrs. Sarah's home is as fine as a home can be, and she is wonderful.

Mrs. Sarah buys Mary, JJ, and me new outfits and shoes. She even buys some clothes for Daddy. She enrolls me in elementary school, drives me there, and drops me off and picks me up in her new red and white Chevrolet convertible with the top down. Mrs. Sarah helps decide which new outfit to wear and she ties my shoes. Thanks to Mrs. Sarah, I attend school in new dresses. I don't know who enjoys it more – her or me.

She prepares and serves hot oatmeal with cream, and pours me a glass of orange juice for breakfast, before we are off to school. I carry my new "Wizard of Oz" tin lunchbox with Dorothy's picture on it. Regardless of what she packs in my lunchbox, she always includes an apple.

We arrive in front of the school; she

brings her pink plastic brush from her fancy purse and gently brushes my wind blown hair back out of my face. She digs into her purse again, finds a colorful hair band and places it on my head. Mrs. Sarah wears red plastic cat-eye sunglasses, candy apple red lipstick, and a silky red head scarf over her dark curls, all of which enhances her uniqueness. Everything about Mrs. Sarah is glamorous, even the sweet scent of her perfume. She says it's "Chanel" and that it is the very best.

In front of the school, the girls wave to me and greet me with eagerness and compliment my clothes. The boys gawk at the fancy car or maybe they are gawking at the fancy Mrs. Sarah. They accept me without too many comments about the pronunciation of my name. I figure your name can be anything, as long as your clothes are in style, and your Mother drives a sporty convertible. They assume Mrs. Sarah Luther is my mother, and I tell them no different.

Mrs. Sarah's car radio blares the music of Patsy Cline and Loretta Lynn, and with such hits as "Walkin' after Midnight" and "I'm a Honky Tonk Girl". On the way home, she offers me a piece of Bazooka bubblegum. I gaze at her with envy as she blows large pink bubbles between her red lips. I chew the delicious stuff, and Mrs. Sarah makes me promise to spit it out, and to not swallow it. I imitate her blowing bubblegum with no success. She pops a bubble with her hand, and it sticks to her lips and face. She laughs and sings along with the radio. She parks at her house; I feel disappointed the ride has ended. It is a thrill to ride with Mrs. Sarah; the wind flies through my hair and strands of hair slap me in my eyes.

We enter her front door; our laughter abruptly comes to a halt. We hear Daddy holler, "Which one of you did this?"

Mrs. Sarah hot foots it down to the basement, and takes the steps two at a time. I follow close behind.

"John Joseph, did you do this?" Daddy screams and beats the wall with his fist several times. JJ's and Mary's bodies become rigid; stiff as two dead animals on the side of the road. Caught in Daddy's line of fire, they do not twitch a muscle. Immobilized by fear, Daddy's fist beats on the wall and is only a swing away from their faces.

"Wait a minute, Abe! It's just a crayon mark on the wall. It will wash off. Don't make such a mountain out of a mole hill, for heaven's sake. A little soap and water and it'll wipe right off," Mrs. Sarah says. Daddy loosens his fist.

Mrs. Sarah wraps her warm arms tightly around JJ's and Mary's bodies. She rubs their backs and kisses their heads until the freeze thaws; and their stiff bodies limber up in response to the heat of Mrs. Sarah's strong embrace.

Later, Mrs. Sarah lugs a gigantic roll of brown wrapping paper, a roll of scotch tape and scissors down the steps. I help her tape the paper to the wall, beside the steps. Every four steps or so, she draws a straight vertical line with a crayon to divide the paper into three equal sections. With colored crayons she labels the section at the bottom of the steps "JJ," middle section "Mary" and at the top steps "Estie." She gives us each our own box of eight Crayola crayons. "There, now this should move the mountain. Have at it. Enjoy!" she says.

It is our drawing paper wall and she doesn't care how much we color on it. And when we have colored all over it, she will gladly plaster the wall with fresh paper for us. "A simple solution is to reduce the size of the mountain, really," she says. We start right away. In my section I draw a simple red apple and a red heart and scribble "Thank you, Mrs. Sarah."

That night while we are asleep, I wake up to the intrusion of Daddy's loud voice. He and Mrs. Sarah argue upstairs. I hear Daddy as he tiptoes up the stairs on other occasions, after we go to bed. Daddy and Mrs. Sarah often talk a while, before he returns to the basement. But tonight, he shouts and Mrs. Sarah shouts back, tit for tat. I've never heard a lady yell at anyone before. Yea, Mrs. Sarah!

"You can stay as long as you want to, but you will never hit or threaten those children in my house," she says.

"And you will not tell me, what I will and will not do," he says.

"In my house, oh yes I will," she says. "And I will tell you again, you will never, you got it, never raise a hand to harm those children, not in my house. Got it? You understand? That's the way it will always be," she screams. Mrs. Sarah is one tough lady. Wow, Daddy has met his match, and I'm proud of her. Eventually, I sleep.

Later I hear Daddy come back down to the basement. "Get up Estie, let's skedaddle," Daddy whispers. He wakes Mary and JJ and carries his duffel bag and tattered Bible. We go out the basement door that leads to the side of Mrs. Sarah's house. We disappear into the cool night. We walk. Mary, JJ and I, still sleepy, ask no questions, only obey.

I wonder if Mrs. Sarah sees my thank

you note written on the coloring wall, and the apple and heart I drew for her. I imagine she sees it, and she cuts it from the rest of the brown paper on the coloring wall and tapes it on her refrigerator door or puts it in a frame, beside her bed.

She is one person who wins my love and adoration and with a little more time, she could possibly wipe away the pain and erase the longing in my heart for my family.

Mrs. Sarah may not give me a second thought; but I will never forget her — a glamorous God-sent angel!

Show proper respect to everyone…
Peter 2:17 NIV

Chapter 13
Sleeping on Kudzu

Daddy's ridiculous midnight escape from the home of Mrs. Sarah Luther in Norfolk, Virginia, now finds JJ snoozing with his head in my lap on a Trailways bus headed to Mount Airy, North Carolina. Mary and I play "Count the Cows" which graze in the pastures, on the side of the road, and we bury them when we pass by a church with a cemetery. Then we count them over again. Mary is tired and sleepy and she lays her head in my lap beside JJ's.

I intently gaze at the road signs as they zip by the bus window. I play the "Alphabet Game," trying to locate each letter in the proper alphabetical order, as I read the signs. I see an interesting series of six red and white Burma-Shave advertisment signs. These small signs are posted consecutively along the highway at the edge of the road, and are spaced far enough apart to allow travelers to read easy when passing by in vehicles. Each sign has a phrase on it:

"A peach / Looks good / With lots of fuzz

But man's no peach / And never wuz' / Burma-Shave."

I think the signs are clever; however, my stomach turns flips in my mouth. I feel squeamish from motion sickness. I intently stare at Mary and JJ while they doze in my lap; I hope to calm my mind and ease my stomach. Their breath is slow, easy, and simultaneous. I breathe slowly to match the rhythm of their long inhales and exhales.

I glance toward Daddy who sits across the aisle from us. Lo and behold, as I live and breathe, Daddy has his pocketknife out and scratches "Jesus Saves" in the gray paint on the metal back of the seat in front of him, which fortunately no one sits in. Oh, dag gum it! My loco Daddy, does such loco things. I'm sure I'm gonna' puke and stink up the whole bus. Oh no, I swallow it back and manage to move Mary's and JJ's heads out of the way. I stand

and move to the aisle. Daddy puts his finishing touches on "God is Love." Uh-oh! I can't help it. I throw up in Daddy's lap; I see his horrified face as he realizes I have thrown up all over him and his "message board." I am startled beyond belief, as I see my throw up splatter and drip all over "Jesus Saves" and "God is Love."

The bus driver sounds frustrated when he announces, "Okay, try to sit back and relax. It smells as if someone has had an accident. We'll be pulling into Danville momentarily – within five to ten minutes. Just hold your breath and you won't smell the odor. Ha! Ha! Of course, if you hold your breath that long, you'll not smell anything any more," he laughs again. The passengers stay quiet, not finding the driver one bit clever. "Everyone can leave the bus in Danville and get some fresh air. We'll stay for about ten minutes. The bus will be cleaned and freshened up, and then we'll load back up and be on our way to Reidsville, North Carolina," he says.

I lean back in my seat, as clean as I was before becoming sick. Not a drop of puke on Mary, JJ or me. Daddy, on the other hand, is drenched in my puke. It is on his chest and puddles of the stuff are on his lap; not to mention the upchuck I sprayed over his "message board."

No one has ever set me down and taught me the proper care and respect to have toward other's property, except for the Golden Rule. Yet somehow, I recognize that my throw up is an accident and Daddy's malicious damage to the bus is intentional. Accidentally harming someone else's property is not good, but it's not as bad as doing the damage on purpose. I didn't mean to get sick; however, Daddy fully intended to scratch the paint off the back of the seat. I am so sorry my vomit is all over Daddy, the back of the seat and the floor; and the passengers are uncomfortable because of the odor. It's my fault, even though it was an accident. I didn't deliberately decide to stink up the entire bus. I feel humiliated, but still it was an accident. Daddy sees the wrong I have done, but he doesn't recognize his own sin. Of all the folks on the bus, and God in heaven, only Daddy is mad as hell fire at me.

In Danville, the bus driver buys me a small bottle of Coca-Cola and he drops a dab of "medicine called ammonia in it to calm your woozy stomach," he explains.

We load back on the Greyhound and it smells clean – the scent of Lysol. The driver, more or less, orders Daddy to take the front seat, behind his driver's seat and for Mary and me to sit across the aisle from Daddy. We do and JJ bounces to the seat with us.

"Rev. Culler, with all due respect, there's no proof; however, I know you maliciously and unlawfully damaged this Greyhound Bus, which is defined in the Federal Code as a commercial motor vehicle. It is a crime to deface or tamper with this bus in any way. The only reason you are allowed on this bus is because you travel with three minor children; otherwise, your ass would be in a police car and hauled off to jail," the driver says.

"Sir, as you said 'there's no proof' of that false allegation, and I travel with my little children, one of whom has been sick and we wouldn't want her to vomit again, would we? We are on our way to Pilot Mountain to visit my aunt," Daddy says.

"Just sit down and shut up," the driver orders. Then the driver directs his attention to me, "Child, when you travel on a bus, it is always best to sit in the front seat, so you can see out the front windshield. See, the windshield goes across the whole width of the bus." He steps aside and points to the windshield. "You will not be as likely to become sick watching things in front; but when you ride for miles and stare out the side windows, you see trees, poles and traffic zoom by and this can spin your stomach upside down. I think you will feel better here.

Remember to look out the front or, better still, close your eyes. There's not anything to see out there that's worth making you throw up again. Okay? Do you understand? I'm not mad or angry with you. It was an unavoidable accident. I'm trying to give you a few hints that may keep it from happening again. Okay?" He smiles at me.

"We need to get off the bus in Pinnacle," Daddy tells the driver.

"Guess what, Rev. Culler, there is no bus station or scheduled bus stop in Pinnacle. Next stop is Mt. Airy. You can get off there," the driver says.

"We expect our ride to pick us up in front of Pinnacle School across those railroad tracks on up there a little way," Daddy says.

"So, like I said, next stop is Mt. Airy."

"My precious children don't need to go to Mt. Airy. We can get off any time now. See, there's the school and our ride either waits on us or will be along momentarily. So, for the sake of the precious children, especially my daughter who has already thrown up once on the bus, please stop here in Pinnacle."

The driver says not a word, but pulls the bus over on the gravel at the shoulder of the road, and opens the door. Daddy grabs his duffel bag and Bible from the seat beside him. He herds his three precious children off the bus in a hurry. We don't linger a second, in case the driver changes his mind.

We stand on the side of the road and watch the bus taillights disappear in the dusk of nightfall.

We follow Daddy to the bank beside the railroad tracks. He climbs down the bank covered in kudzu vines; he struggles and stumbles, but never loses his footing completely. He stands and reaches both his arms up to take hold of JJ, then Mary. "Estie, you can get down that bank by yourself. You're a brave girl," Daddy says. So, I take one step down the bank, fall on my butt and slide the rest of the way down; I grab and hold on to kudzu with both hands to slow me down. At the bottom of the bank, I land on my feet.

Rooster crows wake me, the sun filters through my closed eyelashes, and kudzu tickles my face. I smell trash and taste old vomit in my mouth. I struggle to open my eyelids and make a strenuous effort to balance myself on the slanted bank. Then surprise! What to my wandering eyes appear – the majestic Pilot Mountain. Darkness covered it last night.

"We're at Pilot Mountain! We're at Pilot

Mountain! We're at Pilot Mountain!" I sing and wake up Mary and JJ. They are as surprised as me to see Pilot Mountain!

"Daddy, are Matt, Mark and Luke at the Lord's Mission? Is Mama there too? Are we all gonna' live here together again?" I ask. I am so happy and excited. I move a few steps away and squat to do a "number one" behind some kudzu growing up a thick cable line which is attached to a telephone pole. Mary follows me and she does "number one" and "number two." I pick a couple of kudzu leaves and pass them to her. JJ pulls off his pants and pees right where he is standing.

"No, we are going to see Aunt Martha. You remember her and Uncle Lebert, don't you? They live on down the road from the 'Lord's Mission.' Mary Lou, my cousin, is their only child who still lives at home. The rest are grown and married. You do remember Aunt Martha and her delicious homemade biscuits, sausage, and gravy? She also has jars of every kind of jelly and jam there is in the world. She makes delicious blackberry cobbler. I can hardly wait to eat some. Let's get going. Over there is the school Matt, Mark, and Luke went to," he says and points to a nearby one story brick building.

"I want Mama and my brothers to be

here," I whine.

"Me too!" Mary says.

"Mama, Mama, Mama," JJ cries louder.

"Now, Estie see what you went and did? You got both of them upset. No more talk about your Mama; and your brothers are not here either," Daddy scolds me.

Daddy helps Mary and JJ up the bank to the road.

"Estie, you scooted down there by yourself. How's 'bout you trying to climb back up?" Daddy asks.

I look around, searching for the easiest way to climb the bank. I see it! I walk a few steps down the track to a gravel and dirt path leading up the bank to the road. I climb the path with no problems at all.

"Come on smarty pants. This is the way to Aunt Martha's and we've got a long row to hoe," Daddy says.

When the Lord saw her, his heart went out to
her and he said, "Don't cry."
                                        Luke 7:13 NIV

Chapter 14
Chickens and Blackberry Pickin'

The narrow black top road winds in curves.
They start with short smooth banana shaped
curves, expand and stretch into long thin
goose-neck bends. The road narrows and the
swerves sharpen – black rick-rack zigzagging
across the hills. Some curves are so sharp in
places; you can meet yourself coming back!
The paved road – long black crayon marks –
scribbles every which a way and swirls deeper
into the countryside. As the lay of the land
levels and flattens, the black crayon lines
straighten. Houses, on the sides of the road,

spread further apart. Tobacco grows thick in field after field, acre upon acre. Surry and Stokes County meet on the left at the large tree. A red dirt road intersects with the paved road. This area is "Culler Country." My Grandfather, Daddy and a bunch of other Cullers were born and raised near this intersection at the foot of Pilot Mountain. In fact, there were so many relatives belonging to the Culler Clan that the town of Pinnacle used to be called Culler, North Carolina.

I broadcast, far and wide, chicken feed and seed on the red dirt in the front and on the side of Aunt Martha's house. The chickens follow my bare feet, peck at my toes and seem unable to tell the difference between their food and my toes. I keep my distance – a good arm's throw. I scatter the feed in a complete circle around me. The chickens – mean and cocky biddies – scramble at my toes and peck away.

I panic, jump, squirm, and squeal. Hopelessly, I am scared to death of the beady eyed biddies. I drop the tin can holding the feed and run. "Help, help," I holler. JJ and Mary have a good laugh at my embarrassing and seemingly dangerous predicament.

"Calm down! For heaven's sake, calm down!" Mary Lou shouts. She is coming out of the house to the back porch and at the same time I run inside the house, the screen door slams shut between the two of us.

Mary Lou, my second cousin, is not yet twenty years old and is tall, thin and beautiful. She has shoulder length, long, black hair. She can holler louder than anyone I know. Her shouts can wake our dead relatives, who are all buried miles away in the cemetery of Shoals Community Methodist Church.

Mary Lou can whistle 'bout as loud as she can shout. If she aims for you to hear her, she has no problem getting your attention. Her whistle is louder than the whistle of the train passing through Pinnacle. Whether Mary Lou shouts or whistles, one thing you can depend on – she is consistently loud. In the kitchen, I swing my arms and legs and fight off the chickens (that in my mind, still cluck and peck at my toes). Mary Lou gives a whistle and yells, "Estie, you best get back here this minute, not a second later." I peep through the screen door and watch Mary Lou confidently teach Mary and JJ the proper way to feed chickens.

I quietly slide out the door without letting it slam behind me. Trying to observe Mary Lou's expertise, without her being aware of me spying on her, is ludicrous.

"Estie get off that porch and come

here," she says without turning around.

I swannee, that girl has eyes in the back of her head. I notice the mean biddies are more interested in their food than they are in me. I step off the porch and hide beside and peep around the well to have a closer, yet cautious look.

"Estie, keep your eyes on the chickens when you feed them and don't turn in circles; always walk away from them and cast the food way out in front of you," she explains.

Daddy calls to me, as he strolls from the front of the house. "Estie, grab a couple of cans from the porch. We're going blackberry picking," he says.

Mary Lou tosses out the last handful of chicken feed. "Here Abe, this can is empty and you can take it with you."

Mary Lou shoos the chickens away; as if chickens can hear and see. She bangs her hand on the bottom of the tin can. "Shoo, shoo, scat, get on out of here. Can't you see there's no more food in here? Scat, skedaddle!" she says. She slaps her hand on the bottom of the tin can a time or two more. I suppose the chickens do hear and see Mary Lou because they obey her and scamper off in different directions. They cluck like happy birds.

"Estie, if you want your own can, grab

one from the porch and let's go blackberry pickin," Daddy says.

"Oh Abe, you go ahead and pick blackberries. Leave the kids here. You'll get through quicker by yourself. Hurry and I'll bake you a cobbler."

I hesitate, feeling confused, not sure what to do. I had rather stay with Mary Lou and the mean toe-pecking biddies than to go anywhere with Daddy.

"I'm not taking JJ and Mary. They're young and will slow us down. Only Estie and me are going this time. Come on Estie, let's go," he says. He waves his hand at me and motions me to speed it up. I move in the general direction of where Mary Lou stands and, as I do, Daddy takes a few long strides in front of her and takes my arm and pulls me toward him. "Shake a leg. Hurry,'" he says.

"Can I pick blackberries, too?" Mary asks.

"Mary, you help Mary Lou take care of JJ. Estie and I will be right back. It won't take us long," Daddy says.

"Abe, what the heck do you think you are doing? Sneaking off with Estie and leaving Mary and John Joseph here? I am not dumb; you can't take Estie and leave the little ones here for me to raise. No, you ain't," Mary Lou yells and I tremble.

"Now, calm down Mary Lou. Estie and I are going blackberry picking – nowhere else. I don't have my duffle bag. We're not leaving for good," Daddy reassures her.

"Well, if you are gonna' pick berries, why are you totin' your Bible under your arm?" she asks.

"Mary Lou, you know I carry the Word of God with me everywhere I go. Jesus is coming again soon. Jesus will split open the eastern sky with a shout and the sound of the Angel's trumpet. I will be caught up with Him in the heavens. I always have my Bible with me. When I rise to meet Him in the sky, it will be with Bible in hand," he snaps at her. "Estie and I will be back soon. I will never leave any of my children. The four of us will always stay together. Let's go Estie."

Daddy is in a far away place – in a trance. His eyes are wild, bizarre and focus on nothing in particular. His pop eyes dart around from hither to yonder and never rest. "Estie, take off your blouse and give it to me," Daddy says. He unbuttons my shirt and lays it on the ground beside him. "Estie, lay your lovely head on your blouse," he says.

I obey. He runs his fingers through my

hair and rubs his hand on my head.

"Behold thou are fair, my love; behold thou are fair. Thou hast dove's eyes. You are a lily growing among thorns. Your fruit is sweet to my taste. The flowers appear on earth; the time of the singing of the birds has come, and the voice of the turtledove is heard in our land. Do you hear the sweet chirping of the turtledoves?" Daddy asks.

Daddy is some kind of serious loco. I am paralyzed with great fear. Fear that robs me of my voice and steals all my strength. "No," I answer silently, scared shitless, unable to budge a muscle or utter a sound

"Behold thou are fair, my love; also our bed is green. The vines, with tender grapes, give forth fragrance. Thou are fair my love. There is no spot on thee. Thy lips are like a thread of scarlet. Thy neck is like the tower of David," Daddy says. He rubs his hot hand over my lips, face, and neck. He moves his hand over my flat chest. "Thy two breasts are like two young roes that are twins, which feed among the lilies. How fair is young love? How much better is thy love than wine? Thy lips are like honeycomb drops. Honey and milk are under thy tongue. I have eaten my honeycomb with my honey. I have drunk my wine and my milk." Daddy chants on and on. I am petrified. A lifeless body. "Oh thou fairest among women. Your mouth is most sweet. Yea, you are altogether lovely. You are beautiful my love. Thy banner over me is love. How beautiful are your feet. The joints of your thighs are like jewels. Waters cannot quench love, neither can floods drown it, nor can John Edgar Hoover, his FBI or the CIA destroy it. I teach you all things. I will not allow J. Edgar Hoover, or anyone else, to ever touch you." Daddy raises his face above mine, moves his monstrous head down and aims straight toward my lips. I scream loud.

Daddy screams louder and he jumps up from the ground to his feet, shoves his shirttail in and buckles his belt back at the waist of his pants. Now my screams scare him. I am thankful to Jesus for restoring my voice to full strength. I scream loud, long, shrill shrieks – a frightened kitten scared by a malicious mountain lion.

"Alright, Estie, enough is enough! If you know what is good for you, you will shut up, straighten up, and fly right," he threatens. He yanks me to my feet, slaps my mouth, grabs my shoulders and shakes the daylight out of me.

I quickly shut up and put on my shirt.

"Estie, these words I have spoken were not meant to frighten you. They are from the

Song of Solomon in the Old Testament of the
Bible. King Solomon wrote these words which
describe you today. However, one of these days
your titties will grow full and sweet as melons
and John Edgar Hoover will track you down
to rape you. I will never let him touch you.
That's why I'm teaching you these things. You
can always tell him, any other men, or boys,
as far as that goes, that you belong to Daddy."
Sickening! Daddy makes me sick. He's odd
and says gross things. He talks like a crazy old
fool. He is "loco."

>   We do not pick any blackberries and we
do not have any cobbler for supper.

>   We leave Aunt Martha's before the sun
rises the next morning.

>   It's insanity on the road to glory. I
don't know who I hate the most, Daddy, King
Solomon, or John Edgar Hoover.

Foxes have holes and birds of the air have nests,
but the Son of Man has no place to lay his head.
Matthew 8:20 NIV

Chapter 15
Sleeping in a Filling Station

I am warm as a kitten bathing in the August sun stretched out and then curled up behind a jet black pot belly stove. It's cold, dark and thunder storming. Our last ride drops us off in the drenching rain, at a "y" in the road with a well lit Texaco filling station in the center. I am not sure what city or state we are in. The rough looking man, working at the station, had greeted us warmly.

"Come in, come in – get out of the rain. You kids are soaking wet," he says. The man, who has on a green shirt with the word

"Texaco," a red star, and the name "Bill" sewn on the pocket, is the only person in the station. Cold rain blows and drums a loud, steady beat as it splashes against the large front plate glass window. Through the wet window, the reflections of the headlights from the passing cars twinkle like huge clusters of shiny diamonds.

Mr. Bill scurries about and arranges a couple of chairs in the crowded room. "I know," he says, directing me with a nudge on my shoulders. "Why don't you three little ones scoot right in behind the stove? It'll dry your clothes and warm you up real fast. Don't burn yourselves, that stove can heat up hotter than hell." The huge black stove rests on a brown metal stove mat. Mary, JJ and I sit down and prop against the wall. We tug off our well worn shoes and pour the rain water from them onto the stove mat. I watch the water drip from my shoes and roll under the stubby black stove legs. It spits, sputters, and disappears as it contacts the hot heat.

"I'll put your socks on top of the stove to dry," Mr. Bill says. Mary and I roll off our icky, wet socks, which are folded and tucked under our toes because they are too long for our feet. JJ has no socks on and his cold toes look blue.

Daddy stands with his face toward the stove and rubs his hands together to warm them. He backs up to the stove and warms his backside. Mr. Bill removes a greasy cloth from his hip pocket, and uses it to wipe the dust off the seat of a turquoise plastic chair. "Here, have a seat," Mr. Bill offers. The friction of the chair's rusty chrome legs makes a shrill, grating sound as Daddy scrapes it across the concrete floor and places it smack dab in front of the hot stove.

He introduces himself to Daddy and sticks out his greasy hand. I notice his fingers and fingernails are as black as his pot belly stove. "Sorry for the grease, I was working on that old truck out there until that dag-blame storm rolled in. My name's Bill Kirby, short for William. Me and my wife, Mary, own this little place. Why on earth are you out walking on such a stormy night with these kids?" Mr. Kirby asks. Before giving Daddy a chance to answer he continues, "Bet you young-uns are hungry. How 'bout a pack of peanut butter crackers and a bottle of Coca-Cola?" And before we can answer, he pulls small green glass bottles of Coca-Cola out of a red ice box and removes the lids with an opener attached to the side of the box. He hands each of us a Coca-Cola bottle and a pack of Lance cheese crackers, which have a teensy dab of peanut butter between them. "Here you go, little ones," Mr. Kirby says and smiles at us.

"Thank you," we chime in unison.

He turns his attention to Daddy. "I'll make you some hot coffee. What'd ya' say your name is anyways?" he asks.

I rip open JJ's and Mary's crackers with my front teeth and pass the crackers to each of them. I hang onto JJ's bottle of Coca-Cola to keep it from spilling and to help him hold it when he wants a swallow. To enjoy the crackers as long as possible, I only munch on tidbit size bites. The salty cracker melts on my taste buds. I drink a nose-tingling, swig of Coca-cola with a tad of cracker in my mouth and the fizzing bubbles of the Coca-cola soak the cracker crumbs, and condenses them to soft, soggy mush. I eat my crackers with pleasure, no not exactly chew or eat, but hold the delicious cracker in my mouth until it slowly melts away to nothingness. Oh, so good!

Mary and JJ make little pigs of themselves; they almost swallow each cracker whole and wash it down with huge gulps of Coca-Cola. They both finish eating and drinking before me. My belly growls with hunger pains, but I enjoy every grain of salt on every nibble of the crackers. JJ and then Mary fall fast asleep, with damp heads and warm feet. I lean back and listen to the men talk.

Bill tosses me a flat cushion that is in the seat of the chair he sits in. "Here, that floor has gotta' be hard, use this." Bill checks on us a time or two and smiles.

I wonder where we are, and I also wonder if anyone else wonders where we are.

I have been doing a lot of wondering lately. I had no idea that taking a Sunday afternoon walk with my Daddy from my Grandma's house in Greensboro, North Carolina, would take me on a journey of a zillion steps, or that now I would be trying to fall asleep behind a pot belly stove in a filling station. As my body warms up, my brain starts simmering. I wonder the number of miles we have thumbed and how many thoughtful truck drivers have picked us up and given us rides.

Daddy has coached us to say "Thank you for stopping" to the driver. The driver's response is usually, "Where are you going with these kids? Are you hungry? There are Wise potato chips, Little Debbie Oatmeal Cookies, and chocolate moon pies in the sleeper compartment. You kids eat all you want."

Why does Daddy think he must spout the good news of the Gospel of Jesus Christ at every opportunity, whether appropriate or not

– on crowded street corners, in spirit filled tent revivals and in country churches that happen to be in our path? He usually arrives on the church scene in plenty of time to locate the pastor and speak with him before the service begins. He informs the minister, "God laid it on my heart to share my personal testimony with the good folks of this congregation. God has given me an urgent message and surely some dear soul in our midst is in need of hearing God's message," Daddy says. Before leaving their meeting, Daddy and the minister have a long, wordy prayer on their knees. They pray for power from above to rain down miracles and for God-fearing folks to display a tremendous generosity in their giving. Amen! They both pray at the same time and the piano begins to play the out-of-tune notes of "Standing on the Promises." Together the minister and Daddy step to the platform. The minister introduces Daddy as a "Messenger from God." My Daddy is welcomed warmly and delivers God's message of hell fire; he humbly accepts the kindness bestowed on him with the generous gift of the congregation's hard earned money.

Why does he preach to every trucker who stops to give us a ride? Often times, when Daddy detects the roar of a truck or car in the distance, he steps back into the shadows of the woods, or he scoots down in a ditch and leaves us to hitchhike by ourselves. Apparently, he assumes we can hitch a ride quicker without him at our side; as a rule, we do. Daddy steps out of hiding when the truck slows to a stop. He carries JJ and we run the short distance to the truck and hop up beside the driver. Daddy has warned us to keep our mouths shut and let him answer any questions. We have learned to speak only when he tells us to. For the most part, he expects us to quote from memory Bible verses, especially John 3:16, and sing "Jesus Loves Me." Mary and I can quote this with a breeze, like second nature.

When I quote John 3:16 and Psalm 23, the truck driver hands me two one dollar bills. My eyes bulge with disbelief. It is my first experience touching paper money. The dollar bills are all mine to have, to hold, or to spend. I roll them together in one tight roll and squeeze them in my sweaty palm. The friendly driver compliments me on doing an excellent job. "Keep the money or buy yourself something special," he says.

When no eyes notice, Daddy snatches the damp bills, like a Venus flytrap devouring insects. "I don't want you to lose them," Daddy says. Once he seizes the money from my hand, it's gone, forever lost to me.

I hear Daddy explain to many drivers that his mission in life is to reach Long Beach, California. "The Holy Ghost has been poured out on me and has divinely anointed me to organize efforts of Project Free Bibles. I will oversee the collection of Bibles and load them onto ships in Long Beach, California. I will smuggle the Bibles into Communist China, and deliver them to Chinese Christians, who will spread God's word to the poor lost souls in China. Most Chinese cannot read the English language, but the Holy Ghost will teach them to read, speak and understand the Word of God. Their tongues will become flames of fire, like on the Day of Pentecost," he says.

Daddy often says, "John Edgar Hoover" (whoever that is) "is really a communist" (whatever that is) "and Mr. Hoover is trying to stop my mission. The Federal Bureau of Investigation trails me, spies on me, and keeps files with all sorts of lies and false allegations. The entire force of the FBI works for Mr. Hoover, who is the most powerful man in the world and even greater than Ike Eisenhower, the President of the United States of America. More than likely, Mr. Hoover is the Anti-Christ prophesied in the Bible," he says.

Daddy's comments are way over my head leaving me puzzled and confused. He insists our Mama abandoned him and us children. She walked in the ways of the devil, satisfying the desires of the flesh, and she has joined the Communist Party. I wonder if Daddy thinks we are asleep, but I am not. And I cannot, for the life of me, imagine my Mama at any party.

Lost in my own mind, I hear Daddy's voice, and realize he tells Bill about Mama – so I try to listen. "She is dead – burned to death in a gambling house fire. The house was burnt to the ground – nothing but ashes," Daddy says. This shocks and startles me. I cannot believe my ears. Surely I misunderstand his words. I am in the midst of swallowing coke, I gasp and Coca-cola goes up my nose and then spews out of my mouth along with a spray of orange cracker crumbs. I choke. Mary and JJ stir around at the noise I cause but they continue to sleep. I put the thin seat cushion over my head and, with my hands, press the sides of it tight to my ears.

I cry and my body shakes; I am scared. My Mama has been burned to death in a fire! Not so! Couldn't be! First, I determine I will never tell JJ and Mary about this. Second, I realize my Mama cannot be wondering where we are when she is dead, burned to ashes.

I try so hard to conjure up a memory

of my Mama, to visualize her in my mind. She is tall, strong and soft with long brown hair that she twists up on her head. Her hands are rough. She cries a lot. She listens to Liberace play the piano, and Babe Ruth play baseball on the radio. She can hold JJ, Mary and me, all three, on her lap at one time. I quietly sob myself to sleep.

...We were harassed at every turn, conflicts
on the outside and fears within, but God
comforts the downcast...
Corinthians 7:5- 6 NIV

Chapter 16
Eat My Texas Grits

I intently watch the black and white keys spring up and down to the tune of "Bye, Bye, Blackbird" and then to "Somewhere, Over the Rainbow." Mr. Skitter's fingers never touch the keys. Magic. Mr. Skitter, tall and boney, has an adam's apple that protrudes and bobs up and down as he speaks. He promises to teach me how to work its magic. "Look, but don't touch," Mr. Skitter explains.

We live downtown in an apartment above Skitter's, an old brick grocery store in Houston,

Texas. The apartment has three rooms, but each room, like Texas itself, is extremely large. The store's original purpose, I am told, was Skitter's Saloon, a rip-roaring honky-tonk in its hey-day. Time has clouded the antique mirror, covering the length of one of the side walls, and the mirror's beauty and clarity is dull with layers of tobacco smoke. Neither powerful Windex glass cleaner, nor loads of elbow grease return the sparkle to the mirror. The long solid oak bar that served whiskey, now serves up hot dogs, fried bologna sandwiches, and Coca-Cola in green glass bottles. The dark wood floors have deep grooves and cracks, which are full of Texas soil and oil, from the boots of cowboys and politicians who stopped in for rest and relaxation. The sagging old floors are worn and creak when they are walked on.

In the back of the store, behind the coolers of meat, cheese and glass bottles of milk, steps lead up to the only entrance into the apartment. Stored in the space under the stairs is the old black magical piano.

The apartment has white linoleum floors throughout. The bedroom has a double bed and the only window in the apartment. The view from the window is the exterior brick wall of Southwest Laundry and Dry Cleaners, a two story building beside Skitter's store. The laundry and dry cleaners operates twenty-four hours a day, except on Sunday. The unbearable hot steam heat pours continuously from the large, louvered, metal vents, and the loud clanging racket from the machines make it intolerable to open the window, day or night.

The apartment is completely furnished including the simple basic furniture, kitchen appliances, iron and ironing board, white dishes with a brownish-gold wheat design in the middle of each plate, clean peanut butter glasses for drinking, a light green plastic AM radio, a pot, a frying pan, forks and spoons, sheets and towels. This is far more than we are accustomed to having. You name it, we have it.

I wake up early, hungry. It is a Saturday morning and no one else is awake. I drag a chair up close to the kitchen counter, stand on the chair, and then flop my bare feet on top of the smooth white counter. I open every cabinet door, and finally find some grits in a brown Quaker Oats paper sack. I read, as best I can, the cooking directions on the label. Sounds simple enough, so grits it is.

A hazy mist of steam rises from and hovers above the oversized pot of grits boiling on the stove. I wear one of my socks on my right hand to improvise a much needed potholder. I stir the thick, bubbling grits with a small teaspoon. I suppose, if we are really rich, the huge pot would not be the only pot in the kitchen, the teaspoon would be a long handled ladle, and socks would be on my feet, not on my hand, and padded potholders would be readily available.

I cling to the spoon and my knuckles burn. The grits begin to stick to the bottom of the pot. I am bound, bent, and determined to scrape up the gobs of scorching grits. I stir with the spoon; my knuckles burn. As the grainy grits boil in the water, their consistency becomes runny; then they turn mushy. Soft and mushy grits are good to eat. But, before I can switch off the burner and remove the blazing hot pot, the grits are overcooked. They are now a solid, white, rubbery, circle stuck in the bottom of the pot. I scrape the rubbery circle of grits loose and mash it into hot lumps.

I lift the hot pot of my grits from the burner. "Estie," from behind me my name is spoken. My Daddy simply speaks my name. That's all it takes. Startled. Shaken. Scared shitless! Spontaneously, without a thought or a plan of doing so, my arms and hands automatically jerk in a quick involuntary spasm, fly up and toss the hot pot into the air. Burning hot grits spill on my hand and drop on my bare feet. In all the commotion, I lose my balance, and to prevent myself from collapsing face first on the stove, I quickly cross my arms to protect the front of my face, and I tumble with my open palms landing on the bright red hot coils of the electric burner.

"What kinda' mess you making over there, girl? Don't you know cleanliness is next to Godliness? Clean it up, now. Hop to it," Daddy shouts. "I need you to iron these pants of mine," he says and tosses a pair of his pants over the upright ironing board.

I squat and scoop the grits from the floor back into the pot with the teaspoon. I place the spoon and pot of grits on the counter. Daddy opens the refrigerator and removes a half stick of butter and drops it in the pot, and stirs it in the grits.

With blisters forming on my trembling fingers and hands, I slowly glide the heavy iron around the huge waist of Daddy's pants. When I look up from the ironing board, Daddy watches me through his squinting eyes. He leans and props his back against the kitchen counter. He casually has one bare foot crossed over his other bare foot at his ankles. He eats the grits out of the pot, and he greedily gobbles down the last bite. He smacks his lips loudly and he puts the empty pot in the sink. He keeps his eyes focused on me, his long tongue stretches out of his mouth; he slowly licks each side of the spoon making sure he doesn't leave a smidgen, not even a smell. His lips turn up in a wicked smirk. His eyes are open wide and he glares at me. He appears evil, obnoxious and gross.

"Estie, wash this pot," he orders. He picks up his pants from the ironing board and leaves the kitchen.

I shake from the hair on my head down to the nails on my toes. I realize the extent and magnitude of my petrifying fear of Daddy. Yet, when the immediate fear subsides, my hands still tremble.

This is why I weep and my eyes overflow with
tears, no one is near to comfort me, no
one to restore my spirit.
Lamentations 1:16 NIV

Chapter 17
Playing Dodge Ball – Dodging Daddy

I see him. He lurks behind the trunk of a dark
shadowy cottonwood tree. Intuitively aware of Daddy's
sinister presence, I am unexpectedly overtaken with
intense fear, gloom and dread. That's him; I am sure,
snooping around outside the chain link fence. The
school and the fenced in playground is my safe territory.
He's intruding. What's he up to now? Why doesn't
he get lost?

I dodge the brown rubber ball. Way to
go! I am fast on my feet.

I will not even glance in the direction of his

hiding place. If I pretend I don't see him, then maybe he won't see me.

Uh oh! Watch out for the ball. It's flying in my direction.

He's moves from the shield of the tree trunk. Now he squats beside a low green leaf bush. He is definitely "loco," an imbecile. He sneaks around, hides behind trees and bushes.

Whew! It misses me. I better pay attention to this game. After all, I want to keep up my reputation.

A full grown man, short and stout, round but also robust, not enough hair on top of his head to mention; however; he takes pride in the two inch band of wavy, blond hair that remains along the edge of his head, from ear to ear, in a semicircle. None of his teeth are missing or obviously rotten; but, it matters little, since he seldom cracks a smile. From his appearance he looks normal, but he ain't. He's anything but normal. No, a normal person doesn't sneak around a school playground, hide behind trees and under bushes. Normal, no. Weird, yes. Why does that dingbat have to be my Daddy?

Great, I manage to dodge the ball again!

Well, now he stands in full view, wiggles his index finger impatiently and motions me to come to him over by the fence. But, I don't see him; or really, I don't acknowledge having seen him or the motion of his squiggly demanding finger.

My goodness, Lord, please swat him away, or else, please give me some angel wings, so I can fly away. Please don't let him start preaching, jumping and shouting. If he does, God, please don't let these kids or Mrs. Murphy know he is my Daddy. I send up some quick, silent prayers. Ignore him, maybe he will vanish.

Three kids remain in the dodge ball game. Move it, duck my head. Wow! That was close! I better pay attention.

Please don't let him drop on his knees, throw both of his hands high in the air, and yell at you God; demanding you, the Almighty and Powerful God, to rain down fire on Landtrip School and to pour out locusts on this playground.

Now it's down to two, me and that tall boy, who appears to be too old for the second grade. He'll never beat me. I move, run, duck, slide or jump constantly; whatever it takes to dodge the ball and not let it clobber me.

What if Daddy gets on a rampage because of "the corruption in the FBI," or "because of the lying bastards in Washington, DC," or what if he gets angry and shouts and swings his fist at the invisible, but perverted, John Edgar Hoover?

In less than a week, rumor has it, I am the new dodge ball champ of the second grade at Landtrip Elementary School in Houston, Texas. I may be slow in arithmetic, but that's

about all. I'm a speeding bullet on the ball
field.

*I see him again. Fear, unwanted and
uncontrolled fear, possesses my body.*

Wham! I might as well have been shot
from close range with a semi-automatic rifle.
Simultaneously, my heart stops beating, my
breathing shuts down and the side of my face
explodes and rattles my brain. My hands fly
to my chest and to my head. My body leans
forward slightly and my jaw gaps wide open. I
know I have been hit, and don't know what has
hit me, I am stunned by the blow to my face.

*I see movement. A long finger, stretches and
expands, wiggles, curls and motions to me. Daddy is
peeping around a tree.*

The dodge ball smacks me in the face
with too much force. Why didn't I see the ball
coming and then skedaddle? Get out of the
way. Dodge it. After all, that's the name of the
game, Dodge Ball. My face stings.

Movement, again I see movement.
Now I don't see it. Now I do. Escape. Fly.
Run. Do something. I spot the outside door
that leads directly to my classroom from
the fenced-in playground. I run back in my
classroom door. I spin in circles and search
for a hiding place. The supply cabinet under
the counter will have to do. Quickly, I yank

the cabinet door open. Round containers of finger-paint in the eight primary colors and jars of white paste are neatly stacked in the cabinet. With a strong shove, I cram the supplies to one side of the cabinet, wipe my nose and eyes on my sleeve, bend down and contort my whole body to fit inside the cabinet. I stick my pointer finger through the narrow opening of the cabinet door and slowly pull it closed.

Mrs. Murphy trails after me into the classroom. "Estie Culler, come out wherever you are. Estie, what on earth is the matter with you?" Mrs. Murphy anxiously calls to me. I dare not move, not even a single muscle. I try not to breathe.

I dread the thought of leaving Mrs. Murphy, and I simply hate the idea of hitchhiking on with Daddy, walking down the highways, thumbing. I prefer to stay here in school. Before this week in Landtrip School, it has been months, lots of months, since I have been in school. School is fun and I want to stay. I am sure Daddy is pulling me out of school today and I have no idea if, or when, I will return. I intend to hide in this stuffy little cabinet, as long as it takes. Maybe he will up and leave town without me.

My classmates hurry back inside. "Look for Estie," Mrs. Murphy instructs the students.

I hear chairs shuffle, doors open and close, and children's shoes squeak on the hard floor. Rapidly a slim stream of light rays shines into my corner of the cabinet.

"Estie's in here," shouts Red, a red headed boy with freckles all over his face and arms. "Look, see," he shouts. He smiles at me. "I found her," he exclaims, so proud of himself, like he has discovered the golden egg in an Easter Egg Hunt. Red swings the cabinet door wide open for everyone to have a look at me all wadded up inside the cabinet.

Mrs. Murphy, crouches on the floor, pokes her face inside the cabinet, and her Bugs Bunny teeth glow. Her extremely white teeth constantly protrude over her bottom lip and creates a permanent smile plastered on her face. She is young, vivacious, and bubbly. She has auburn hair, brown eyes, and long eyelashes.

She pulls me by the hand, unfolds my body. "Estie, we were only playing dodge ball. It's a game, and you can't run off and hide because you were hit with the ball. Sooner or later everyone gets hit. That's the object of the game." She bends her head down to examine my face and she notices I am crying. "Okay, Estie, tell me, what is really bothering you? Why are you crying so?" Mrs. Murphy asks. "You can tell me."

"He's come to get me," I whisper.

"Who?" she asks.

"My Daddy. Please don't make me leave with him. Please," I plead.

"What makes you say that? No one is here to get you," Mrs. Murphy reassures me.

"Oh, yes, he is. I saw him hiding on the outside of the fence behind a tree. He motioned for me to come to him. It scared me, and that's the only reason I got smacked by the dodge ball," I explain.

"No one is taking you anywhere. Now, now, Estie, calm down, you are alright," she says.

"No, Ma-am, I know he is here to get me. When Daddy shows up at a school or anywhere else, it is always unexpected and he takes me away. We move on to somewhere else. We always leave. We have to get the Bibles to China. I don't want to move on any more. I will not leave you," I say.

"Honey, you're not going anywhere," Mrs. Murphy promises.

Mrs. Murphy guides me, her hand on my shoulder, to my desk. She insists all us kids settle down, and rest our heads on our desk tops. I cross my arms and place them on my desk top and drop my head on them. I hide my face in the bend of my arm, near my elbow.

When all is quiet, Mrs. Murphy begins reading <u>Hansel and Gretel</u>. I am quiet, not making a sound; my silent tears soak the long sleeve of my blouse.

The loud speaker of the public address system screeches abruptly, and all heads pop up and all eyes spring open. The speaker produces a continuous high-pitched shrill sound. Mrs. Murphy stands and shuts the book. The speaker crackles and sputters with static. When the shrill noise subsides, a female voice with a slow Texas drawl asks, "Mrs. Murphy, Mrs. Murphy, are you able to hear me?"

"Yes, I can hear you," Mrs. Murphy replies.

"Mrs. Murphy, please send Esteeee Culler to the office."

"Okay," she answers.

Crying, I run from my desk to Mrs. Murphy. "Please don't make me leave," I beg. I wrap both my arms around her and cling tightly. I stick close to her, as peanut butter sticks to bread.

"You've gotten yourself in a tizzy." She pulls herself free from my arms, steps back and holds both my hands. "Estie, your hands are trembling. Take a deep breath. You'll be alright. Why are you afraid? I promise nothing scary is going to happen," Mrs. Murphy says.

A promise she can't keep.

She gives me a quick hug. "You are wrong," I whisper in her ear.

"I'll see you tomorrow," she says. She opens the door, my clue to leave. But before I walk out the door, I make my last ditch effort. "Please, I don't want to go with him. Please I don't want to take a ship to Communist China. I only want to stay put. Please," I beg.

"You're not going anywhere, much less to China. You are being difficult, aren't you? We'll talk later, okay? I'll see you tomorrow." Mrs. Murphy flashes me her best smile and closes the door.

In the empty corridor, I feel small and lost. I know I will never see Mrs. Murphy again. I want to remember Landtrip School, Mrs. Murphy's protruding teeth, being good at playing dodge ball, and the odor of finger-paint and white paste. I want to read <u>Hansel and Gretel</u>. Looking down the hall, I walk slowly toward the office.

At the front door I see Daddy, Mary, and JJ. Mary is holding the old duffle bag. Daddy has JJ's hand and the old Bible is tucked tightly under his sweaty armpit.

I feel hopeless and oh, so sad. My heart hurts. My heart screams, yet no one hears.

Night falls. We sleep in the woods again, kinda' like Hansel and Gretel, minus the bread crumbs.

...tell them to take up twelve stones from the middle
of the Jordan from right where the priests stood and
to carry them over with you and put them down at
the place where you stay tonight......They are to be a
memorial.
Joshua 4:2, 7 NIV

Chapter 18
A Reprobate in Timbuktu, USA

Mary, JJ and I are asleep in the back seat of
a cozy, warm car. I sit between them. They
stretch their feet and legs toward their side of
the car and my lap is a pillow for their resting
heads. I sit up, rest my head and sleep with my
back against the seat. Up and down, side to
side, my droopy head bobs and nods, and then
nose-dives and I slump either over JJ's body, or
the other way over Mary's. When the weight

of my heavy head and my sharp shoulder bones are on Mary or JJ too long, they begin to stir and wiggle uncomfortably, so I switch positions and use the other one for my pillow.

The setting of the car heater is on high; the volume of the car radio is down low and plays soft, slow music for the pleasure of the late night listeners. The songs are clear and strong, without any scratchy static, live from the Grand Ole' Opry in Nashville, Tennessee. Daddy and the driver chat, "What's your name? Where you from? Where are you heading?" The usual get-to-know-you stuff. I feel warm and safe, at least temporarily, sleep robs my consciousness.

Simultaneously, several turbulences occur: brakes squall, wheels swerve and Daddy shouts, "What the hell! You SOB." JJ topples to the floorboard and Mary screams. Alarm, my resting body jerks abruptly. My tranquil, peaceful mind automatically shifts from sleep mode to high gear, charged full of energy and panic. My steady heartbeat, quietly doing its routine thumping and pumping in a smooth rhythm, abruptly stops and explodes into chaotic spasms. Unexpectedly Daddy opens the passenger's front door of the moving car, and he holds on tightly to the door handle. Cold air swooshes into the car.

"You are an abomination in the eyes of the Lord. A repulsive reprobate and a sinner in the worse possible degree! You might as well curse God and die!" Daddy hollers at the driver. The tires screech and the car swerves to an abrupt halt. Daddy swiftly slings the car door open. "God have mercy on your sinful soul," he shouts. Daddy snatches the back car door open, grabs Mary and sets her on the edge of the road. "You allow your sinful nature to control you. Your sinful lust damn you to eternal hell fire!" Daddy shouts. He lifts JJ off the floorboard and I scoot out behind him. Daddy slams the back door behind me.

"Please get back in the car! It's freezing! I will drive you to a safer place. You and your kids will freeze to death out here. I'm sorry. It won't happen again," the driver pleads, as he leans across the front seat, and reaches for the door handle to keep the door open. "Don't let the kids freeze. Get back in the car where it's warm."

"Reprobate!" Daddy shouts.

"For Christ sake, hop back in the car." The driver's voice is trembling. He sounds scared and sad, like he's crying.

"A low life reprobate!" Daddy shouts.

"There is no traffic on this dark road. There will not be another car along this road tonight. Get in," the driver pleads.

"Reprobate; a snake crawling on your belly. Jesus will crush your head. I would rather we freeze to death, right here in the middle of...of... uh...well...of....right here in the middle of nowhere, than to burn in hell with you! I flee from your evil presence and will not linger a minute longer. Jesus will protect us from all harm, and his angels will take charge of us and keep us warm and safe. But you, you will burn in hell!" Daddy slams the front door. "The Bible says to flee evil. And that's exactly what I'm doing!" Daddy shouts.

Not a light anywhere, except the fading red glow of the taillights on the car driven by the "Reprobate," now miles down the flat-as-a-flitter road.

I stand in absolute darkness and I squint my eyes to shield and protect them from the sting of the wind and the gritty sand. I slowly pivot in a complete circle and deliberately peer into the cold night. Carefully I scan all four directions, and survey the wide open expanse of dusty, dismal desert. Huge, round tumbleweeds are weightless; they swirl and spin in the mighty rotating force of the untamed gushing wind. The strong whirlwind circles of sand whips our bodies and burns our eyes. I take firm grips on Mary's and JJ's hands and guide them back off the road. (Wouldn't you know of all the places for Daddy to go berserk, work himself into a frantic frenzy and to act out-and-out "loco," is in the middle of nowhere?) The sandstorm rages and Mary and JJ are too scared to be sleepy. We stumble against the wind and within a few minutes we happen upon a small, low (no more than five feet tall) lean-to. Beside the sturdy three open-sided shed, several planks of wood are neatly stacked.

Under the lean-to, Mary, JJ, and I move to the back and immediately flop down close to each other. The lean-to blocks the wind some. Mary and JJ, in no time, appear to be asleep. I lean back against the one wall, and I watch Daddy. He kneels at the woodpile with both arms lifted high above his head. "Holy and Almighty God, Jehovah, Savior, it is You, I praise. It is You, I worship. You watch over me and provide my needs. I praise you for this lean-to. This stack of wood I dedicate as a monument to the Glory of God. You are worthy of all praise and honor. You are my refuge and my help…" Daddy prays in a loud, clear voice. I don't care to hear any more.

I scoot down and snuggle between Mary and JJ, and close my eyes. I wonder why Daddy stays out in the blowing sand. He oughta' pray under the shelter – the very shelter he thanks and praises God for providing? When God gives, you ought to use the gift. Oh Lord, Heaven knows, this cannot be normal. Surely no other families live, day in and day out, like we do. We are honest to goodness, genuine hobos. And my Daddy is "loco." I can't think about it or I'll cry and I am too tired and too sleepy. Life is complicated.

"God, take us home," I pray.

We are in Timbuktu, USA, camped out in a Greyhound bus station. Stale cigarette odors stink and the haze of blue-gray cigarette smoke is as thick as fog. It blurs vision, and is nasty to breathe. We sit in the "white only" waiting room; use the "white only" restroom and drink from the "white only" water fountain. All of this "white only" stuff makes no sense and will soon be changing, according to my wise Grandma.

Wooden bench seats are hard on the butt. Wooden arm rests are spaced every couple of feet, and make it impossible to stretch out my body and lie down. The seats are not designed for comfort but are intended to be occupied for a few minutes before boarding a bus. Stuck here forever, I am certain we have lingered beyond the usual amount of time for waiting on a bus. We sit and do nothing. Mary and JJ sleep lightly and when the public-address system abruptly announces a departing bus, they wake with a quick jerk and then drift immediately back to sleep.

Daddy is in the seat at the end of the row on the other side of JJ. I zero in on him for a while as he dozes too. I notice his hair is thinning on top, that he has lost his blond curls and he has his hair combed over to disguise his balding head. The gray felt hat that he has recently added to his apparel is lying on top of his Bible in his lap. His aging face has creases and wrinkles around his eyes and several long horizontal lines cross his forehead, and deep grooves are on each side of his nose to the corners of his mouth. He has accumulated a load of weight, mostly in his round belly. He appears unhappy and seldom, if ever, smiles or laughs. He appears angry or sad; his lips sag downward in the corners.

Daddy stands, stretches and walks in circles around the waiting area of the bus station; he strolls back and stops in front of me. "Estie, I am leaving. Stay put and watch them," he says and glances at JJ and Mary.

"Alright," I nod and yawn sleepily. He walks away, carries his duffle bag, places his hat on his head and sticks his Bible under his arm.

Maybe he won't come back. This will be my opportunity to take JJ and Mary and hide out in the restroom. I could go outside where the Greyhound buses are lined up and ask the drivers to please drive us home to our Grandma's in Greensboro, North Carolina. I look out the glass window, notice Daddy talking with a driver and the driver points down the street in the opposite direction of the bus station. I wonder what he is up to, where he's going. I stretch my neck to see, but it is too dark. I don't want anything to happen to Mary and JJ. I touch each of them with my hands, so they cannot make a move without my knowing it. I close my eyes, slump down in the seat and try to sleep. I feel burdened down with the heavy load and responsibility of caring for Mary and JJ. It seems I am always watching them sleep. I'm afraid to sleep myself for fear of something happening to them. But, sleep wins.

Someone softly wakes me by patting my shoulder and I rub my eyes with my fist. First I spot JJ in front of me with his pants that have holes in the knees pulled down around his feet and he is peeing on the floor with a cute, lop sided smile to show how proud he is of himself for a job well done. Then I notice a pair of shiny black shoes. I look through partly closed eyelids, I see they belong to a man in a dark uniform, a cap, a silver badge on his chest and a gun in a holster on his wide black belt. I play opossum. I would like to sleep through this. He pats my shoulder again, shaking me slightly, in an attempt to wake me up. "What's your name child?" he asks with a growl.

"Estie Irene Culler," I say.

"Effie, is this your brother?" he begins.

"My name is Estie!"

"Thought you said Effie."

"No sir, I said Estie Irene Culler. Yes, that's my little brother, John Joseph. He is called JJ. That's Mary, my sister," I announce with pride and point to her. She's asleep and her head leans on the hard armrest of the bench.

"How long ya'll been here?" he asks.

"Only a few minutes," I say.

"Long enough for you to nap," he says.

I straighten myself up. "I am not asleep; I am just resting my eyes."

"Oh, and while you are just resting your eyes, your baby brother pees on the floor," he says with a chuckle.

An older black gentleman with wiry, gray hair shows up rolling a beat up galvanized bucket with a heavy string mop. He wrings out the excessive dirty water through the wringer attached to the side of the bucket. JJ tugs his pants up. The old gentleman with the stringy mop cleans the floor. He has a grin on his thin face as he hums "Swing Low, Sweet Chariot." He seems happy as a clam, as if he has no worries in the world.

Mary wakes up, confused like she has forgotten where she is. She and JJ sit and look at me and the policeman.

"My Daddy is coming to get us," I offer to the policeman.

Then Daddy shows up, clean shaven and speaks to the officer like they are old buddies. "Hope they've been no problem. We're on our way to my Mother's house in North Carolina."

The officer flashes a disapproving glare at me. "They look like they have been here a long while," the policeman says.

Oh thank heavens, I think surely this policeman will see through Daddy's lies and take us to find our Mama and Grandma. A policeman is supposed to help lost children find their way home.

But he did not.

Go and make disciples of all nations...
Matthew 28:19 NIV

Chapter 19
No Boats – No Bibles

"Praise the Lord, Glory to God! We are here. God has led us across the United States and He has provided all our needs and has kept us safe in the palm of His hands. Hallelujah!" Daddy shouts and immediately, he falls on his knees and lifts both hands high above his head. This is his favorite prayer position, no matter where we are or how inappropriate it may seem, on the shoulders of roads where speeding cars and trucks zoom by or on a busy sidewalk in town where people stare at him. Nothing distracts Daddy when he is on his knees, with his eyes closed, and he talks out loud to his Lord.

We stand at an entrance sign, white with neat black letters, to "Believers in Christ's Coming Again Village." Daddy kneels and it sounds like he aims to spend a while in prayer and conversation with God. The sign is in the center of a well kept flower bed of golden poppies in full bloom. Wooden railroad ties form a square border which encloses the flowers. Mary and I balance ourselves on the ties, and stretch our arms out straight on, like airplane wings. We have barrels of fun, until JJ copies us, trips, tumbles off and skins his knees. He cries; I gather him in my arms, and we sit down on one of the railroad ties. I hold him on my lap and wipe off his legs, which makes him scream and cry louder. Daddy keeps talking to God. He stays on his knees with his hands still held high, and his eyes still closed tight. He doesn't stop long enough to check on why JJ is screaming and crying to beat the band. The louder JJ cries, the louder Daddy prays.

I decide to sing to help JJ forget all about his scratched knees. "John Joe, John Joe, where ya'll gonna' go-e-o," I sing. Mary joins me, and there's no doubt she and I are loud, as we blur out the noises of JJ's screams and Daddy's 'Gloria's'. "John Joe, John Joe, what ya'll gonna' do-e-o. John Joe, John Joe, where ya'll gonna' go-e-o. Goin' down the road to see your little girl-e-o," Mary and I sing together. It doesn't take long for JJ to stop screaming and to simmer down, and when he does, Daddy quiets down his voice also. Mary and I make monkey faces at JJ. We cross our eyes, keep our lips closed, stretch our tongues over our top front teeth, and pull our ears out on each side of our heads. We try not to laugh, but all three of us laugh and giggle at our monkey faces.

A shadow appears over us and blocks us from the warm sun. Daddy stands and looks down on us as we sit on the railroad ties. "Wipe the monkey faces off now! I've told you before, your eyes will get stuck and you'll be cross-eyed forever. You brown eyed girls, like your Mama, are ugly enough, as it is. Now get up, we're here to do God's work, gotta' load Bibles on ships to China," he says. We are on our feet before he finishes his sentence.

Daddy walks down the narrow gravel road into "Believers in Christ's Coming Again Village" and we hurry to to keep up with him. I take it all in; watch everything, my eyes roam and don't miss a thing. I realize that I haven't thought about the color of my eyes in a long time, if ever; and it irks the dickens out of me, that Daddy has said Mama, Mary and I are ugly.

I notice there are no other people in

sight, only us. According to the neat white signs with black letters on the cinder block buildings, there is a "Dining Hall," "Meeting House," "Shower House," and several larger houses labeled "Men" and others labeled "Women and Children." The "Meeting House" sign is in the center of the flowers. I spot still more railroad ties laid in a long rectangular shape with a sign that reads "Vegetable Garden." Beside the vegetable garden is a rough, unpainted building labeled "Tool Shed."

Daddy points to more railroad ties bordering more golden poppies, which he calls "Cups of Gold." "Sit your butts down here and wait for me. John Joseph, you best sit down before you fall down and break your scrawny neck. Do you understand me?" Daddy asks.

"He'll be okay. I'll mind him," I speak up. I distract Daddy and hope he doesn't notice that JJ pays him no attention. "We'll all sit here and wait," I say.

Daddy turns and enters the "Meeting House." A black Pontiac is parked in front of the building. JJ, Mary and I follow instructions and keep our butts on the railroad ties. At this location I can survey the entire gravel circle road and all the buildings. "Why are there not any other people and only one car?" Mary asks.

"Well, I don't know but at least we

are in California finally," I point to the sign. "According to the 'Believers In Christ's Coming Again Village' sign, the people at this village believe Jesus is coming here soon," I answer.

"Looks like Jesus has already been here and He took everybody but us with Him," Mary says. Her voice trembles.

"No, Mary. When Jesus comes again He will never leave children behind. Jesus loves all children and will take us with him; especially little children like JJ. As long as we have JJ with us, we know Jesus hasn't come here yet. So we're okay. You don't need to worry about Jesus ever leaving you," I reassure Mary.

Mary and I pick up gravel off the ground. We take turns throwing one rock at a time. Without saying so, we watch to see who can pitch their rock the furthest. "It's 'bout time we got here," Mary says.

"We've been gone from Grandma's house forever and ever," I say. "Maybe, after Jesus does come, we can go back to North Carolina to see her." I sling my rock and watch where it lands.

"Mine went the furthest," Mary squeals. Proudly, she jumps up and down and laughs with delight. We can always take nothing, which is all we have, and come up with a fun game to play.

"No way. Not so. You are kidding me," I say. But, I am almost certain, Mary's rock travels as far as mine, and possibly further.

"Oh, yeah, I'm positive this time mine went the farthest," Mary brags.

"We'll see." I throw a rock as hard and as far as I can. "I wonder how far away the beach is? It would be more fun to play in the ocean and sand than in this hot gravel. I miss playing in the sand pile under the crepe myrtle tree at Grandma's. You do remember us playing in Grandma's sand pile, don't you?" I ask Mary.

"Yeah, I remember JJ kicking in the sand with his bare feet, and us not wanting to get stung by bumble bees," Mary answers. "Those bumble bees were fuzzy and black and made loud, scary, buzzing sounds as they swarmed in the flowers. You remember?" Mary asks.

"Yeah, they were scary," I answer.

"I'm glad none of them ever stung us," Mary says.

"Daddy said one whole side of California is on the beach with seashells and the blue ocean, and rich movie stars live in mansions and they own giant boats called yachts," I say.

Mary and I watch with interest as JJ rears back, with a rock in his hand, winds up his right arm, and practices his throws – a little pro.

"I wonder if Daddy is mistaken. You reckon we are at the wrong place? Or are we too early or too late? Where are the Bibles? Have we missed the ship bound for China?" I ask to no one, and no one answers.

JJ proves to be strong and he hurls his rock clean out of sight. Surprisingly, Mary and I agree, JJ pitches his rock the farthest – out distancing both of ours.

As soon as we realize that JJ outshines us Mary and I promptly lose interest in the rock throwing. We remain on the wooden railroad ties and wait patiently for Daddy.

Daddy and another man finally come out of the "Meeting House" building. Daddy motions, waves his hand and directs us to come to him. The other man is well-mannered, in a dark suit, white shirt and necktie. He smiles weakly and wastes no words. He opens the back door to the car for Mary, JJ and me to jump in; Daddy slides in the front passenger's seat. Without any introduction to the driver, the three of us in the back seat keep quiet, and come to think of it, so do the two in the front seat. They are too quiet for comfort, especially Daddy, who is always ready to share the Gospel story of Jesus Christ, and he does so, whether anyone wants him to or not. But now, not a word is spoken.

More than a year, we have been traveling, thumbing, walking, constantly in the process of reaching our destination – California. In particular, Long Beach, California, so I assume we are now headed to the coast, to load Bibles on the ships and to do the Lord's work. I am thankful for the gentleman and his car, and I anticipate being at the beach soon. I am excited to be a part of the secret organization helping to send Bibles to the poor lost people and children in China.

When the driver shifts the car into park, I am taken aback. There is no ocean in sight. Without any explanation or any reason whatsoever given to us, the man has driven us straight to a Greyhound bus station. There he purchases an adult and three children's nonrefundable one-way tickets to Houston, Texas. My mouth drops open and I am speechless.

Daddy and the gentleman shake hands, and he hands Daddy the tickets and a ten dollar bill. "Have a safe trip, Brother Culler," he says. With no further comment, he leaves us in the café at the bus station.

Sing to the Lord, praise his name; proclaim
his salvation day after day,
Declare his glory among all nations, his marvelous
deeds among all peoples.
Psalm 96:2-3 NIV

Chapter 20
Preaching and Singing in the Bus Station

The café is full and there are no seats available in the booths, on the bar stools or at the tables. While we wait for a place to sit, I realize I didn't ever hear the gentleman's name. I wonder if it's because he works for the secret Bible smuggling organization.

Daddy teaches and quizzes me on what he considers to be important and valuable facts; such as, the names and number of books in the Bible, the names of the states in America and their capitals, the name of months in a year, and about the big hand and little hand that travels slowly around the face of a clock, (which is a timepiece) and hangs on the wall in the cafe. There's a giant clock named Big Ben in England, and a timepiece is also called a watch. I listen; but, most of Daddy's lessons confuse or bore me. Perhaps it's more than I can understand because we don't own a watch, a clock, or any such timepiece. Anyways, I don't believe anything named Ben, with two hands wiping circles slowly around his face, can tell me anything, much less the time of day. How can he without a mouth? Again, I realize the genuine meaning of "loco." My Daddy is "loco."

Daddy tells me it has taken us more than a year – five hundred days – to follow the Lord's "Holy Calling," (and that's a mighty long time to me). We hitchhiked slowly, but surely, and made it to California. As Daddy says, "Like the US mail, we never fail. We must go in rain, snow, sleet or hail."

It is crazy, loony as all get out, for Daddy to thumb from North Carolina to California (or anywhere else for that matter), without any money, without a job, and with Mary, JJ and me tagging along. What's even more absurd, ridiculous, and totally insane, is that within fifty minutes of our arrival, we make a complete u-turn and high-tail it back across the United States. I am dumbfounded. It's insane. This is pure lunacy; and my Daddy is a lunatic. "Loco, loco, Daddy is loco," I whisper softly to myself, and can't help but smile, remembering that my older brothers, Matt, Mark, and Luke had told me so. They knew, and now I know for sure; loco, loco, my Daddy is loco.

After five hundred days of my life, what's the big fat rush? What's one more day? If I had my druthers, we would stay, at least one day, long enough to see the Pacific Ocean.

When we get an available table, Daddy orders three grilled cheese sandwiches, which drip in butter, a few potato chips and a slice of pickle for Mary, JJ and me; he orders a cheeseburger and hash browns for himself, along with four small cokes.

"Eat up. Hurry, we've got a bus to catch. Our bus is already here and it will be the next one to leave. Finish eating and make a trip to the toilet. Estie take JJ with you and Mary," Daddy says.

"Daddy, I want to see the long beach. Is the bus going to take us to the long beach?" Mary asks.

"No, and it's not the long beach. It's Long Beach. The name of the beach is Long

Beach," Daddy says. Mary looks at Daddy confused. I am 'bout as confused as Mary is, if not more so.

"If we aren't going to the long beach…" Mary starts, but is interrupted by Daddy.

"Mary, you don't get it," Daddy says. "It is not the long beach. It is a beach. The name of the beach is Long Beach." Daddy raises his voice, and his face turns red. "It doesn't make any difference. We're not going there," Daddy says.

"Oh, is the bus going to take us to China? I want to help deliver the Bibles and…" I say.

"Sure, yeah, right, of course, we're riding the bus to China. Now shut up, eat and go to the bathroom," Daddy shouts. He slams his open hand on the top of the table where we sit. We eat fast.

Mary, JJ and I hurry to the restroom, and when we are returning to the table where we left Daddy, we all three stop. Daddy stands in the center of the café preaching. "My children and I don't have much time here. We are taking the next bus out. The Lord has called me to assist in a special project in Key West, Florida. I am going to help load Bibles on a ship and deliver them to Cuba – to the poor, lost and dying souls of Cuba. We must beware. There are those in our government who try to interfere with the spread of God's Word to all the world. The FBI's leader, John Edgar Hoover, has made it a priority to stop the teaching of Jesus as proclaimed in God's Holy Word, the Bible. In the gospel of Matthew, Jesus gave his command to the disciples to 'Go into all the world and preach the gospel.' This is what God has called me to do.

"I know there are those of you who are Believers of Jesus Christ and in His second coming, and you want to see Jesus proclaimed to every nation. Beware of false prophets and leaders, like John Edgar Hoover - Yes, John is his name. He goes by J. Edgar but I know his name is John Edgar. He thinks he is almighty and he tries to stop the growth of Christianity in the world. But, this Bible," Daddy holds his old tattered Bible high above his head, "this Bible, the Word of God, commands me to go into the entire world and preach the gospel. That's exactly what I am going to do. Glor-ia! I want you to know John Edgar Hoover and all his forces of evil make it a priority to stop the Word of God from spreading to a lost world. I feel led to give you the opportunity to help me in this divine mission. My children standing there," he says and points to me, Mary and JJ. "My three precious children are with me and they help me in the Lord's work. Estie, you and your sister, Mary, sing a song for these folks. Sing 'We've A Story to Tell to the Nations' and sing loud," Daddy demands. Everyone turns and looks at us "precious children." Daddy doesn't say another word.

Mary and I barely know the song. We look at one another and wonder if we'll remember all the words. However, we both realize we are not given a choice in which song to sing. "Lord help us," I whisper. I take Mary's hand and give her a smile, and we both smile at all the people who smile at us. We appear comfortable and confident, like we sing songs in crowded bus stations all the time. A smile tends to be contagious and yields confidence, even if we lack ability.

"We've a story to tell to the nations, That shall turn their hearts to the Lord. A story of truth and mercy, A story of peace and light, A story of peace and light. For the darkness shall turn to dawning And the dawning to noon day bright. And Christ's great kingdom shall come to earth -The Kingdom of love and light."

Mary and I sing our best as loud as we can. And we smile and smile. Whew! We remember all the words! The people clap their hands. "Amen," "Praise the Lord," "Glory to

225

God!" Shouts of praise to God are plentiful. We continue to smile. Daddy continues to preach.

"Yes, God is leading us to Key West, Florida, and we are going to load Bibles on ships headed to Cuba. A secret Christian organization, 'Operation Free Bibles,' is behind the movement and the goal is to reach the whole world for Jesus. Amen. Let me hear an Amen," Daddy yells.

Most of the people in the café shout "Amen!"

"My children and I leave on the next bus to proclaim the Word of God." Again Daddy lifts his Bible high above his head and he shouts, "This is the Holy Word of God. Now if you believe, if you are a true believer of Jesus Christ, let me hear all of you join me in a big Amen!"

"Amen!" Everyone shouts "Amen!" and waves their arms high in the air.

"Now, we must be leaving, so as my little ones, God's precious children, walk by you, please open your hearts to the lost and dying people of Cuba. Please give your money and give generously, your offerings to these my children to help spread the Word of God. Mary, straight down this way," Daddy says as he motions to Mary. "Walk slowly so these wonderful people of the Lord can give you their gift of money to help spread the Word of God to the poor lost and dying souls of Cuba. Estie, you and JJ, ya'll come around this way," he says. He motions the opposite way from Mary's. "JJ, please hold out your hands and these kind folks will place money in them so we can help others know and love Jesus."

Someone hands me an empty Coca Cola glass with money already in it. JJ and I walk slowly around the café; JJ, with his hand out to the people, and me, holding out the Coca Cola glass. People are filling the glass with change and a few dollar bills. We slowly walk toward Daddy and Mary; they now wait for us at the door of the café that leads into the bus terminal.

Someone begins and others join in singing, "Amazing Grace." I notice that the colored people in their cramped waiting room stand and clap their hands and sway from side to side as they sing, "Amazing Grace." A young black boy leaves their waiting room and runs over and hands JJ a coin.

"Thank you," I say. I look the colored boy in the eyes. For a few seconds we gaze into each other's brown eyes and sing, "through many dangers, toils and snares, I have already come. Tis grace that brought me safe so far, and grace will lead me home." Our hearts connect briefly, ever so briefly, but long enough for me to see his courage and God's love. He diverts his eyes to the floor and hurries back to the "COLORED" waiting room. We climb onto the Greyhound. On both sides of the bus is a picture of a greyhound dog running with legs stretching the length of the bus. It stinks of diesel fuel and cigarette smoke. We head back to Houston, Texas. Since we aren't staying in California, I am glad we are going back to Texas. I look forward to returning to Landtrip Elementary School and grabbing and hugging Mrs. Murphy, and never ever leaving her. This gives me something good to think about, along with playing dodge ball.

On the bus ride I feel motion sickness and I throw up my grilled cheese sandwich in the aisle and stink up another bus. The bus driver pulls the bus over and stops on the shoulder of the road. The driver lets me get some fresh air to calm my upset stomach.

While the driver takes care of me, Daddy stays on the bus and again scratches "Jesus Saves" and "Prepare to Meet God," in the paint on the back of the metal seat directly in front of him. Because of this, he comes close to being arrested and having us tossed off the bus. However, before we reach the next stop, the bus slips in a snow blizzard and slides off the road down a slight incline. We spend the night sleeping on the bus which, to me, is a welcome spot of safety and comfort after all the nights we've slept in the woods and by railroad tracks. We have had one-night stays in homes of a preacher or two, but, we often are without food for days, and then only wild blackberries, pecans, peaches, and grapes, depending on the state we are traveling through.

After we arrive at the bus station in Houston and Daddy has the three of us line up with him and stomp the dust of California off our feet, he immediately walks us to the highway, where we poke out our thumbs and hitchhike again. Apparently, Daddy has decided it is God's will for us to head to Key West, Florida, immediately.

"And, Estie, the capital of Florida is what?" Daddy asks.

"Tallahassee," I answer. "I want to stay in Houston."

"Too bad, God wants us in Key West, Florida. We have a boat to load," Daddy says.

If anyone will not welcome you or listen to
your words, shake the dust off your feet
when you leave that home or town.
Matthew 10:14 NIV

Chapter 21
Doing the Hokey Pokey

We come to a stoppin' place most *every*
Sunday morning at a rinky-dink church along
the way. Often these churches are far from
the main highways and down an off beaten
country road. "This *very* church," (Daddy
says of *every* church) "is divinely placed at this
intersection by the All-Knowing God, Himself.
God predestined it," Daddy explains. "This
means God planned it all ahead of time for me
to preach right here and right now."

Daddy introduces himself as "Rev.

Culler" to the preacher, who is most likely the only man around with a suit and tie on. He informs the earnest preacher of his tragic story. His wife abandoned him and their three children. "She sought and followed the pleasures of her flesh and was burnt to death in a gambling house fire. Furthermore," Daddy tells the man in the suit, "God has placed on my heart a message from His Holy Word." Daddy brings his old sweat stained Bible from beneath his left armpit and then waves it up and down in the preacher's surprised and bug-eyed face. Daddy declares loudly, "This is God's Holy Word. God has commanded me to deliver His message to the fine folks gathered here on the pews of this church. They starve, and desperately need to be fed upon God's Word. More importantly, they will be given the opportunity of a lifetime – the marvelous chance to be blessed, through giving a love offering, to me to help me and my children to travel to Key West, Florida. God has called me, and time ticks away. We must hurry before time runs completely out. God's purpose for my life is a secret mission of distributing Bibles to the lost and dying souls in Cuba."

The preacher, (who can't be much older than my brother, Matt), is speechless.

Daddy quickly interprets his silence as a

"Yes, welcome, come on in now and bring us a message from our Lord."

"Well, Bible college didn't teach me how to handle this kind of situation," the preacher says, rubbing his temples with both hands.

"Of course not. Bible College can't predict the workings of the Holy Ghost. But, you can rest assured that the Bible teaches us to welcome all who come in the name of the Lord. I do humbly come in the blessed name of my Lord and Savior, Jesus Christ."

"Yes, of course," says the young preacher, whose cheeks are red. "This is my first church and I'm still learning." They shake hands. "Welcome to my church."

After all the proper introductions and announcements, Daddy sets the stage by calling on us "his three precious children" to sing. Mary, JJ and I, in our dirty glad rags, stand straight, smile and sing softly and sweetly:

"Jesus loves me, this I know, For the Bible tells me so;
Little ones to Him belong,
They are weak, but He is strong. (At this point JJ raises both arms and flexes his imaginary muscles)

Yes, Jesus loves me, Yes, Jesus loves me,
Yes, Jesus loves me, The Bible tells me so."

The men sometimes shout "praise the Lord!" and "hallelujah!" The "I feel so sorry for them" tears flow from all the soft hearted ladies. We then take our seats on the front pew; JJ and Mary on either side of me. When Daddy begins to preach, I always stop listening.

The pages in his Bible are well-written on – almost every sentence is underlined with red, black or blue ink pens or pencils, and flips easily to where he wants it to open. And then Daddy begins to quote from memory (he hardly ever reads the verses, he knows them word for word), "go ye therefore and preach the gospel to all nations, baptizing them in the name of the Father, and of the Son, and of the Holy Ghost. Teaching them….." I zone out and Daddy shouts on.

After a long while, Daddy winds down his message with: "Yes, my dear brothers and sisters in Christ, Jesus loves all the children. Amen! He loves all the children of the world! Hallelujah! Glor-i-a! Now I call my three precious children to the platform to sing," he says. He motions to me and up we go again; we know the routine well – stand straight, smile and sing.

I wake JJ, whose head is flopped over on my lap, take his hand in mine, and Mary grips my other hand tight, and we saunter sleepily to the stage. Since we are moving slowly, Daddy continues, "My children are precious to me and your children are to you – but we must take the love of Jesus to the lost children in Cuba. As Mary, JJ and Estie sing the closing song, come to the altar with your love offering. Be generous." Daddy looks at me, my clue to start singing.

"Jesus loves the little children, All the children of the world;
Red and yellow, black and white, They are precious in His sight.
Jesus loves the little children of the world."

We sing. We know the song by heart. As soon as we sing the last note, we switch back to the last verse of "Jesus Loves Me."

"Jesus loves me! He will stay, Close beside me all the way;
If I love Him when I die, He will take me home on high.
Yes, Jesus loves me......."

We continue to sing "Jesus Loves the Little Children of the World" and "Jesus Loves Me" over and over again. We, three precious children, have moved the faithful Christian ladies and some of the men folk to tears. Tears loosen purse strings. The more tears fall, the more money falls into the offering baskets. Happens every time.

Finally, when all the tears are dried, all the money has been finagled that can possibly be finagled from the congregation, and prayers of thanksgiving have been offered, Daddy accepts the generous love offering and praises God for His provisions. The young preacher proclaims a benediction with his hands held over our heads. Today the church is having dinner on the grounds and everyone insists that we stay and eat the delicious home cooking prepared by the church ladies. Tablecloths and blankets are spread on the grounds and the ladies serve up plates of fried chicken, potato salad and chocolate brownies for JJ, Mary and me. "What precious children you are!" several of them say to us. Daddy stuffs himself with lots of everything there is to eat. We say our thank yous and goodbyes and head down the road; however, before we are out of the town, Daddy hits another church at their Sunday evening worship service. Same songs – different verses.

Daddy's opinions of how others have treated him affects some of his actions in weird ways. For example, when we reach a road sign which indicates the city limits, the county line or a state's boundary line, if Daddy believes the fine citizens of that particular place welcomed him with a warm meal, money or sandwiches, or if he thinks the congregations in the churches have given to him generously, he kneels beneath the road signs on the loose, rocky gravel. He lifts his arms high and stretches his hands toward the heavens and in his loud preachy voice, he thanks his Heavenly Father for the Godly people in this good city or state.

Otherwise, if the preachers, police – or anyone for that matter – makes it known to Daddy that his loitering, begging and his presence in general are not to be tolerated, Daddy reacts totally different and even weirder. He lines JJ, Mary and me, like stair steps, under the road sign. He kicks his shoes off his feet and he insists we do exactly what he does. He repeatedly stomps his bare feet in the dirt and rocks and then hops on the hot black top road, stomping his feet fast. Barefooted, we slowly move to the steamy road, stomping our little tootsies faster. We sweat from the blazing sun, and squirm from the hot road below our feet; we dance around in agony. We look plum stupid. Ridiculous! This can't be normal. My

Daddy is really "loco." We appear to be doing the hokey pokey, "put your right foot in, put your right foot out… and shake it all about."

Ain't no one gonna' offer us idiots a ride anywhere, except maybe to the nearest "loco" hospital. But, never fear, Daddy reads us verses from the Bible to support our actions. "And whoever will not receive you nor hear your words, when ye depart out of that house or city, shake off the dust of your feet, as a testimony against them." So the Bible says, according to Daddy, it is good and proper to stomp the dust off your feet, do the "hokey pokey," barefooted in the highway. I ain't believing it! Daddy knows a Bible verse to support all his weird actions.

My daily task has been to read and memorize verses from Daddy's old Bible. Now Daddy includes geography lessons. Often when there are no vehicles to thumb down, Daddy digs his road map of the United States from his banged up duffle bag. He squats on the ground, opens the folded map, and spreads it out on the side of the road, in the gravel and dirt. Daddy puts a rock on each of the four corners of the map. He seeks and finds the location of the state we are traveling in, and points out its capital. Diligently he moves my hand over the map, identifies each state we have been in, and each state we are going to be in. Daddy forces me to pronounce and to correctly spell the capitals of each state: Raleigh, North Carolina; Columbia, South Carolina; Atlanta, Georgia; Tallahassee, Florida; Baton Rouge, Louisiana; Austin, Texas; and Jackson, Mississippi. (He taught me to spell Mississippi by using the rhyme M – I - crooked letter, crooked letter, - I, - crooked letter, crooked letter – I, hump back, hump back – I.)

"Estie, you are getting a good education. Only a few children get to see the world in person. You can only see pictures in a text book, if you are in school; but, you are seeing first hand, with your own eyes, the important places and landmarks as we are traveling," he says.

He uses a blue ink pen to trace the roads and highways we have traveled on. I am curious about the white letters on the dark blue pen. "What do those words on your pen say?" I ask.

"O' Henry Hotel, Greensboro, NC," he answers. "That's where your Grandma, Matthew, Mark, and Luke are," he adds.

"Can we go this way?" I ask. I point to North Carolina on the map.

"Of course not. We are on a journey

for the Lord. We have been all the way over here," he indicates with his index finger, "to the state of California, and the capital of California is Sacramento. Key West, Florida, is our destination; maybe we'll go on to Cuba. God has anointed me to load Bibles on ships bound for Cuba. I've told you that. Once you put your hand to the plow you can't turn around. You must push forward to the prize of the high calling in Jesus Christ," he says.

"Oh, okay," I sigh. "Can you show me where Cuba is?" I ask.

"No," he says and folds his map.

"Okay." It did not slip by me that my Daddy said Grandma and your older brothers are in Greensboro and that he did not mention my Mama. I don't know if I should dare ask any more about my Mama. Daddy keeps saying that she's been burnt to death. I don't believe that. I can't.

"Is Mama waiting in Florida for us?" I ask.

"No, she is not. She left us and you will not ever see her again. Dead, I've told you. Burnt to death. Now, let's thumb a ride. We've got some miles to travel," he says.

I don't ask about Mama any more; the reality of her death sinks in slowly and leaves me heart-broken.

JJ stands in front of me, he lifts both arms up to me, and begs me to carry him as we all plod down the lonely highway. I pick him up and carry him in my arms. With his dirty little hands, JJ wipes my tears from my face. Even though my Mama's dead, it occurs to me my Grandma, my Daddy's mother, Estie, whose name I have, may be searching high and low for us. Of course she is. We are two peas in a pod.

Almost daily Daddy fishes deep in his pants pocket for his folding pocket knife and in his neat lettering he carves "Jesus Saves" or "John 3:16" on the bark of trees in the woods; he carves on telephone poles, park benches, bus station benches and on sign posts along the way. He prints "Man shall not live by bread alone," "Jesus Loves You," or "God is Love" on café menus and the covers of magazines for sale in display racks. Daddy's logic for tampering with the property, damaging trees and writing on magazines he does not intend to buy is simple: "Someone lost, without Jesus, will stumble upon the tree or the signpost and will come to know Jesus as their Lord and Savior, and great will be my reward in heaven," he explains.

Daddy walks right up to complete

strangers and asks "Are you saved?" or "Have you been born again?" or "Is your name written in the Lamb's Book of Life?" At which, most good hearted strangers look down, make no eye contact, and shake their heads in disbelief. Daddy kneels on the public streets and prays for their lost and dying souls, or he stomps the dust off his feet. I can't help but remember my brother, Matt, teaching me the meaning of "loco" – real crazy in the head.

I secretly pray that Jesus will grab Mary, JJ and me, and take us away to a safe place. A place, where someone will keep us, and will not let us leave town with my Daddy again. I doubt God loves me, because He does not answer my secret prayer. I cry and beg, but He doesn't hear me

I remember my sores and my wandering,
the bitterness and the gall.
I well remember them, and my soul is
downcast within me.
Yet I call to mind the Lord's great hope
and therefore I have hope.
Lamentations 3:19-21 NIV

Chapter 22
Mosquitoes and Mrs. Stevens' Garage

Foul smelling swamp odor is nasty – really worse than nasty. Nasty is hog farms in North Carolina, chicken farms in South Carolina and the rotten boiled egg smell of paper mills in Georgia. Cattle ranches in Texas stink; however, you will never get a Texan to say so. But nothing is as repulsive (unless it is the johnny house at Pilot Mountain) as the Florida swamps. We are in south Florida and the stench of decay permeates the hot air. Rotten dead fish odor, causes me to vomit. I bend at my waist, placing a hand on each knee. My dizzy head hangs low; I cough, gag and have the dry heaves.

Then there are mosquitoes. Mosquitoes galore! Millions, billions, zillions of these disease carrying, flying insects are all over Mary, JJ, and me. Our bare legs, ankles, face, arms, eyelids and every minute pore of our skin is covered with mosquitoes. The mosquitoes have buzzing wings, which I hear constantly on, around, and in my ears.

We tramp through the home of mosquitoes, through their breeding beds in the soggy, stagnant water-logged swamps of the Everglades. Mosquitoes attack and assault us with their painful bites. For occasions as this, God gives each mosquito a slender tube snout, their individual drinking straw for sucking and drinking my blood. How nice of You, God to create these wee-little blood sucking vampires! You had the entire universe to fling into space, and You created all things, including the stinky swamps and thirsty mosquitoes. It is beyond my comprehension why You would endow mosquitoes with the equipment to feast upon my blood or why You would be inclined to furnish mosquitoes with large, swampy homes.

On second thought, I suppose it is their privilege and also their responsibility to bite us; after all we are the ones invading their homes. I've no idea of our real dangers – like gators and crocodiles. I'll choose little nibble bites and sucks of mosquitoes any day rather than be swallowed whole and alive by an alligator.

I hold Mary's and JJ's hands which prevents me from swatting and slapping mosquitoes. Finally, Daddy gives JJ a ride on his back. This frees up one of my hands to swat at the buzzing insects that cover Mary and me. "Mary, our legs are black. Mosquitoes have covered every bare spot of our legs and we look like we have on long black socks," I say. Mary doesn't reply. And now, I realize why Mary is not talking. Mosquitoes, no lie, fly into my mouth. I immediately learn that spitting and spewing mosquitoes out of my mouth only provides an open mouth for more mosquitoes to invade. I swallow a mouthful, and thereafter, keep my lips closed tight. Not a word out of me. I am exhausted.

Finally, as the sun goes down and we are covered up by total darkness, our feet hit solid ground, not mushy marsh. Daddy collapses on his stomach and JJ rolls off his back and lies on the hard ground. Daddy uses his duffel bag as his pillow. Mary and I fall to the dry road, and we quickly zonk out. We sleep, or pass out, in total exhaustion. I never know which; nor for how long. It could have been minutes or hours, or maybe overnight, before we stir.

We all wake and come alive at about the same time. We discover our resting place, the solid ground, to be a paved black topped surface road; which evidently is rarely traveled. No good Samarian has passed our way.

Not far from our resting spot, on the road not traveled, is a busy intersection with Highway 1. Would you believe a busy tourist road? Highway 1 is scattered with motor courts, motels, restaurants, and truck stop cafes. We aren't moving anywhere too fast, but our feet (which are yucky from the gunk of the swamps) pick up speed as we approach the first place serving food. It's a drive-in burger joint, however, we walk up to the screened in window; and Daddy orders ten hot dogs, all the way, for a dollar, and water to drink. We sit on benches that are permanently attached to a picnic table, eat hot dogs from white wrapping paper and drink water from paper cups. It is mouth-watering delicious. While Mary, JJ and I are still eating at the table, Daddy walks to a telephone booth, drops change in the telephone machine, and talks to someone on the phone. When he returns, we follow him and step a little peppier, down Highway 1.

We stop at a house, built beside a Baptist church, the parsonage. The sweet little preacher's wife gives us some clothes from the church's clothes closet. Daddy explains to the Preacher his mission and the secret organization's plan to smuggle Bibles to Cuba without Batista or John Edgar Hoover ever knowing about it. Daddy, with a new suit of clothes, is set to preach the next day at the Sunday morning worship service.

We are finally in Key West, Florida. Same story as California, there are no Bibles to load, and no ship to be loaded. I reckon Daddy missed the boat – again. Where does he get all this misinformation? Since God is delivering this information personally to Daddy, why can't Daddy keep the departing time schedule straight? I wonder, and then I decide to ask Daddy.

"Daddy, when God told you to go to Key West and to load free Bibles on ships bound to Cuba, why didn't you find out the time the ships were leaving?" I ask.

Without the slightest warning, Daddy slaps me across the center of my mouth, which

I am not expecting.

"Estie, that's for blaspheming," he shouts.

"For what?" I am truly puzzled and hold my hands to my stinging lips.

"For blaspheming, that's what! You have no right, none at all, to question God's timing! You got that, Estie? Never, never again, let me hear you speak disrespectful of the authority and wisdom of the Almighty God," Daddy says.

I catch my breath, my mouth stings, and hot embarrassing tears flood my face. I feel ashamed. I did not ever intend to be disrespectful, or to blaspheme God. I want to have God's approval. "I am sorry," I say softly. "Daddy, I am not questioning the authority or the wisdom of God. Never. I only asked if you have the correct time. If there really was a ship in California going to China or a ship here sneaking into Cuba, then why…"

The force of the slap across the side of my face sinks me to my knees; my bare knees skid on the concrete floor; and I place my hands on the floor and try to stand back to my feet. Daddy kicks my butt, and I cave in flat on my stomach.

"When are you ever going to learn to honor your father? You are slow to learn,"

Daddy yells at me. He is hyperventilating and sweating. He stomps across the floor, out the door, slamming the door behind him, leaving me with his handprint bright red on my face, and his dirty shoe print on the back of my shorts.

We stay a few days in Key West, in a garage behind a white house. Cots line the walls on the inside of the garage. The cots are narrow strips of canvas material, stretched over wooden, collapsible frames. The cots are fine with me. I've slept on much worse. Mrs. Stevens, the landlady, rents the cots by the night. The rent includes breakfast in the dining room of her house at six o'clock in the morning and supper at six o'clock in the evening and use of her bathroom facility until nine o'clock at night.

Daddy has rented two cots for the four of us. Although it is still daylight, he makes Mary, JJ and me go to bed while he sits on Mrs. Stevens' porch enjoying her company.

Mary, JJ and I sleep together on the same cot. Much later, after dark, when Daddy decides it is his bedtime, he quietly enters the garage, picks me up and puts me on the other cot with him. I wake up, but I pretend to be asleep because I don't like it and I don't know what to do about it. He wraps his hand firmly over the top of my hand and rubs himself. He groans, grunts and sweats. I hear his heart pound fast. He releases my hand. He carries me back to the cot with Mary and JJ. I feel dirty, ashamed, and wonder what I did to deserve this treatment that just doesn't feel natural. Why doesn't he leave me alone? What do I do to provoke this?

On the sidewalk in front of Mrs. Stevens' home, I draw square boxes with white chalk for Mary and me to play hopscotch. We are beginning our game when three boys, who look about twelve years old, come swaggering down the street with smirks on their faces. The tallest one has a lit cigarette in his mouth and, as they approach us, they grin, like a cat that has swallowed a canary. They look mischievous – like they know a top secret or they've got some prank hidden "up their sleeve."

"Girl, you look like you have better things to do. Why don't you take a walk with us?"

"No thanks. I'm taking care of my little sister now."

The three of them are acting obnoxious. The boy drops his cigarette butt and grinds it with his foot in one of our hopscotch squares. He lifts his left hand into the air toward me and forms a circle by placing the tips of his thumb and index finger together. The other two guys think it is fun and do the same thing. They point the other three fingers of their left hand up in the air. They touch each of these fingers with the middle finger of their right hand and all three of them say "kiss my ass hole." When they say "hole," they insert their finger into the circle formed by their thumb and index finger. They are all chiming in, chanting, "kiss my ass hole. Kiss my ass hole."

I have a rock in my hand that I plan to toss in our hopscotch game. I throw my rock as hard as I can, and aim at the tallest boy. The rock hits him in his belly. Then I run, holding Mary's hand, to Mrs. Stevens' front porch and retreat into her house. We stay quiet until we see they have gone on out of sight.

Puzzled. Are these the boys I hear playing outside at night? Did they see Daddy take me to his cot? Why else would they want to say something dirty to me? I don't understand. This makes me nervous and causes me to wonder if everybody in the world thinks bad things about me. I am confused.

Across the street from Mrs. Stevens' house is a stone Presbyterian Church. "Just another rich Roman Catholic Church, regardless of what name is on the sign. And besides, there's not a nickel's worth of difference between the two. Both churches, Catholics and Presbyterians, are full of rich sinners. They love money, the root of all evil, more than God," Daddy says.

We are sitting on Mrs. Stevens' front porch, on a Sunday evening and watching young people, high school and college students, park in the parking lot behind the church and enter the church. Daddy raises all kinds of "cane" to Mrs. Stevens, who is an attractive, elderly widow, the spitting image of Aunt Bea on the Andy Griffith Show. She has thick gray hair pinned up on top of her head, a plump little lady, well-dressed and well mannered.

After a while, unexpectedly Daddy shouts, "Something sinful is going on inside that Roman Catholic Church. See, I told you, just a bunch of sinful Catholics. Why in God's name, would Christians ever need to turn off the lights during a church service?"

"Mr. Culler," Mrs. Stevens says.

"Reverend Culler," Daddy corrects her.

"Mr. Culler," Mrs. Stevens clears her throat and continues to speak calmly, "I have been a member of that God-fearing Christian church for more than forty years, and so were my parents before me," she says, all prim and proud.

"Maybe so, but you are headed down the wrong path, the wide path leading to hell. Of all the audacity, turning off the lights in church! Sinful. Sinful," he shouts.

"Mr. Culler, it was announced this morning at our worship service, a missionary from Africa would be presenting a slide show depicting the work of the Lord being accomplished there. Therefore, the lights must be lower to be able to see the slide presentation. Now, Mr. Culler, you and your children will kindly leave my front porch. You may stay in the guest quarters, for the night only, because it's the Christian thing for me to do, since you travel with these children. In the morning, I'll drive you back across the bridge, and you can leave like you came," she says. Mrs. Stevens smiles, very satisfied with herself.

*Ask and it will be given to you, seek and
you will find;
knock and the door will be opened to you.
Matthew 7:7 NIV*

Chapter 23
Scratching With a Fish

Mrs. Stevens swings her 1952 green and white Ford into a gravel parking lot on the left side of the road at the north end of the "Seven Mile Bridge," and slams it to a screeching stop in front of the "Bridge Bait and Tackle Shop." Daddy bounces out of the passenger's front seat, opens the back car door, and Mary and JJ scoot out; Mrs. Stevens turns and lifts her arm over the back of the seat. Her hand holds a small brown paper sack with the top neatly folded down.

"Estie, dear heart, please take this bag. Strawberry jelly biscuits are inside it for you, your sister and your brother," she says. I take the sack and smile.

"Thank you so much!" I say. I am grateful because my belly is already growling. I smile again and slide from the back seat.

Daddy, who hasn't spoken a word for at least seven miles, is now ready to talk to Mrs. Stevens and leans in the open car window. Mrs. Stevens is not ready to talk or to listen. She changes the gears of her car, and the tires spin, shooting gravel and spitting sand all over the legs of Daddy's pants. The Ford makes a wide turn out of the parking lot and speeds onto the "Seven Mile Bridge" back toward Key West.

We copy Daddy and stomp the Key West sand and dust from our feet. "If anyone will not welcome you or listen to your words, shake the dust off your feet when you leave that home or town. Yeah, you three know how it's done," Daddy says. He is proud of us. He smiles and stomps his feet; likewise, our sandaled feet join in, and we all stomp, one foot after the other, faster and faster.

"You put your right foot in. You put your right foot out. You put your right foot in, and you shake it all about. You do the hokey pokey and you turn yourself around. That's what it's all about!" Daddy sings loud.

Holy moley, Lord, help us all! Daddy, my loco Daddy, is doing the "hokey pokey dance" with all the motions. "Okay, kids get in line. Here. No. Let's form a circle," Daddy says. With his hands on each of our shoulders, one at a time, he guides Mary, JJ and me to form a circle and he fills the gap.

"Again, let's sing. Sing it loud and try to copy all my motions," he shouts. Then he has a better idea. "Well, I'll tell you what! Let's do first things first. Listen and repeat after me, okay," he instructs us. "If anyone," he says, and smacks his hands together three times. Clap, clap, and clap. "Will not welcome you," he says. Clap, clap, clap. He puts his hands together. "If anyone," clap, clap, clap, "will not listen to you," clap, clap, clap, "shake the dust," he says, and shakes one foot and leg high in front of him, with his hands on both sides of his waist, shake, shake, shake, "off your feet," he says, and lifts his other foot and leg, and shakes it hard. Shake, shake, shake.

Then to my surprise, Daddy leads us again in the "hokey pokey dance." He does all the motions and this time he exaggerates the moves more. On the "turn yourself around," he sways his big butt from side to side several times as he turns his body around in a circle.

Good glory, this is getting embarrassing. Bless patty and jumping Jupiter's, here we are beside Highway 1 doing the "hokey pokey." Daddy is having fun. Impossible! I've never seen him behave like this. My Daddy is loco, and I am copying all his words and motions; maybe I'm halfway loco too. Mary, JJ, and I need to get away from him before all his loco-ness rubs off on us. I don't want to be loco, so I stop singing and dancing; and I carry Mrs. Stevens' sack of biscuits with me and I stray a short distance away from Daddy. Mary and JJ leave Daddy dancing and come on with me.

Daddy grabs his duffle bag off the gravel. The dancing is over. "Let's go fishing," he says. We skip along following Daddy, as he gains some of his senses and we wander behind the bait and tackle shop. He takes a fishing rod and reel that is propped against the side of the tackle shop as if it belongs to him and is where he left it. "We're going fishing for a ride to Miami," he says. Sure enough, in no time at all Daddy strikes up a conversation with a fisherman about the same age as he is. The fisherman, a thin man with deep wrinkles in his suntanned face, is smoking a corncob pipe and wearing a White Sea captain's hat. His bib overalls remind me of what the farmers wear at Pilot Mountain; he is just missing the checked flannel shirt. The fisherman is friendly enough, and nibbles at the bait Daddy is casting in his direction.

JJ, Mary and I sit in the sand and eat the strawberry jelly biscuits which Mrs. Stevens had wrapped in waxed sandwich paper. Six warm biscuits, drip with sticky strawberry jelly. Mary and I eat two each and JJ eats one. We finish and lick the red jelly from our fingers and circle our sticky lips with our tongues. I leave the last biscuit wrapped and in the brown sack.

We play in the sand, look for seashells, and kick around a coconut that appears to have been tossed back and forth in the rough ocean, since the time of Adam and Eve. The slick brown outer coconut hull, shaped like a football, is tough, and hangs loose from the brown stringy hull. I can see the monkey-looking face on the inner shell and I try to pull the loose outer hull completely off, but I can't. So I hold the coconut to my ear and shake it, and not hearing any liquid, I determine it is empty. No coconut milk in this one. Dry as a bone. It is only good to kick around.

Daddy tells the fisherman, whose name I've not heard, that Florida has been our home for years, and his wife of nearly twenty years has left him and their three kids. He tilts his head in our direction. "Oh, how could their mother up and leave these three precious children?" Daddy asks. He hangs his head and rubs his eyes. "It's so sad. Heart breaking," Daddy says slowly as he shakes his head.

There. Got him. Mr. Fisherman snags the bait. He is caught completely in every slick lie that drips off Daddy's tongue; hook, line and sinker.

"I need a ride to the other side of Miami, where my sister and her family live," Daddy says.

"I'd be much obliged to drive you there, but I am driving 'Honey,'" Mr. Fisherman says.

Daddy's face is blank and he looks confused. "Honey?" he asks.

"Sure, 'Honey' is my pick-up truck. I call it 'Honey' because it looks like a wad of honey with its orange and brownish color," Mr. Fisherman says.

"Well, that sounds like an unusual color to me. I've never seen trucks, or cars either for that matter, to be honey color," Daddy says.

"Oh well, you'll see. I've fished all night and only caught three fish. And I haven't had a nibble in hours. Let me fish a few more minutes and then we'll leave," he says.

I listen intently as they talk of fishing, the kinds and the sizes of a variety of fish. Mr.

Fisherman has a galvanized bucket filled with ocean water for his few fish. The bucket is in the sand a small distance behind him.

Red, angry whelps from mosquito bites have popped out over my body. The irritating, itchy whelps swell in the heat of the sun and cause me to be restless and annoyed. I scratch my arms, legs, and ankles, wishing my fingernails were not gnawed off to the quick. I sit down in the sand beside the fisherman's bucket and scratch. I wish for eight more hands, with long pointed claws, to dig into my skin. I dip my hands into the bucket of warm, cloudy, fishy water and slip them over the slimy, scaly fish. Poor, pitiful things have been cramped in the bucket for hours. Well, I can't think about the poor pitiful fish because of poor pitiful me, itching all over. I lift my hands and stir both of them around in the grainy sand. Now, I'll scratch what itches. With sand clinging to my damp hands, I rub them up and down my legs. I dip my hands again in the fishy bucket and then coat them again with the rough sand. I rub the sand on my arms and legs, as hard as I can. My sandy hands are coarse, like sandpaper, and stink of fish. The itching of my skin settles down a little. I stand and slap my hands together, knocking the sand off, and I wipe them dry on the legs of my shorts. My legs are still screaming to be scratched! The itch is still itching to be itched! So I sit back down quickly in the sand by the bucket. I put both my hands in the bucket and grab the first fish my hands touch. I stare into its glassy black eyes and watch the sucking movements of its mouth. Rapidly, an idea flies into my mind. That's all is takes – just a quick thought. I prop the scaly fish to my knee and with all my strength, I push it down my leg. I never look away from its glassy eyes and sucking mouth. The scales on the fish scratch my legs as I continue to mash and push it against my skin. I rub the sharp scaly fish down to my ankle, and then put it back to my knee and slide it down my leg again. As I scrub the fish down my leg, I pick up speed and add more muscle. I switch to the other leg and scrub it. My itchy legs, a scrub board; the fish, a scouring pad; and, finally relief! Just in time too, because the friendly fisherman is coming toward me. "Thanks for scratching my legs. I feel much better!" I say to the fish, and I put it back in the bucket.

"I'm going to empty the bucket into the ocean, and let the fish swim free," Mr. Fisherman says. After emptying his bucket, he gathers up his rods and tackle box. We all follow him to "Honey." He places his fishing gear into the back of the truck.

"Your pick-up is not orange or brown. Yeah, it's the rustiest hunk of metal I've ever seen. 'Rusty' describes this thing to a "t"; not 'Honey'. You should call it 'Rusty,'" Daddy says.

"Well, I don't call it 'Honey' only because of the color. If you will quit criticizing, I'll give you a ride," Mr. Fisherman says.

"Sure, I meant no harm. I am only making an observation," Daddy says.

"Well, get in. And, when you see how slow 'Honey' runs, you'll know why I call her 'Honey'. She is slower than molasses, but I like 'Honey' better."

He and Daddy help the three of us climb into the back of the pick-up with all the fishing gear and "Honey" chugs slowly away. The wind is chilly and we lay flat in the bed of the pick-up truck to stay warm. "Honey" drops us off at Aunt Janet's and Uncle Warren's house on the outskirts of Miami.

The angel of the Lord appeared to him in
the flames of fire within a bush.
Moses saw that though the bush was on
fire it did not burn up.
God said, take off your sandals for
you are standing on holy ground.
Exodus 3: 2, 5 NIV

Chapter 24
That's No Burning Bush

Their rambling, ranch style house sets in the center of a small horse farm with stables and a white fenced riding ring. There are horses, dogs and cats a plenty.

Aunt Janet and Uncle Warren have two sons, Kenny and Eddie, a little older than me. I remember we had fun when they visited Grandma on Mother's Day for the annual

Culler family reunion or during the Christmas holiday. We ran races across Grandma's yard, played tag and climbed trees. I was competitive and could beat my girl cousins in races and often left some of my boy cousins lagging behind; but never Eddie. He was my favorite cousin and we became fast friends. He was cute, with brown, wavy hair and hazel green eyes. He kidded me about me being his kissin' cousin. No way. Now, we are at their door and I am embarrassed by the thought of seeing him again. Daddy knocks and neither Eddie nor Kenny opens the door; but Aunt Janet does. I am relieved, yet disappointed.

Aunt Janet's hair is jet black, shoulder length and curly. With harsh, but also sympathetic brown eyes, she gives Daddy, Mary, JJ, and me a quick once over from head to toe. She instructs us to walk around to the back of the house. "You can wait at the picnic table, and I'll make you some sandwiches. I'll be right there in a jiffy," she says, and closes the door.

Three brown and white beagle puppies scamper and nip at our feet as we slowly make our way around to the back of the house. Mary and JJ throw sticks and have the puppies retrieve them; they run in circles so the puppies will chase them. We find the wooden picnic table and two wooden benches, sitting directly under an outdoor light which is attached to the top of a telephone pole. Sure enough, Aunt Janet is standing in the open doorway at the back of her house. I assume she will swing the screen door open and spread her arms open wide to hug us, but she doesn't. "Estie, you can play with the puppies too. They're friendly. Be back in a sec with something good to eat. How does that sound?" she asks. She vanishes from the doorway; she does not invite us to join her.

All three of the beagles are the spittin' image of each other. Mary and JJ play on the ground with the cute puppies. They giggle as the beagles wiggle, roll over, climb on their faces, and lick their mouths, eyes and noses. I am sad. Miserable. I remember my baby puppies and their senseless suffering and deaths at Pilot Mountain, because of my Daddy's heartless cruelty and his downright meanness and wickedness. My heart crumbles and my tears fall. I wipe tears from my eyes with the backside of my hand, and look around to make sure no one sees me cry. Mary and JJ are doing fine, and Daddy is kneeling on his knees by a large blooming bush with red flowers. As usual my tears are unnoticed.

Daddy's shoes and socks are off, and

his hands and arms stretch high. I wish he'd get stuck in that position and not be able to move. Let him be forever stuck on his knees! There are worse things I could wish. Like my brother, Matt, told him on the day of the big fight, he should be chopped into pieces and dropped into the shit of a shitty shit house.

"Sandwiches. Sandwiches are ready." Aunt Janet's voice, a life jacket, rescues me from sinking deeper into the stinking crap in the bottom of the out house at the "Lord's Mission;" it gently places me on the picnic bench in her back yard.

"You kids wash your hands under the spigot by the back door. Be sure to scrub them clean with the cake of soap that's on the step. You too, Estie." We do as Aunt Janet tells us and then we wipe our hands dry on our dirty clothes.

Aunt Janet sets a platter of sandwiches and some napkins on the table. "I'm going in to get you some milk," Aunt Janet says. Mary and JJ come and sit with me on the bench. Our eyes are on the platter of sandwiches, chicken salad and peanut butter and jelly. The sandwiches are cut in triangle slices and are in neat, high stacks. I am certain they will tumble over, but they don't. On the bench, we swap places a time or two, until I am in between Mary and JJ. Now, they are both content. Aunt Janet returns, carrying red metal drinking glasses and a matching pitcher, full of cold milk. She pours each of us a glass.

"Where's your Daddy?" Aunt Janet asks. Yet, she keeps on talking and doesn't wait for me to answer. "I hope he didn't abscond and abandon you children here. Warren and the boys are away, on a Boy Scout camping trip; so, it's up to me to tend to the horses, and that's a tough job in itself. Sure don't need anybody else to look after," she says, opening a new bag of Lay's potato chips.

Finally, Aunt Janet stops talking and looks at me. "Well, Estie, now tell me. Where did Abe go?" she asks. I point to Daddy kneeling by the bush.

"Abraham, if you want something to eat, you best get off your knees and get your butt to the table. These sandwiches are going fast!" Aunt Janet shouts. Daddy doesn't budge, and after a few minutes, she tries again. "Abe, I know you can hear me, so listen good. Okay, Abraham Culler, come on over here. That bush is not 'The Burning Bush', mentioned in the Old Testament. Those red oleander flower blossoms are not burning flames. That bush is not on fire! So get off your knees and come and eat." Aunt Janet shouts louder.

She eats half of a chicken salad sandwich and chomps on some chips. With a napkin, she dabs at mayonnaise on the side of JJ's mouth. "You kids must be starving. Eat all you want, but be sure to save room for watermelon," Aunt Janet says.

Happiness is in my mouth, and my taste buds are having a blast! Homemade chicken salad on slices of fresh, soft bread – out of this world delicious! I'm starved and can't eat them fast enough.

We have eaten nothing, as much as we have eaten peanut butter, since walking away from Grandma's house with Daddy on that Sunday afternoon. Mary, JJ, and I eat the chicken salad sandwiches and leave the peanut butter and jelly ones. I enjoy my last bite, swallow it, and wash it down with gulps of milk. We leave no evidence, not even the smell, of chicken salad. I wonder if Aunt Janet has forgotten Daddy is kneeling over by the bush, or is she waiting for us to eat all of the chicken salad sandwiches before she calls Daddy to the table again.

Aunt Janet gives us each a slice of cold watermelon, smiles and winks at me. Then she nods her head toward Daddy. "When you snooze, you lose," she says.

"Abraham, the red flowers are still on

that bush, but guess what? The homemade chicken salad sandwiches are all gone. And besides Abraham, it was Moses, not old Abraham who saw God in the burning bush! Do you understand? You are Abraham, not Moses! And, that's no burning bush! Put your shoes back on your feet. This is not holy ground! For heaven's sakes, it is only my back yard! So come on and eat!" She shouts loud.

Gazing at me, "How in the name of our good God, can anyone remain in that position and keep their arms lifted high for so long, without collapsing and rolling over?" she asks.

"I have no idea," I say, shrugging my shoulders.

"Abraham, all the chicken salad may be gone but God has sent you His special manna from heaven. God has given it especially for you. I've gathered it up. God's delicious manna from heaven for no one but you is here on the picnic table," Aunt Janet says in her sweetest, but loud voice. There is no movement. Daddy must be stiff – like when a person dies and rigor mortis sets in.

With little concern about Daddy, Mary, JJ, and I eat the watermelon carefully, trying not to slurp the juice or drip it all over us.

"Don't worry about your clothes; they're 'bout as dirty as dirty can be. A little watermelon juice won't make any difference. Besides, you're getting a rub-a-dub-dub in a hot bathtub, as soon as you finish eating," Aunt Janet says.

Daddy decides to join the picnic and to partake in his manna from heaven. With bare feet he gingerly tiptoes to the picnic table; he carries his shoes and socks in his hands. He sees the peanut butter and grape jelly sandwiches that remain on the platter.

"Bath time," Aunt Janet announces. "Come on Mary, and Estie. I'll bring JJ. It's time for a bath. Abe, you eat all these sandwiches and there's more milk in the red pitcher, if you want some," Aunt Janet says. She carries JJ toward the back door.

I hold Mary's hand, and we linger. We turn and see Daddy, as he raises his hands toward heaven. "Oh, praise the Lord! Praise the Lord! Peanut butter and jelly sandwiches! My favorite!" Daddy exclaims enthusiastically. He couldn't have been any more grateful, no matter what was setting before his hungry eyes, watering mouth, and growling stomach. We enter the back door as he chooses a sandwich, and bows his head in humble thankfulness.

Now we are allowed in her lemon-scented clean house, and directed straight to the aqua blue tile bathroom. She fills the tub with hot, not warm, water. She pours in liquid bubble bath and lays her instructions out to me. JJ and Mary can shimmy out of their dirty clothes, which Aunt Janet calls "a crying shame." "I am sure you will feel ten pounds lighter when all the filth you have been hauling around all over Texas and half of Georgia is washed down the drain. No human being should be so filthy. My horses are far cleaner than you kids! The horses are the ones who sleep in the barn and you younguns are the ones smelling like it!" Aunt Janet says. Oh, to have the comfort of a barn. If she only knew.

"Mary and JJ can bathe together. Here's a tin cup. Pour water over their cruddy heads; and here's the shampoo. When was the last time your heads were washed? JJ let me look at those ears." She bends and pulls his ears and scrapes her glossy red fingernail in his ears, then behind his ears. "As I figured, your ears have layers of black crust!" she says. Poor JJ's ears are red from her scraping. "Estie, I'll be back. Scrub them really good. Get the dirt from between their toes. Okay?" she says. She looks at me to determine if I follow the instructions.

"I don't know," I say.

"You don't know what?" she asks.

270

"When our heads were last washed," I answer.

"I am sure you don't. That's okay. Get them clean now," she says. Aunt Janet pats the top of my head ever so gently, but fast; she fears bugs or lice might jump out on her.

I recognize the scent on her wrist in the seconds she pats my head. "Mrs. Sarah Luther," I whisper.

"I'm sorry. Did you say something?" she asks.

"I like the smell of your perfume," I say.

"Thank you. You have good taste. It's called 'Chanel' and it's the very best," she says.

Ding-a-ling, a bell rings in my mind. I've heard the same words before from Mrs. Sarah Luther.

Aunt Janet leaves the room and closes the door behind her. And I turn my attention to the job waiting for me in the bathroom. I scrub Mary and JJ with a clean white washcloth and a cake of Ivory soap. I scrub their heads vigorously, using thick Johnson and Johnson shampoo.

I fill the tin cup with water from the faucet and dump it on their sudsy heads, over and over again, until all the bubbles are gone and their hair squeaks when pulled through my fingers. When I'm certain they are clean, all crud and crust off their pink skin, Aunt Janet steps back in the bathroom with pajamas belonging to her son – one of our cousins. She hands me clean, white towels. I help JJ dry off and Mary helps herself.

"I can't believe you don't have one change of clean clothes. I'll have to see to that," Aunt Janet says. She helps Mary and JJ into boy's baggy pajamas, and uses diaper pins with yellow duck heads to hold the bottoms up. We follow her down the hall to our cousin's bedroom. It is almost as long as the ranch house, with a wagon wheel bunk bed at the end of the long room, made up with matching cowboy and Indian bedspreads. The two windows have matching cowboy and Indian curtains. Framed pictures of horses are on the walls. I examine them closer, I notice the pictures are of Eddie and Kenny, in riding clothes sitting on the backs of champion horses. A bookshelf, without any books, fills the length of one wall. It displays the family's prized photos, trophies and ribbons.

"The boys won't mind you sleeping in here. Anyway, this is their week to camp and sleep on the ground in their sleeping bags. JJ, you oughta' sleep on the bottom bunk 'cause you wouldn't want to roll off the top. It's a long way down," Aunt Janet says. For the first time since she's seen us, she draws Mary and JJ into her arms and holds them tight.

"You smell good and clean. I bet you'll sleep fine tonight. Especially since a ton of filth is off your little bodies. My goodness, you are both really blond headed. JJ, your hair is almost white. I'd never known, under all that matted crust, you both have soft, very blond hair," Aunt Janet says. She releases her hug and turns down the covers for JJ.

"Mary, you wanna' crawl up to the top?" she asks.

"Maybe later, but I'll stay with JJ down here for a while, if that's alright?" Mary asks.

"Sure. That's fine. And I'll leave the light on for you; at least until Estie has had her bath and is ready for bed," she says.

I hug them, and reassure them I'll be back in a few minutes. Aunt Janet pulls the door almost shut. "I'll leave the door cracked a little, if you want."

I follow Aunt Janet back to the aqua tile bathroom.

"Estie, tell me, what in the world did you get a hold of, or what in the world got a hold of you? You kids stink to high heavens! You smell like you have been rolling in the mushy carcass of a rotten skunk. Whatever it is, and wherever it is from, it is the foulest, nastiest stench known to mankind. You need a hot bath, and while you are at it, shampoo your hair too. When you are finished, you can stand and turn on the shower and rinse all the suds and dirt off your body and down the drain, and then you can go to bed," Aunt Janet says.

Before I can take my bath, Aunt Janet sprinkles the tub with white powder from a round can with tiny holes in the top. She gets down on her knees, bends over the tub and washes it with a rag. When she stands up, she explains how to pull the shower curtain closed and how the faucet works.

Then, to my surprise and complete astonishment, Aunt Janet startles the pee-pee out of me. She slaps my hand and grabs it away from my mouth; which now hangs open. "Estie, you cannot chew your nasty fingernails!" she exclaims.

"My fingernails are not nasty, they have been in that tub with hot soap for the last...I don't know how long," I say as I yank the aqua blue toilet paper to wipe my eyes and nose, causing it to spin, fast forward.

"Estie, I'm sorry. You're probably right. Your nails may not be dirty now. But Estie," she says and takes my hands, "Estie, never, never put your fingers and hands in your mouth. It spreads germs we can't even see and besides, it is bad manners and young ladies want to have good manners. It can become a habit, and from the looks of your nails, it already appears to be a bad habit. Your nails are chewed down to the quick. Now, what on earth gnawed on your wrists, your arms, and your legs? You have scratched the ever loving daylights out of them. You've clawed so much, you brought the blood. Then you turn around and stick those same fingers in your mouth," Aunt Janet says. "What has eaten you alive?"

"Mosquitoes," I answer.

"Mosquitoes, my eye. It looks like an army of mosquitoes made themselves at home on your arms," she says.

"You got that right. They drank so much of my blood; I thought I might have to crawl away from the swamp."

"Estie, this is serious and not the least bit funny. These sores are infectious and contagious, and it can spread on you and Mary and JJ."

"I didn't say it was funny. Do you want to know what I think is funny?" Not waiting for her answer, I carry on. "What is funny is that Eddie and Kenny, are sleeping on the ground in the woods and I am going to sleep on their bed. Are Eddie and Kenny uh, you know a little loco?" I ask. I take my hand from hers, and raise my pointer finger to my temple and draw circles in the air. "Who in their right mind would give up a bed to sleep on the ground; with all the outside creatures and critters, large and small, like big wild bears and small blood-sucking mosquitoes?" I ask, with the tone of a smart aleck, which I am turning into. I do the "loco" sign with my finger beside my temple again.

Instantly my thoughts kick back and wind into reverse – into my past. *Daddy climbs a cherry tree to wire up a loud speaker, and Matt teaches me the sign for loco and snickers and giggles with me. "Daddy's real loco," he laughs. I laugh too, and laugh some more. The tears of laughter sting my eyes. I continue to laugh so much it makes me cry. Then, the pointer fingers on both my hands are spinning in big circles at my temples. "Loco, loco. Estie is loco. Loco, loco, loco. Estie is loco," I cry.*

All of a sudden, the dam breaks and my warm tears gush and flood my face. I am afraid – so scared I'll become loco like my Daddy. I wipe my eyes with both my hands and shake and sling them to get rid of the salty tears.

"Snap out of it, Estie! Estie, nothing can be so amusing, or so sad, especially not at the same time," Aunt Janet says. She stands next to me with an empty tin cup in her hand. "Now, Estie, straighten up. Here now, what's come over you? Get control of yourself. Scrub up, shampoo your hair first. If you need anything just give me a holler." Out the door she goes.

In the bathtub, I use a soapy washcloth to scrub my body clean and to scratch the hard to reach itchy places. Relief. I scrub my already tender skin so hard it splits and brings the blood to the surface in several places.

When Aunt Janet returns, she finds me clean from head to toe, in boy pajamas, and brushing my wet hair with her brush.

"Okey, dokey. You're all clean. Here's a new toothbrush. Put some toothpaste on it and brush your teeth. You can keep the brush, and I have two more new brushes for JJ and Mary to brush their teeth in the morning," she says.

I've never owned a toothbrush. It is embarrassing to me, because I don't know how to use the thing. I hope Aunt Janet will leave the room and give me some privacy. I can figure this out by myself. I wonder if Aunt Janet can hear my thoughts.

"Estie, I'll leave the bathroom. You finish brushing your hair and then brush your teeth. Okey, dokey," Aunt Janet says again as she leaves the room.

Brushing my teeth is a new fizzing

experience for my mouth – not a bad experience, only different and spicy.

Aunt Janet returns and says, "It could be fun having a girl around. Tell you what," she says and she reaches in a cabinet. "Promise me you will keep your fingers away from your mouth. Your nails and cuticles are in terrible shape. You must stop biting them," she says and shakes her head in disapproval. "The tips of your fingers are raw as hamburger!"

I stand and look at her.

"And stop clawing at those mosquito bites. You have mountain size whelps, and red circles around the open sores, and they appear to be infected. Red circles indicate infection. And that's not good. You need some medicine. I have calamine lotion, which could help dry up the oozing and stop the itching. It's in the first aid bag that I always keep handy, but, wouldn't you know, it's gone camping with the Scouts. It wouldn't be enough to begin to cover all the places on your body anyway. It would take gallons. You would need to bathe in the pink stuff. At least you're clean and that'll help. Give me all your dirty clothes. I'll wash them and have them dry for you in the morning," she says.

"Someone at church gave us some hand-me-down clothes while we were in Key

West. Maybe they are in Daddy's duffle bag," I say.

"I'll check. Now, I'll tell you what. Let's make a deal. No more scratching and, no more gnawing. And look," she says and holds a tiny bottle, squeezes the top of it and it sprays perfume mist on me. "It is 'Chanel'," she says.

"I smell like fresh flowers and I don't stink like a dead skunk anymore," I say.

"Now let me give you a hug." She throws her arms open. I step in the circle of her warm hug and wish it could be my home forever. When was the last time I was hugged?

After a few warm moments, she releases me and steps back to have a look into my eyes. "Estie, you're as cute as you'd ever want to be. I want you to take care of yourself. You are the only you there is, or ever will be. That makes you something special. You're the only one of your kind." She smiles and hugs me.

"No, Grandma, and I are both one of a kind. She's Estie and I'm Estie. Two peas in a pod," I say.

"Well, you're sure right about that. Mama is so proud of you, Estie. I'm going to let her know that you're okay," she says.

"Please tell her I love and miss her," I say.

"Sure will. Now, you sleep tight. And if

you, Mary or JJ need anything, call me. Okay?" she says.

Yawning, I stumble to the bedroom with bunk beds. There JJ and Mary are almost gone to the world in the bottom bunk. I tiptoe and head toward the roomy top bunk.

"We are waiting on you," JJ says.

"You smell good," Mary says.

"I'll take the top bunk bed," I say.

"No, no," they both plead. "Get in the middle, that way you will be beside us, both of us," Mary says.

"Okey, dokey, make room." I grab a cowboy pillow off the top bunk.

The three of us twist and turn, trying to sleep, two too many, in the small bunk. But hey, I'm not bellyaching, compared to the bare ground or the sleeper in a transfer truck, the bunk is giant size; and smells better too.

We say our "Now I lay me down to sleep" prayers and we drift to sleep, like the children we are. And in the early hours of morning, someone wets the bed. I manage to switch our wet, soiled sheets for dry ones from the top bunk. Goodness, don't you know, a couple of Boy Scouts are going to be good and pissed off when they return home to a wet bed. Like the story of the three bears, they will whine "Who's been sleeping in my bed?"

I wish this bedroom was ours and that I could bathe in soapy water and use Chanel perfume every day. I pray to God that Daddy will leave me alone every night for the rest of my life. If not, I pray God will hang a millstone around his neck and throw him into the deepest sea.

Hold them in the highest regard in love
because of their work.
Thessalonians 5:13 NIV

Chapter 25
Miss Goldie

"Oh como amo la Christo, Oh como amo
la Christo, Oh como amo la Christo, porque el
primero me amo." Lucino sings.

"Oh, how I love Jesus. Oh, how I love
Jesus. Oh, how I love Jesus, because He first
loved me," I sing. Then she sings the chorus
in English, and I stumble over the words in
Spanish.

During the week long program at
church, called "Heavenly Highland," Mary, JJ,
other kids from the projects, and I have the
best time skipping down the concrete sidewalk

to the church. We learn each other's names; many speak in Spanish, sounding exactly like the older ladies at the tent revivals, speaking in unknown tongues.

Happy as two doodle bugs, Lucino and I are leaving Highland Park Baptist Church, a sandy beige stucco building. All the kids in the projects are invited to attend the event at the church. It is similar to Vacation Bible School at Manley Avenue Baptist Church at Grandma's. Highland Park Baptist Church is where we attend church on Sundays, if the Spirit so moves Daddy. It is almost within sight of our little yellow square house. Thanks to our Aunt Janet, who makes the necessary arrangements and pulls all the right strings at the Welfare Division of the Housing Authority, of Dade County, for us to live in the low income house. Unlike the housing projects in North Carolina, which are brick two story apartments, this housing project is made up of single story, one family units.

Saying our "goodbyes" and our "thank yous" to Aunt Janet is brief and before I have time to scratch an itch on my elbow, lo and behold she is gone.

The little yellow square houses are lined up in straight rows, each within spitting distance of the next. Some houses are backing up to each other and some are facing each other. All are identical, with a screened-in front room. This is where Daddy sleeps on a roll-away bed that is never rolled away. It is the most comfortable room because breezes flow through the screen and stirs and cool the air. Mary, JJ, and I sleep in the one bedroom on an old scratched up brown iron bed, with uncovered metal springs under the mattress. Across from the simple kitchen is a small basic bathroom. There are no halls in the square house, so we pass through the bedroom from the front screened porch room, to the kitchen and bathroom in the back of the house. The wooden back door has no screen, so it stays closed most of the time.

The kids think it is necessary to poke fun at my name. "Estie Irene ate a pinto bean," jeers Heraldo, a dark skinned, knock-kneed boy. The other kids laugh and repeat, "Estie Irene ate a pinto bean."

"Shoo, pinto beans stink," says Lucino, a cute Spanish girl, with long dark hair and shiny white teeth. I observe that dark skin people's teeth appear to be whiter than the teeth of people with light skin.

Trying not to be out done, I say, "I would rather be Estie Irene who eats pinto beans, than to be Heraldo, who is a silly face doe-doe." This gets a giggle from the other kids. Lucino's top lip curls up on one side of her mouth and she grins the fake smile of a trouble-maker, snickers and begins to speak in Spanish. Most of the kids are having fun and laughing, apparently at me.

"What? What's Lucino saying that makes ya'll laugh so much?" I ask. I don't see any humor in anything at all.

"She is saying, 'Estie Irene ate a pinto bean,'" answers Maria, a snaggletooth girl who is younger than most of us.

"So, I got that already. Is that all she is saying?" I ask.

"No, she is also saying, 'pinto beans are good for your heart...'" Maria begins and I interrupt her before she can finish her sentence.

"I know, in fact, I've known all my life. The more you eat, the more you fart." Laughing, I finish the rhyme for her. I have brief thoughts of my brothers, who had taught the rhyme to me, over a bowl of pintos, in the long ago and far away past. All the kids begin to laugh with me. Now, the joke is on Heraldo and Lucino and not on me since I'm the one who says the punch line before Maria.

"Well, Heraldo is a doe-doe," I say, which makes them all laugh again. With no further comments from any of them, I say,

**Our Yellow House in the
Housing Projects, Miami, Florida**

**Estie and her younger
sister and brother,(ages,
8,6,4) at housing projects,
Miami, Florida.**

"Yeah, Heraldo is a silly face doe-doe, and Lucino is a loopy loco." We become friends and they learn the one ground rule: Do not laugh at my name because making fun of my name is making fun of my Grandma's name, and I won't allow that!

A different game begins. We jump over the lines in the concrete sidewalk, trying to jump the furthest. I am off the sidewalk, in the midst of a jump, when I hear one of the kids saying, "Step on a crack and you'll break your Mama's back." Suspended in midair, I am motionless, as still as a fly sleeping on a rusty farm tractor. Frozen in space and time, the mention of the word "Mama," spoils the fun and I land on my knees and not on my feet.

A team of missionary people come to Highland Park Baptist church to tell us Bible stories in Spanish and in English. They serve us lunch, a bowl of homemade vegetable soup, crackers and cheese, and milk to drink. I am excited about the last activity planned for us. We all stand around two huge boxes; the size cantaloupes are packed in and sent to curb markets and fruit stands. One of the huge cardboard boxes is for boys and the other is for girls. We are instructed to form a circle around the box, and to reach into the box without looking and pull out one item. The one item we pull from the box is our gift to keep.

So, here I stand, with approximately twenty-five girls around the same age. A lady circles the box and inspects to make sure we are not peeking or reaching into the box before she gives us the signal. She announces, "On your mark, get set, go." All our hands reach deep in the box to grab our surprise and lift it from the box. What happens next, happens in a flash. My hand feels something that is soft, smooth, and silky. Satisfied with my selection, I hurriedly pull my gift out of the box. I'm sure my hand grabs and pulls out the cream of the crop, the best of the rest. Boy, what a disappointment! To my total surprise, I realize I am standing there like a dummy, with a pair of pink frilly girl's under panties in my hand. I feel embarrassed by such a personal item being in my hand for the entire world, including the boys to see. I hear the joyful sounds of the other girls gushing with delight over their gifts. Rosetta, a dark haired girl with wide black eyes, stands next to me. She holds and admires an elegant, magnificent, lacy, silky pink ruffled dress. Wow! It takes me about half a second to decide what to do. And in the other half, without any premeditation or discernment of right from wrong or without any thought of consequences, I commit the crime.

I snatch that awesome dress away from Rosetta and cram it snuggly under my shirt. I throw my gift – the stupid pink panties – toward Rosetta and run. I run faster than a scared deer, fleeing harm. I run all the way to my little yellow house – run in the screen door, to the screened in room with the roll away bed and I flop on it breathing fast and sweating. I pull the dress from under my shirt and I spread it with care on the mattress beside me. I stare at the beautiful dress and gently touch its softness with my shaky fingers. I have never seen anything so fancy! Why did I do such a thing? I took it – I actually stole it – right there in front of God, the missionary ladies, and everyone in the church yard. Instantly I feel guilty and wish I could erase the incident. I want it to be a terrible dream and to wake up and start the day over.

A loud knock on the screen door sends me off the bed. I swing the door open and step outside. I see a crying Rosetta, one of the missionary ladies, and Miss Goldie, my Sunday School teacher, whose hair is beginning to turn white. She was a golden blond when she was younger; that's how "Miss Goldie" became her nickname.

"We want you to return the dress to

Rosetta," Miss Goldie says.

"Okay," I say. What else can I say? How about, no I just don't believe I want to return it to her today. Please come back tomorrow and we'll see. I quickly go inside, grab the dress and toss it out the screen door to her.

"Do you know you did wrong?" she asks.

"Yes," I reply.

"Do you know Jesus loves you anyway?" she asks.

"No," I say, my eyes tearing up.

"Well, He does. I do too, and you be sure to come back to church tomorrow and you will learn more of His love," she says.

"Will I get a new dress?" I ask.

"No, probably not," she says.

"Then Jesus doesn't love me," I answer and close the screen door behind me. I don't return to the program the missionaries are having at the church the rest of the week.

I am swimming in guilt, a black murky pond; and I don't know how to get out of the mess.

A couple of days before Christmas, Daddy brings home a used string of Christmas lights. He says he got them at the Salvation Army Store but regardless of where the lights came from, I am happy we have them. I wind them around the top of the metal headboard of the bed JJ, Mary, and I sleep in and plug the cord into an outlet. We lie in bed and sing Christmas songs, like "Away in a Manger" and "Silent Night" and stare at the colorful lights.

Mary asks, "Estie, is there really a Santa Claus?"

"Sure there is," I answer.

"What do you want from Santa Claus?" she asks me.

"I'm not sure, what 'bout you?" I ask.

"I want a baby doll," Mary replies.

"Well, I'm glad we have these lights to watch at night," I say and notice that the color is peeling off a few of them. We gaze at the lights and snuggle until our eyes grow heavy, and I unplug the lights.

The next day, the day before Christmas, Miss Goldie from Highland Park Baptist Church comes to the screen door of the little yellow house. I am looking at a <u>True</u> <u>Detective</u> magazine of my Daddy's when I see Miss Goldie tapping on the screen door.

"Merry Christmas, Estie," she says.

"Oh, me, I haven't done anything wrong, have I?" I ask.

"Oh, no, of course not. Don't be afraid. I've been thinking about you, and I have a present for you. May I come in?"

"My Daddy doesn't allow me to open the door for anyone. He will not let anyone come in our house," I say. I slip out the screen door to talk with her. I notice a bag in her hand.

"Estie, this is for you," she says as she hands me the brown bag with red yarn tied in a bow around the top. "I hope you have a Merry Christmas. Jesus loves you, you know," she says as she slowly walks away.

I open the brown paper bag and drop it to the ground. With my eyes and mouth wide in disbelief, I see a gorgeous silky pink dress with ruffles, lace and a long sash tied in the back at the waist. "Wow, Jesus does love me," I squeal and hold the dress up in front of me. I laugh and cry at the same time; I run after Miss Goldie. She stops and stoops down; I grab her and hug her around the neck with all my strength.

"Thank you, thank you, and thank you again," I say and bounce up and down with delight. I twirl around, hugging the dress to me. "Isn't this the prettiest thing you ever did see?" I babble on.

"Estie, it's a darling dress for a precious girl! It will look good on you," she says with a smile.

"Is Santa Claus real?' I ask.

"Yes he is. Why do you ask?"

"Mary, my little sister, asked me last night if Santa Claus is real. This is proof he is real," I say.

"Yes, its proof Santa is real and also proof Jesus loves you," she says.

"How about Mary and JJ? Santa has to be real to them too. How will they ever believe Jesus loves them if Santa doesn't?" I ask. Tears drop on my dress.

"Estie," Miss Goldie says. "Do you think you and your little brother and sister will not get anything from Santa for Christmas?" she asks.

"Well, we never have," I answer.

Miss Goldie holds both my hands, looks me in the eyes, and then turns her head to hide her tears, splatters of tender affection. "Estie, put your dress inside your house and hurry back," she says.

I skip with my beautiful dress to the house, my heart happy. I hurry back. I'm afraid Miss Goldie will be gone, but there she stands, an angel in disguise.

"Estie, come walk with me to the church. Santa Claus has left several toys there. Maybe you can help him by selecting a gift for Mary and JJ. Would you like that?" she asks.

"Yes ma-am, I would love it!" I exclaim.

Before going to bed on Christmas Eve, Daddy tells me to recite the Christmas story from the Gospel of Luke:

"And there were in the same country, shepherds abiding in their fields, keeping watch over their flocks by night. And, lo, the Angel of the Lord came upon them, and the glory of the Lord shone round about them, and they were sore afraid. And the Angel said unto them, 'Fear not: for, behold, I bring you good tidings of great joy, which shall be to all people. For unto you is born this day in the City of David, a Savior, which is Christ the Lord....."

By the time I am through saying the Christmas story, I sure miss my brothers, Matt, Mark and Luke, and my Mama.

Then Mary asks, "Daddy, will Santa Claus bring us a toy tonight?"

"No, of course not. Estie just finished telling us the Christmas story from the Bible. God gave us Jesus. Jesus is our gift. Our everlasting gift," he says. "You'll get no other gifts, so go on to sleep."

He leaves the room and I plug in our one strand of Christmas lights.

"I want Mama," Mary whimpers.

"Me too," JJ cries. "I want Mama."

"Well, that makes three of us," I say.

They are quiet for a while and watch the glow of the lights; still awake and still wishing.

"JJ," I whisper.

"Yeah."

"Mary?" I ask.

"What?" she answers.

"Santa Claus is real and Jesus loves you too," I said. "You'll see." I promise.

When they are asleep, I crawl out of bed without a sound. I reach under the bed and carefully slide out my pink dress, then Mary's baby doll, and JJ's fire truck. I place their gifts on the foot of the bed; and I put a bottle of Old Spice after shave for Daddy on the table beside the bed. I am positive they will be happy in the morning. I hold my dress close, shut my eyes and whisper, "Thank you Jesus for loving me, and thank you for Miss Goldie."

On Christmas Day, there is much happiness. Mary loves her baby doll which can cry "Mama." The red fire truck, with its siren blaring, is a hit with JJ. Daddy splashes on Old Spice and he never asks how it got there. So far this is my best Christmas. Thank you, Miss Goldie, thank you Santa, and most of all, thank you Jesus.

And God spoke all these words:
Thou shalt not steal.
                              Exodus 20:1, 15 NIV

Chapter 26
Robbing Peter

We eat mangos, oranges, and coconuts....
and ketchup sandwiches. In the kitchen,
I stand on a chair, climb to the counter top,
reach in a cabinet and bring out a 'bout empty
glass bottle of Heinz Ketchup, only because
there is no peanut butter or anything else.
After crawling back down from the counter,
I find a Merita bread bag containing one slice
of bread and the two heels. JJ and Mary are
watching me with hungry eyes and growling
bellies. There is not enough thick red ketchup
in the bottom of the bottle to smell, much less

pour. So making a ketchup sandwich is not an easy task. It takes forever and a day to hold the bottle in one hand and beat the sides and bottom of the bottle with the other hand. The ketchup doesn't budge, it clings to the bottom, so I run a few drops of water from the spigot into the bottle, shake the bottle, turn it upside down and slap on the bottle some more. Only a smidgen of ketchup trickles from the bottle. It is no longer red but a rosy pink. I watch it slowly crawl from the bottom of the bottle and drip onto the bread. I share with Mary and JJ.

They begin to shove their watered-down ketchup sandwich into their mouths. Then, of all things, I notice spots of green and gray fuzz growing on the edges of the slices of bread. I immediately grab it away from them so I can pinch off the fuzzy growth with my fingers. They both scream to high heavens!

"Okay, okay, already! My goodness gracious!" I say. I wonder why do they scream, yell and cry so much. They aren't the only ones hungry, I think. Immediately I feel selfish, then feel guilty for having selfish thoughts.

Daddy listens, and makes us kids sit and listen, to "The Old Fashioned Gospel Hour," Billy Graham, Oral Roberts or to someone preach or sing gospel songs on the radio. He sits in an upholstered chair and orders us to sit on the floor at his feet.

None of this interests us. In fact, it bores us, but if we were to fidget, squirm or move around on the floor from the spot where we are supposed to sit, Daddy slaps us back in place. He often shows us money: one, five, or ten dollar bills that he places in an envelope and mails to these radio evangelists.

Does God really want Billy Graham to have this money while I make moldy ketchup sandwiches for my little brother and sister to eat? I don't think so! In fact, I may be young, but I'm not stupid. I am no moron. I don't even believe Billy Graham or anyone else wants to take food out of little children's mouths. My Daddy is loco. A man in his right mind feeds his kids, buys them soap, clothes and medicine, the basic needs in life, before making contributions to the pockets of radio evangelists.

Often I am left to do what I want to do, when I want to do it. Problem is, I don't know what I want to do. So, it can be easy for me to get myself into bad situations. Idle hands are the devil's workshop.

I prove myself to be a leader of the kids who live in the projects. Hardy's, a small grocery store sells a little bit of everything. It is only a hop, skip and jump from our yellow house in the projects. Mr. Hardy, an old gray haired man with thick, wide, black framed glasses that sit on his bulbous nose, is the owner of the store. He generally mans the store alone. He spends much of his time in the back of the store at the meat counter. He carves and slices meat with his old, but steady hands. Mr. H., as he is called, has his regulars who order and purchase fresh meats daily.

Some friends, Mary, JJ and I, head to the store. I have a dime and five other kids with me. We enter the store with a definite plan, our mission. "Come in the store with me. The ice cream freezer is right inside the door. Be real quiet. Mr. H is usually in the back of the store. He knows me, so he'll stay in the back. You don't make a sound and when I get my ice cream, all of you reach in and get one too. Got it?" I ask.

"Sure," they nod in agreement.

I open the door and the others quietly step inside with me and the screen door slams.

"Hi, Mr. H, it's me, Estie," I yell toward the back.

"Hey, Estie, be right with you," he answers, "I'm slicing some pork chops."

"That's okay. I'll put my dime on the register and get a fudge sickle." I leave my dime on the cash register and hurry back to the ice cream freezer beside the front door. I slide the door on the ice cream freezer open and motion to the others, four hands reach into the freezer pulling out one ice cream each. All except JJ, he cannot reach one so I hand him a dream sickle.

"Estie, what's all the noise?" Mr. H asks.

"I've got it. Thank you. See you later," I say and ignore his question and shoo the kids out the door.

To avoid being caught, we run as fast as we can and as far as we can down the street; for sure Mr. H is close on our heels. When we are too tired to run any further and we don't see Mr. H anywhere in sight, we sit on the curb to enjoy our ice cream. Well, surprise, there is no ice cream to eat. I look at the bandit of thieves, out of breath and each of us holds an empty little ice cream stick. Sticky melted ice cream streams down our arms and legs and sticks on our shirts and shorts. All of the evidence is proof of a crime committed. It dawns on me; I ought to have bought and paid for one fudge sickle. After all, I had a dime to cover the cost. If I had purchased one fudge sickle and divided it into six equal shares, each of us could actually eat and enjoy at least a couple bites. Are we goof balls, or what?

When I explain to the other thieves the stupidity of our actions, they laugh. I laugh too. But, I do learn a few sobering lessons from this experience; not that it will prevent me from ever making dumb choices again. For one thing, I learn that crime does not pay. Not one of us reaps anything good, not even a good lick of ice cream by stealing from Mr. Hardy. I also learn ice cream melts faster than I run. I definitely learn I don't feel good when I do what is wrong; or, put another way, I can't do wrong and feel good about it.

I wander the streets of my neighborhood by myself and I soon realize I'm beyond the boundaries of the familiar and I lose sight of the rows of little yellow houses. The neighborhood changes; there are liquor bars on both sides of the streets, and the people roam the streets are filthy and drunk. They are all older adults, no children.

A man, only half a man really – because he has no body from his waist down is strapped on a wooden board which has skate wheels on all four corners. He has a dirty, matted, long gray ponytail with a rolled up toboggan on top of his head. His dirty sleeveless t-shirt shows gray hair escaping out from under his armpits. Both arms have tattoos running from his shoulders down to his fingers. He has L-O-S-T tattooed on the four fingers of one hand and L-O-V-E on the four fingers of the other. He has a yellow rectangular cigar box without the lid, in front of him on his board. He constantly moans and asks passers-by for change. In each hand he has a small round handle (about as big around as a broom stick, and six inches long) with a skate wheel on the end of each. He uses these to push himself around on his board. It is the way he moves from one place to another.

I stroll around the block and watch him. On the third time around the block, I slow down. "Change please," he moans. Lord help me. I don't know why, but without any advance plan, my hand, with a mind of its own, is in the cigar box and snatches out a coin. I run. But I cannot outrun this man with no legs.

He pumps both arms and moves his hand rollers so fast sparks fly. "Stop. Stop, right now, you little twerp," he shouts. But I don't stop. I run into a bar. I have never been in one before. It has a high counter and high stools to sit on. There are no customers, only one man with a white apron, who is wiping off the counter with a wet cloth. He looks at me, I run in, grab his legs. Hide behind him, as the man on the wheels rolls in cussing. "Damn, you little urchin. You stole from me."

Before I say or do anything but hide behind the stout black man who has positioned himself firmly, with legs spread and hands on his hips. "Peter, get on out of here. Leave her alone," he says.

"She stole my quarter," Peter shouts.

"Well, maybe she needs that quarter worse than you," he answers.

"She has no right to take my money!"

"I know, I know, but, let it ride this time; get on out of here. She won't do it again," the bartender says.

And Peter maneuvers his board and turns around and rolls out of the door to the sidewalk.

"Child, don't you ever do that again. You hear me?" the bartender asks.

I move from behind him. "Thank you," I say.

"If I ever see you on this street again, I'll whip you good. This is no place for a little girl, especially a little white girl." He stands behind me and holds my shoulders and guides me to a door and opens it. "Now run. Get – and don't you ever come back. You hear?" he asks.

Sounds like wise advice, so I run and I

don't even look back, much less go back.

I hide my quarter in my pocket for a long time. I am sad because of my own rotten behavior and afraid to tell anyone. So the number of my secrets grow. What to do with the quarter? I don't know. If I spend it, I will be asked where I got it, because pocket change is something I don't ever have.

I am back in Mr. H's store again by myself this time. Again, he is busy. "Hi," I say, and walk by where Mr. H is talking with a lady customer.

"Hello, Estie, you doing alright today?" he asks.

"Yes sir, I think I will get some ice cream." I try to make sure he sees the shiny quarter in the palm of my hand.

"Help yourself," Mr. H says.

I smile, and move to the front of the store. I place Peter's quarter on the register and leave the store without any ice cream. Relief! A heavy burden is lifted. I swear, I'll never take anything from anyone again. It weighs too much.

Be kind and compassionate to one another....
Ephesians 4:32a NIV

Chapter 27
Haircuts and Crinolines

How in the world do I manage to be in the fourth grade? It's beyond me. I attend Highland Park Elementary School in Miami, Florida. It's a two story stucco building, within walking distance of our yellow square house. During the last two years or so (all this time with Daddy), I have attended school, little to none. Exceptin' for two weeks in Norfolk, Virginia, and a few days in Houston, Texas, I have not seen a school unless it was while hitchhiking right on by. I am sure I've had a birthday or maybe two, but no one has mentioned it. I have thumbed in thirteen states from North

Carolina to California and back to Florida. I have never seen a report card or had school pictures made.

My teacher, Mrs. Woodell, is wonderful. She is not very tall, however every inch of her being radiates a happy person. I enjoy being in school. I am placed in a high level reading group and I like it a lot. I hate arithmetic and I fit into no arithmetic group; all the groups are too advanced for me. My test scores in arithmetic are so low – they could win a limbo stick competition. My low arithmetic grades make me sad because I love Mrs. Woodell and I don't want to disappoint her. But she is not the least bit angry at me. Through my tears, I can see she is happy and smiles. "Estie, it'll get easier for you. I will teach you. You'll catch on soon." Mrs. Woodell reassures me.

I am the odd ball of the fourth grade; I am the shortest. My sister, Mary, and I are about the same height even though I'm almost two years older than her. All the girls have long, shiny ponytails that swing from side to side when they walk. Daddy experiments with mine and Mary's hair and invents the straight-across-in-the back and the straight-across-in-the-front "bowl-cut" style. Of course, this gives the kids something else to poke fun at me. I'll show them.

I "borrow" the classroom scissors and I keep them hid in the waist of my skirt, as I go down the hall to the restroom. I lock a stall door behind me, sit on the floor, criss-cross my legs and this puts me about eye level with the chrome toilet paper dispenser. I pick up pieces of blond hair on top of my head and snip, snip, snip. I feel around the sides of my head and randomly snatch up already short strands and snip some more. I look at my distorted reflection in the toilet paper holder, and as fast as I can, I cut away on the ends of my hair. I am determined not to have a bowl cut. I whack at my bangs, a snip here, and two snips there. I'm caught up in cutting and have fun doing it.

Surprisingly, I see Carol's upside-down eyes peep under the stall. Her cute face is framed by not one but two long, dangling, brown curly ponytails (which, at the moment happen to be mopping the dirty bathroom floor). Swish! Sneaking she's gone. I think it's a nightmare. But, no it's real. Abruptly, Carol screams like she's seen a two-headed monster. Then quickly her screams stop. "Okay, messy Essie, I'm telling Mrs. Woodell." I hear Carol hurriedly stomp out of the bathroom.

Who's the next person to enter the bathroom? Of course, it's Mrs. Woodell. "Estie, please open the door and come on out."

Mrs. Woodell says, sounding like her normal, happy self.

So, I obey her and when I do, she is waiting with her hand out and I place the scissors in her hand and she puts them in her skirt pocket. No reason to act all innocent – when I've been caught red-handed.

"Wash your hands and let's get back to the classroom," Mrs. Woodell says, as if it's an everyday occurrence to find a student in the bathroom giving herself a shaggy haircut. "We must hurry. Today, we're having school pictures made before we go to lunch." She winks and smiles.

"Mrs. Woodell, aren't you mad at me?" I ask.

She doesn't answer my question, but turns it around and ask me one. "Estie, should I be mad at you?"

"Didn't Carol tell you? Uh…Carol told me she was going to tattle on me for……." I hesitate.

She takes my hand, "Estie, I explained to Carol that when a person is in a locked bathroom stall, it means they want and need their privacy. I told her that smart fourth grade girls don't peep under locked bathroom stalls, especially when another fourth grade girl is in it. I gave Carol a few words of advice – words of wisdom on how, why, and when you do or do not tattle to your teacher. And, since Carol was loud and boisterous in front of the entire class, my response to Carol was spoken in such a way to allow all the students to hear. I'll fill you in on it, only because it may be helpful for you to hear them too.

Estie Irene Culler – Highland Park Elementary School, Miami, Florida
- The day I cut my hair at school

"First of all, if you feel it is necessary to tattle, then it should be done quietly – not loud and noisy enough for the whole class to hear. You don't tattletale if you are only jealous of someone and you hope to get that person in trouble. It is not smart to blabber on someone for doing something different than the way you would – only because you don't understand. If it's not hurting you or someone else, why interrupt the class? No need to rat on someone only to put them down, and to build yourself up. You may think it will make you appear to be better than the other person, but it only makes you look worse. It's not necessary to try hard to find someone to tell on.

"I suggested to Carol and the entire class that if you are on the toilet seat, bent over, hanging your head on the floor to peep into another person's bathroom stall, then you were trying too hard and going to way too much trouble, just to be able to find out something to gossip and tattle about to the teacher and others. I informed Carol what she did to obtain the scoop on you is a far cry worse than what you were doing in the privacy of your stall. Carol will be staying after school today and she will empty all the trash cans." Mrs. Woodell kinda simmers down and let's go of my hand.

"Wow. You said all of that to Carol because she ratted on me?"

"Yes, I did and I hope she understands the intensity and seriousness of my words."

I smile. I smother my giggles behind the palms of my hands, tears sting in the corner of my eyes. "Oh, Mrs. Woodell, thank you. I'm thankful you are not mad at me. Everything has always been my fault and I'm to blame for everything that goes wrong. But, not this time. Thanks."

As Mrs. Woodell opens the classroom

door, she gives me her happy smile and her friendly wink. "Estie, it's time for our class to go to the library to have our pictures made. You stand here and be my line leader. By the way, Estie you have so much talent. I especially like your new haircut. You did a great job. You managed to clip and style it all by yourself. I'm sure your school photograph will be beautiful. All you need to do is show your sweet smile," she says with her hand on my shoulder. "Okay, line leader, lead the way." It's hard to believe she's speaking to me.

I am thrilled! Happy! My lips break apart and spread across my front teeth. My smile is from ear to ear.

My spirit soars to the high reaches of the ceiling (and beyond) of Highland Park Elementary School as I proudly walk down the hall. Me, a line leader! Me, a leader! Unreal!

All the girls wear at least one, if not more, crinoline slips under their skirts. Their skirts stand out exactly right, kinda' like the girls who square dance. I don't have a crinoline, but I do have a slip – a regular straight slip – no ruffles. I have no way to make my skirt stand out and no way to be like, act like, or dress like the other girls. I remember the ladies on Gunsmoke wearing hoop skirts. So, I have an idea, and mentally make a plan.

Crinolines are starched to make them stiff. In the bathroom at our little yellow house, there is a bottle of Little Bo Peep blue liquid starch. Not sure what to do with it, I dab it on my slip which I have spread out on the closed commode lid. I try with all my strength to bend a wire coat hanger to make the shape of a circle. I have trouble bending it into a neat circle, but after pushing and pulling the wire as best as I can, I lay the lop-sided, more triangle shaped than round, coat hanger at the bottom edge of the slip and attach it on with safety pins, the large kind used to pin on diapers. I lay it over the side of the tub, hoping the starch will work miracles and upon drying will turn the petticoat slip into a heavily starched crinoline. I hang it on a towel rack to dry overnight.

The next morning, I put on my homemade hoop slip and slide into my red and blue checked dress. I am so happy to see my dress standing out away from my legs. I think I look exactly like the other girls. I am completely satisfied with my job well done. Now I will fit right in with the girls who wear puffy crinolines under their skirts to school.

As I walk to school, I realize my slip is not cooperating as it should. There are not enough diaper pens to hold the coat hanger in place. I look ridiculous – a real pitiful sight. I head straight to the girl's restroom. Some girls are always in the restroom before the school bell rings. They swing their skirts to show off their crinolines and today is no different. Immediately, they laugh at me and they don't even try to pretend not to. They make no bones about it; I want to spit in their eyes or break their arms. Instead, I move quietly into a stall, lock my door and cry. I am embarrassed and I do not intend for the uppity, highfalutin' girls to laugh at me and my stupid crinoline. I decide to hide in the confines of the stall all day if necessary.

Mrs. Woodell, my happy teacher, comes in and shoos everyone out. When we are alone, she convinces me to unlock the door and to come out of the stall. She promises not to laugh at me or my homemade crinoline. So, I trust her and I come out of the stall and true to her word, Mrs. Woodell doesn't laugh; instead she quickly unsnaps the diaper pins and removes them from my slip. She also removes the cock-eyed coat hanger. I feel foolish and in the bathroom mirror, I see my red face.

"Estie, crinolines are a fad, which means they won't be popular for long. Fads come and fads go. Don't try to be like the other girls. Be yourself. Besides this could be dangerous to you," Mrs. Woodell says. She bends the wire hanger, folding it, and making it small, puts it in a brown paper bag.

I am disappointed. Fad or not, I want to dress like the other girls. I could sure use the help of Mrs. Sarah Luther, who dressed me in neat stylish clothes when I lived in her basement in Norfolk. She would make sure I owned a crinoline or two.

"Estie, please stand in the hall. I'll be there soon," Mrs. Woodell says. Singled out to stand in the hall, I feel embarrassed and scared. Patiently, I wait and silently I pray. I fear Daddy has come to pull me out of school and to start hitchhiking again.

Why does she send me to the hall? Standing in the hall is punishment for misbehaving. What wrong have I done? I bite at my fingertips and fret. Mrs. Woodell finally joins me in the hall. She has a paper in her hand. It is my arithmetic test folded in half, long ways, down the middle. As she unfolds the paper, I see a red 40 written on it. "Estie, I notice you haven't been turning in any arithmetic homework and this test score indicates you lag behind," she says.

I say nothing. I stand there and push thin skin away from the base of my sore fingernails. I wish, like my Grandma, I had white half moons at the base of each nail. "The way you chew on those nails and fingers, you would think they are sugar coated," Mrs. Woodell says.

She holds both my hands. "Estie, stop that!" She examines my hands closer. "Estie, your fingers are gnawed and chewed so much they bleed. Your hands are germy with dried blood and grimy with dirt. You have a sty on your eye, so keep your hands out of your mouth and away from your face."

Sores, some raw and some scabby, on my arms and legs, show signs of infection and have thick, yucky pus oozing from under the scabs. I have a sty on the edges of both my eyelids and a boil up my left nose hole. My eyes are swollen and trapped behind matted lashes, which are stuck with dry, yellow crust — sealed tighter than painted window sashes.

My eyes tear up and burn. I rub my tears away from my swollen eyes. Pus starts oozing. Mrs. Woodell reaches in the pocket of her skirt and brings out a Kleenex and she softly dabs my eyes, but then her hand accidentally bumps my nose. It hurts and tears spring to my eyes again. "Estie, what is wrong, why are you crying now?"

"It's my nose; your hand bumped my

sore nose," I whimper.

She put her hands on both sides of my face and tilted my head back, "Look up at the light and let me take a look at that nose. My heavens, Estie, what on earth," she gasps with a catch in her voice. She releases her hands and I hang my head and look at the floor. "Your nose is swollen and infected. Boils, boils! I think you have boils up your nose. And what are all these sores on your arms and legs? Stay here; you can sit on the floor. Be right back. You'll be okay. Stay put." She hurries down the hall, only to reappear with a man in a dark suit and tie. He has thick, white, curly hair and blue eyes behind his wire rimmed glasses.

"Estie, this is Principal Chapman and I want him to see your sores, your eyes and to look up your nose, okay? Come here," she says and takes my hands and helps me up off the floor. So Mr. Chapman looks me over, takes one quick peep up my nose and shakes his head. They look at each other with looks of shock and disbelief. It's just a sore in my nose and mosquito bites on my arms and legs and a sty on each eye.

"Has your Daddy taken you to a doctor?" he asks. I shake my head no. "Well, we'll have to see about this." He turns and walks away.

Mrs. Woodell takes me to the teachers' lounge, scrubs my hands and fingernails, removing all the dirt and dried blood and puts a hot, wet cloth on my eyes. She explains how important it is to wash your hands with warm water and soap. "Estie, keep your hands away from your face, nose, and eyes." She kindly holds my clean hand as we return down the quiet hall. Her high heels clip-clop each step of the way.

At the classroom door, she sees my test paper on the floor where she had dropped it. She opens it, glances at the red 40, and shakes her head. "Never mind, this is not too important right now. Don't worry about your grade, I will help you after school with your homework. Will that be okay with you?" she asks. She leads me back into the class and to my seat. I take my seat, feel thirty pairs of eyes on me, know they all now think I have cooties or lice or leprosy or some dreaded infectious disease. My goodness, it's only mosquito bites – no big deal!

...anoint him with oil in the name of the Lord.
And the prayer offered in faith will make
the sick person well.
James 5:14b, 15 NIV

Chapter 28
Is This the Great Judgment Day?

After school, I happily skip along the sandy paths that serve as the sidewalks leading to the front door and the backside door of each of the little yellow houses in the projects. Daddy stands on the back stoop with both hands on his hips. And whoa – one look and I know he has it in for me. His anger is obvious; his face is blood red. My feet stop skipping and my heart starts skipping. He grabs my wrist with his strong hand. "Get inside," he growls between clenched teeth. He slings me into the house through the open back door. I land on the floor and he immediately snatches me up to my feet and slams me right back down to the floor, where I fall face first. I sprawl on the floor like a lifeless rag doll.

"Okay. Now, that I've got that settled. Why did you run your mouth to your school principal?" he shouts. Daddy foams at the mouth, loose slobber escapes his lips and his spit flies every which a way. "Get up off the floor. Let me see your nose. Mr. Chapman says you are covered with sores and have boils in your nose and you need to be seen by a doctor. Well, you do not need a doctor. Besides, there is only one Great Physician. Nothing is wrong with your nose that I can't take care of. Come here." He places me on the kitchen table, yanks my hair, pulls my head back and with his humongous hands, he tries to stick his finger up my nose. All the while, I scream and cry in great pain. He pushes my nostrils up toward my forehead so he can look inside. The pain is excruciating and feels like my whole head is being smashed with a car compacter that crushes automobiles into one small hunk of metal.

Through a space between his huge fingers, I see him reaching for a knife. He places the sharp end of the table knife up my nose and he scrapes inside my, oh so tender nose with such vigor and determination. He must think he's digging for gold. However, all he gets is globs of pus – thick, gooey, greenish yellow pus. The weight of his whole body mashes my head to the table. With the rest of my body, I spin all over the table and squirm, everyway but loose – a mouse's head caught in a trap. My body flips and flops uncontrollably. I jerk and try to get loose, with every ounce of strength I can muster up. During this ordeal, which feels like major surgery, I wet my pants right on the kitchen table.

Green gook gushes out of my nose, over my lips, into my mouth, and down my chin. He removes the blade. "Well, I got it all, right down to the core. See, I told you. You don't need a doctor," Daddy says. He moves away from the table to the kitchen sink.

I slide off the table, exhausted and dog tired. I slowly walk to the bathroom, sure I am going to throw up. I squat by the commode, grab a wad of toilet paper, press it to my bloody nose and lay my head on the rim of the seat. I cry and cry, too tired to move. After a good while, Mary comes in the bathroom and finds me lying on the floor with both hands over my face. "Estie, you alright now?" she asks, as she steps over me and takes a seat on the commode.

"Yeah, I'm tired. I hate him so much!" I whisper.

"Yeah, I hate him too," Mary says.

I move my hands from my face and Mary is startled at the sight of my face and she jumps up from the seat. "Oh, Estie, I'm sorry he hurt you so bad. Your eyes are all swollen. They are open only a thin slit and I can barely see the browns'. There is blood on your nose and lips!" she says with her own eyes wide in disbelief.

She runs water in the sink. She sits down on the floor beside me and lays a dripping, wet cloth on my eyes and face. "I want Mama," she whimpers.

"Me too."

We're quiet for a while. "Do you want to come out now?" she asks.

"No, not yet," I answer.

She reaches deep into her pocket and brings out a little army-green plastic toy soldier man. He's about an inch and a half tall and holds a rifle over his shoulder. "Here, you can play with this. I call him Matthew. You can have him."

I take the toy soldier, Matthew, from her and try to smile. "Thanks, I'm gonna stay in here."

"Okay. Call me, if you want me to come back and stay with you longer or when you are ready to play."

"Okay, love you," I whisper as she quietly closes the door behind her.

I squeeze Matthew in my balled up fist and place my fist near my heart. I wonder where my brother Matt is. I hope he is not fighting in a war somewhere. Where are Mama and all my older brothers? I drift to sleep on the floor beside the bottom of the commode.

I am at school, swinging on the playground. The kids are all pointing and laughing at me. I fly higher and higher in the swing, so high that I can't hear their mocking or laughter. As I swing higher, I feel happy. The higher the swing goes, the happier I am. My insides fly high. Not only my body, but also my spirit, is elated. I see the knob of Pilot Mountain. I float on clouds, headed toward the mountain. Then Matt, in his Army uniform, and Johnny Cash dressed in black, are both picking a guitar and singing:

"Because you're mine, I walk the line. I keep my eyes wide open all the time.

I keep a close watch on this heart of mine, Because you're mine, I walk the line."

My Grandma and I clap our hands and wave at them. We want them to notice us as they sing. Then the knob of the beautiful mountain explodes. The top blows off with great force, like a volcano, it erupts and

322

shoots out lava – thick greenish yellow pus. I tumble down and rocks descend on me and pus squeezes out of my whole body.

"Estie, come on out, you've been in there long enough," Daddy yells. When I come out of the bathroom, he calmly holds JJ on his lap and Mary holds Daddy's open Bible and she sits on the bed beside him. "Come here, Estie. You can read to us. Come show Daddy how well you can read," Daddy says. I sit down and JJ bounces to my side. Daddy hands me his open Bible. "Read here in Genesis, the last chapter of the first book. Start right here," he instructs, pointing his finger to a verse.

"And, Joseph said unto them, Fear not: for am I in the place of God? But as for you, ye thought evil against me; but God meant it for good…"

"Stop right there, Estie," Daddy interrupts. "You may think I meant evil against you, that I meant to hurt you, but like God, I meant it for your good." He reaches for an almost empty jar of Mazola cooking oil, which has been placed on the floor beside the bed, pours some on his old handkerchief and rubs the sores on my face and legs. "Jesus said to anoint the sick with oil and they would be healed." Daddy kneels at the side of the bed and calls on the healing power of the blood of

Jesus to heal my sores. "You will feel better now because Jesus Christ's shed blood has healed you. Now you only have to trust Him."

I am too tired to move. I stay and crawl to the middle of the bed and I don't get up until the next morning. My body crashes but my mind runs full steam. I wonder and pray, "how is having my nose ripped apart for my good? . And if it is for my good, couldn't he be gentler? For a while there, I thought he tried to remove my whole nose to get rid of the boils. Before I sleep, I pray, "Jesus, please heal my nose."

At school the next day, around lunch time, a nurse dressed all in white – white hose, thick soled white shoes and her white hair pokes out from under a stiff white cap on her head, enters our classroom. "Boys and girls, I am here to explain the importance of cleanliness. You must bathe and wash your hands with soap and warm water. Being clean is important because it stops germs from spreading. Now Estie Culler, raise your hand." No, oh my God, no, she didn't call my name out in front of the whole class. Surely she does not expect me to lift up my hand. I am horrified. I am sure she is not handing out the "Cleanest Person Award" – might be the "Dirtiest Person." How embarrassing. Chairs squeak, kids move around and get situated where they all have a good look at me – the dirty girl with the ugly sores. I am paralyzed, powerless to move. There is no way I can wiggle a little finger much less lift my whole hand. I am frozen in place – like the statue of Christopher Columbus standing in front of the school. I feel it first sliding down my cheek and then my tongue flickers out and licks the salty tear away.

The nurse starts walking. "Whew!" I think she is leaving, but no, the squeak of her white rubber sole shoes and the swish of her white stocking legs, stops dead still beside my desk. Silence. The kind of silence everyone hears. Silence which lasts forever. She bends over my ear, "Estie, come with me," she whispers. Now, why in the world did she whisper? She has already made a spectacle of me, like a freak in the side show at a carnival. All my classmates watch her every move. My chin down, eyes to the wooden floor, I slowly rise and follow the white stiff-as-a-board uniform out the door, and to the principal's office.

In the principal's office, I can't figure out what is going on, and why I am here. They make me wait in the outer office in a wooden chair on the other side of the counter. I wait and wait. On the counter is a bell. It is round with a chrome dome and a button to push to get attention if you need help. I stare at the bell and am so tempted to mash the button to get their attention, so someone can tell me what I am doing here in the first place. They are behind the closed door with frosted and bumpy glass and has the word "Principal" in bold, black letters.

I continue to stare at the bell, but I am afraid to ring it and ask what's happening, or may I please hurry back to my class because that is what I come to school for, not to sit here in this office with sweaty hands. And Mrs. Woodell wonders why I bite my nails. Well, I bite my nails when I don't know what the heck is going on, like now. So, I sit here gnawing my fingers on one hand and scratching the itchy sores on my legs with the other.

I am stupid, a big red 40 on my arithmetic test; really, how low can you go! I am beyond ugly and no one wants to be near me. That's why they have left me in this chair by myself to stare at that stupid bell.

"Estie, we're leaving. Come with me to the car." So out the door I am ushered to a waiting black four door Buick. Mr. Chapman opens the door and I slide into the back seat. I am going on my first field trip. Problem is I am the only student, everyone else is grown up people; the school principal, the white all over school nurse and another lady I don't know. The nurse introduces the lady to me. I am scared so her name doesn't seem important.

"Where am I going?" I ask. The lady in the back seat with me reaches across and takes my hand away from my mouth and then drops it in my lap. "Estie, don't worry, everything is going to be fine. We need to take you to court so a Judge can look at your nose and sores. He can order your Daddy to get you some medicine before your sores spread any further," she smiles.

"A Judge? Is this the Great Judgment Day?" I ask, my voice trembles and my body shakes.

"No, don't worry, Estie," she smiles. If she thinks her words and smile will make me feel any better – she's wrong. It sounds so important, a Judge – like God, Himself. I am mortified! I might die in the back seat of this car with people I don't even know. I look at my dress, the same one I wore yesterday. I did change panties this morning but the dress is wrinkled, dirty and smells. This is not how I want to meet God.

"Please don't force me. My nose is better now since Daddy scraped it clean with a knife – he got all the stuff out right down to the core. I'm okay now. Don't make me see the Judge. Daddy will not like it. He will be mad. Please. What if the Judge doesn't like me and sends me straight to hell?" I sob. I am in a panic tizzy. My head begins to spin in circles like the lock button on a johnny house door.

"Estie, please calm down, you will not have to say anything but we do have to escort you to court so the Judge can examine you and make your Daddy buy you some medicine."

The courtroom is barely sufficient in size. I think children like me will be lined up for the Judge to look at, but no, there is no one else like me. I am the only kid here. I think the Judge will be old with white hair and a white beard and have on a white robe. But not this Judge; his robe is black and he is young, too young to be God. I am relieved and try to relax and breath normally again.

It is a closed hearing, for the court to determine as a fact that I am neglected. An Emergency Petition has been filed in the Miami, Dade County Family Court, Juvenile Division, by Mr. Dallas Chapman, Principal of Highland Park Elementary School, alleging that Estie Irene Culler, a minor child needs medical attention. The petition requests the court to order Rev. Abraham Culler, father of Estie Culler, to immediately take the necessary actions to procure the proper medical treatment and medication for Estie's infectious sores. My Daddy must not have been invited to come to court or else he doesn't bother to show up. After hearing what the grown-ups have to say, the Judge signs an Order stating that I have impetigo, a contagious bacterial skin infection, and orders that Rev. Abraham Culler buy me medicine.

I am driven back to school. When I get home, my Daddy walks me to Dr. Ruiz's Pharmacy on 7th Avenue, with Mary and JJ in tow, and buys me the required medicine. He storms to high heavens because he has to pay the expensive amount of fourteen dollars for the small tube of ointment.

After all, Jesus heals for free.

Jesus told them: Take nothing for the journey —
no staff, no bag, no bread, no money, no extra tunic.
Luke 9:3 NIV

Chapter 29
Keeping My Pink Dress!

"We are going to see Grandma!" I flit around and dance with joy. JJ and Mary join me. We spin in circles, and flap our arms, three butterflies all-a-flutter. "Oh goodie! We're going to see Grandma," we squeal with sheer happiness. We flit fast and dart dangerously all around!

"Hold it. I told you we are going back to North Carolina to see Mama, your Grandma, but let me tell you why. It is because she is very sick and in the hospital," Daddy says.

Three butterflies descend – sinking

silently. This news is a shocker. It startles and horrifies me.

"My Grandma can't die. Mama is already dead. I want to see my Grandma again," I cry.

"I feel led by the Lord to take care of her," Daddy explains.

This time, Daddy, the Lord, and I all agree. Seeing my Grandma again means the whole wide world to me. After all, we are two peas in a pod.

We have never stayed-put in any one place long enough for me to develop any friends, not even long enough for anyone to learn how to correctly pronounce my name. Often, before the kids find someone else to poke fun at besides me, my clothes, my haircut, or my name, Daddy has his old Bible and old duffel bag in hand, he has stomped the dirt off his shoes and we have already hitched a ride, bound for parts unknown.

Now, for the first time ever, I have a friend or two: kids who live in the same projects and go to the same school. And my happy teacher, Mrs. Woodell, well, I'm positive she more than tolerates me. I think she really likes me.

She insists I remain after school a couple of days a week to tutor me in arithmetic. She pleads, and all but begs me, to please stop my fingernail biting. She threatens to cover my nails with electrical tape and to saturate my fingertips in red hot pepper sauce. Once, Mrs. Woodell places a pair of wool gloves on the corner of my desk. (I can't imagine, for the life of me, how she manages to be in possession of a pair of black, fuzzy, wool gloves, just my size. After all, this is Miami, and people from sunny southern Florida don't have a clue what gloves are.)

"Okay, Estie, you even think about sticking your stubby gnawed-up fingernails in your mouth and you'll wear these hot, wool gloves the entire time you are in my classroom," Mrs. Woodell says in her firm, I—am—so—serious voice.

She also tries bribery. "Let's make a deal. If you refrain from chewing on your nails in the morning, then at lunch time I will give you a small treat, maybe a Tootsie Roll, or some raisins, or a mint. And, if you don't bite them after lunch, then I'll give you a treat when school is out for the day. Only a small treat though, maybe bubblegum. How does that sound?" Mrs. Woodell asks.

She offers the bribe and I take it. "Sounds great to me," I say. Mrs. Woodell holds true to the promised bribe. Most days, her offer influences me and persuades me to keep my fingers out of my mouth.

As for the extra help in arithmetic, Mrs. Woodell has more patience and tolerance with me than I deserve. It is obvious to me; she wants me to have a clear understanding. She wants me to "catch on," to "get it." And try as I may; I can't "get it" or "catch it." She is throwing the ball too high over my head.

To my surprise, Mrs. Woodell doesn't give up on me. She smiles at me and reassures me daily, saying, "Now Estie, don't you worry. It'll come in time."

I avoid eye contact. My way of thinking leads me to the assumption, rightly or wrongly, that if I accidentally or intentionally allow anyone the opportunity to look into my eyes, even a quick glance; then that person will be able to know my thoughts and read my mind, revealing too much information. Not sharing my thoughts, my feelings or my anything, I keep all of me to myself. I learn from life that rejection hurts deep down inside. I will not give myself. No one can reject what's not been given. To hide myself from the scrutiny of Mrs. Woodell's kind eyes is a difficult task. My nervous eyes flit from here to yonder eluding her seeking eyes.

She is patient and calm. To my surprise,

her eyes snatch and tightly surround my eyes. I am caught in the spotlight of her searching eyes. Mrs. Woodell's eyes penetrate deep and I am afraid. Frightened speechless. Her eyes shine brightly, gazing intently into my eyes, and closely examining my heart.

Eyeball to eyeball. Heart to heart. I pray Mrs. Woodell will not reject me, that she will always be close to me. I need her, her encouragement and her attentiveness. No doubt, she aims for me to increase my arithmetic skills; however, her kindness and genuine concern, extends beyond the call of an efficient teacher's duties. If not for Mrs. Woodell, (the combination of her caring nature, perseverance and her persistent determination, together with her ability to jump through any and all hoops and over all barriers) I would not have the medicine needed to heal my impetigo and to keep it from spreading all over my body. Even if it means obtaining a court order, she does it.

We talk and she tries to look me in the eyes. I look anywhere and everywhere but not at Mrs. Woodell's happy face. I am stupid, about as dumb as a stump. I feel ashamed because she has tried her darnedest to help me comprehend the skill of multiplying numbers. I am disappointed in my inability to grasp even the simplest concept of arithmetic, especially, multiplications. (How can two *times* two equal four? When I know good and well, it's two *plus* two that equals four; and how can three *plus* three equal six, and three *times* three not also equal six, instead of nine?) I am more discouraged and disappointed at being such a total failure to Mrs. Woodell, than I am disappointed in my inability to do the arithmetic. I want to learn because she wants me to.

"Estie, you'll catch on, believe me. Where did you attend school before coming to Highland Park?" she asks.

"I don't know." I look toward the window, away from Mrs. Woodell.

"Well, did you receive any report cards with your school grades?"

"No."

"Have you ever received a certificate from any school, promoting you to a higher grade level?"

"No."

"Well, Estie, you are in the fourth grade. Did you get promoted from the third grade to the fourth grade?" she asks.

"No, no and no," is my honest answer. My eyes are cast down to the floor.

"Well, let's forget about long multiplication problems. Let's begin by memorizing the multiplication tables first," she says. "What do you think of that?" she asks.

Wait. Wait a minute! What's that I see in her eyes? Is it disappointment; frustration, pity? No, I don't think so. There are tears floating in the bottom of her eyelids and if she blinks, tear drops will fall. I know its love. Yeah, I see love. Simply amazing. Amazing! Mrs. Woodell loves me.

"Estie, will you help me?" she asks, and draws me from my thoughts. "I need help washing the chalkboard and beating the loose chalk from these erasers. She hands me two erasers; she keeps two in her hands. "Come on," she says.

I follow her out of the classroom, down the hall, and out the school door, to the concrete sidewalks. She sits down on a low step and motions for me to join her. She beats a felt eraser against the concrete sidewalk and I copy her. Here we sit on the warm, hard concrete step and beat erasers. Chalk dust flies. She slams the eraser harder and harder. So do I. She sniffs back tears. No, she is laughing – we beat, we cry, and we laugh, until we are finally exhausted. "I feel a little better now. Keep your chin up. Don't worry. You and I will conquer arithmetic. You'll see. Thanks for your help with these erasers. We may have to beat them again sometime. I'll see you tomorrow," she says.

I look forward to school and being with Mrs. Woodell again tomorrow. She inspires me to seek knowledge and encourages me to never give up. She bubbles with happiness, and I want some of it to bubble over to me.

Tomorrow I will thank her for caring about my ugly fingernails. I will thank her because she encourages me and assures me that I will "catch on" to arithmetic. And, I will look in her eyes again, and hope to glimpse a trace of love. Yep, I think she may love me. I sure love her. She's the best and tomorrow I will tell her so!

"Estie, you are daydreaming again!" Daddy snaps.

"Oh," I whisper. And, Lord help me! Daddy is holding that darn old duffel bag. And his Bible. That means we are leaving and going to Grandma's right this minute. That's exactly what he means. "Come on, we're leaving," he says.

"You mean right now? Can I run and say goodbye to Lucino and all my friends?" I ask.

"No. We obey God and follow His lead," he says.

"I'll get my doll," Mary says.

"No, you will not. Now, all three of you go to the bathroom. It'll be a long time before you use a commode again. Now hurry it up," he says. We take turns using the bathroom. Daddy is waiting with the back door open.

"I want to get my pink dress," I say. "I'll be fast, and I'll be back before Mary is out of the bathroom."

"No, we'll not wait," he says, as Mary comes out of the bathroom door.

"It'll only take a minute," I beg.

"Take no thought for tomorrow, what you will eat or what you will wear. When we leave a city, God instructs us to take only the clothes on our backs," he says. He speaks so preachy and with so much authority.

"Okay, I'll put the dress on my back," I say. I run off before Daddy has the chance to stop me. I find the dress where I keep it, under the bed. I snatch it out and slip it on over my clothes. My eye catches a glimpse of something green sticking out from under Mary's pillow. "Oh, Matthew," I say. I stop and lift the pillow and remove the little rubber army man and squeeze it tight in my fist. Not wanting to provoke Daddy any more than I already have, I run to the back door.

Daddy holds JJ's hand. Mary begins to cry. "Daddy, please let Mary and me find Lucino and the others long enough to say good bye," I plead.

"Estie, stop begging this minute. The answer is no," Daddy says. He drops JJ's hand and jerks my shoulder. "Estie, do you have any idea how stupid you look wearing that silly pink dress over the top of your other clothes?" Daddy snaps at me.

"Why, I am sure God won't care, after all it's on my back," I smart back.

Well, I better leave well enough alone. I try not to think about my friends and Mrs. Woodell. I will never see any of them again, so my heart is torn. I can't wait to see Grandma, but I am also disappointed because we leave in such a hurry.

With no transportation, we hit the highways again. Unlike Dorothy, I have no red slippers; I can't click my heels together and return to my Grandma! We do it the hard way, hitchhiking.

We thumb on Highway 1 through Fort Lauderdale, Cape Canaveral, and Palm Beach. We ride with truckers mostly, eat their potato chips and nap in their sleepers; we also sleep in the woods, and walk for miles.

We make our way, one way or another, to the shores of Georgia. I know my geography well enough to realize that when we are in Georgia traveling north; we have only South Carolina to travel through; then, it's North Carolina, home sweet home. There, I'll reach the warmth and security (not to mention the bed with clean sheets) of my Grandma's house. Just the thought of seeing my Grandma is all I have to ease the horrific pain in my sad heart. I doubt I'll ever see Mrs. Woodell or Lucino again.

Seems I always hurry off in the opposite direction before love can catch me and hold me.

You have been a refuge for the poor, a refuge for the needy....
a shelter from the storm...
Isaiah 25:4 NIV

Chapter 30
Telephone Booths and Tent Revivals

Soaking wet, head to toe, Mary and I position ourselves on the concrete floor of a telephone booth. "My goodness gracious, Mary! for heaven sakes, stop kicking me," I say.

"I can't help it. You're squashing me. Scoot over. How 'bout it?" Mary asks.

I try to inch myself away from her, but I can hardly move a muscle. "We're packed in here like sardines," I say.

It is smelly. One whiff and it is obvious pee has splattered the floor a time or two in the recent past. The concrete floor is littered with umpteen stale cigarette butts and black soot marks where the cigarettes have been stomped out and ground-in with the soles of shoes.

We are the only people walking – forever it seems, near the surf of the Atlantic Ocean. Daddy insists that I learn to spell "Atlantic" and "Pacific," and to know which ocean is on the east and which is on the west. We are somewhere between Miami Beach, Florida and Savannah Beach, Georgia. The sky's heavy, slate gray clouds tilt and solid sheets of rain spill from the heavens above. I am unable to tell where the gray sky ends and the gray ocean begins. My vision is impaired by the rain in my eyes. (It all resembles the color of lead in a No. 2 pencil.)

Off in the distance, I catch a glimpse of the word "TELEPHONE" in white letters on a green background. As we get closer, we discover there are two, three-sided Plexiglas telephone booths with no doors. If not for the bright green color appearing in the gray surroundings, Mary and I would have missed the opportunity for such closeness.

Daddy tells Mary and me to either sit or

lie down on the hard and rough cement floor, in one of the telephone booths, and to stay there until the rain stops. He and JJ take the other booth.

Mary, stuffed in the back of this thing called a telephone booth, rests her head and shoulders against one side of the enclosure and props her feet up on the other side. I lie zigzagged on my side and face the open entrance, with my back toward Mary. Mary's feet continually fall and knock me in the head. The rain slowly seeps in and forms a puddle under my head and around my face. Not too cozy. For a little bit, I think I might drown right here in this telephone booth. Quickly I change my thoughts before I can feel too sorry for myself. I decide to think about my Grandma, the other pea in the pod. I think about her chocolate cake and Juicy Fruit gum. I see her crystal blue eyes. And I close my eyes. Sleep soon swallows me. The telephone booths are our shelter for the night.

The early morning sun rises over the Atlantic Ocean. Mary and I can barely budge. We manage to wiggle our stiff bodies, twist a little this way and turn a little that way, until we are able to stand on our feet, and stretch our sore bodies back into shape. "Up and at 'em," Daddy calls to us.

Mary and I leave the plastic hut, which houses a telephone, and follow Daddy and JJ. I turn around and walk slowly backwards and see the green signs on the telephone booths. We have just spent the night in a telephone booth. Nothing should surprise me anymore. It's like the natural place to sleep on a rainy night at the beach. I wonder, if not for these telephone booths, where would we have found shelter from the rain and slept for the night. I think Daddy may be right, God does provide for our needs; but I don't remind him, 'cause I don't wanna' hear Daddy shout and praise the Lord so early in the morning.

Daddy preaches two nights consecutively at a tent Revival in Augusta, Georgia. The music is loud; and that is to be expected at an "old- timey preachin', sangin' and praising the Lord Revival." It's supposed to be upbeat! The odor of fresh wood shavings spread over the ground and the exciting smell of Revival permeates the cool southern evening. Strands of bare light bulbs are strung from tent posts and trees, beckoning every flying insect in the county to swarm on over and buzz for a spell.

I am familiar with this scene 'cause it's where we often end a day of hitchhiking. Mary, JJ, and I join the insects and sit for a while.

The preacher whoops and hollers, then its Daddy's turn. He whoops and hollers louder with dozens of "Glori-a's" and even more "Hallelujahs."

The good citizens of Augusta are now on fire with the Holy Ghost, and some of their tongues begin to make strange sounds, which the preacher calls the gift of speaking in unknown tongues. Sounds like Spanish to me; kind of like Lucino and her mother when they argue and cry because of some unacceptable behavior of Lucino's – like the time Lucino calls her teacher a "*puta fea.*" The ladies in this tent revival are blabbering and carrying on like Lucino's angry Mother, shouting and throwing her arms in the air and then following it all up with hushed whimpers and nose blowing.

Mary and JJ are sleeping through all the workings of the Holy Ghost; and I am beginning to doze off, thinking of Lucino, Miss Goldie, and Mrs. Woodell. Then, on the brink of sleep, I hear Daddy saying my name. He is pacing back and forth on the wooden platform stage. "Yes, their sinful Mother pranced out of our lives. She left me all alone to bring them up in the ways of the Lord. Brothers and sisters, their mother strayed from the fold and shamefully, she never returned. John Edger Hoover, the Director of the FBI, has spied on her and kept secret files on her. The agency informed me of her horrible death in a gambling house fire. Because of the nature of the activities, harboring and hiding of criminals and communists in the house, it was burnt completely down. Nothing but ashes remain. The FBI thought no one was present in the house, but she was. John Edgar Hoover has told me personally that because of my wife's actions, vicious harm will descend upon my innocent nine year old daughter, Estie, before she is twenty-one years old," Daddy bellows.

The sweaty and hyped-up congregation utters wails of disbelief and disgust.

"My Bible tells me that whosoever harms one of these little children, it would be better for him to have a millstone hung around his neck and he be cast into the deepest sea. So, dear brothers and sisters in Christ, I believe that my children's Mother and John Edgar Hoover, Director of the FBI, should both be drowned in the deepest sea," Daddy shouts.

"Amen. Hallelujah." The brothers and sisters of the congregation are on their feet, shouting "praise the Lord."

"Now, Estie, I want you to step right up here with me. Hop on up here, Estie," Daddy says.

I do as I am told. My loose sandals

scoop wood shavings off the ground and in between my cold toes. Since we sit on the front row, as we always do when Daddy preaches, whether in church or in a tent, it doesn't take me long to reach the platform stage. And when I do, wham bam! Daddy and another over zealous evangelist, both smack me on top of my head with the palms of their open hand. Daddy, one hand on my head and the other arm lifted high, begins to pray out loud to the "Holy God Almighty." And simultaneously the other preacher, not to be out-done, with his hand still on my head, begins praying even louder. Each jerk and rock my head back and forth.

Within minutes, I am surrounded and enclosed in a tight circle of men's legs, all different lengths covered in overalls, blue jeans and cotton suit pants. I stare down and see all kinds of shoes: rust colored brogans, loafers, cowboy boots, and plain black tie ups. I am smothered by bodies of men, in a variety of shapes. Some shout and cry and others make weird sounds and utter unfamiliar words. I look up, in hopes of breathing fresh air. I gulp for air; I see arms. Every arm is the same, white shirt, with rings of sweat and the stench of bad odor under the armpits. Arms reach to my head, intertwine and overlap, like spokes on a bicycle wheel. I am the hub.

Unrelenting pressure weighs heavy on the top of my head. Sweat trickles and drops off their bodies and onto me. So, I decide to keep my eyes down toward the ground. I feel nauseated, cold and dizzy. All the loud prayers of everyone, over my head and ears, makes me wonder if all these grown men think the Holy God is hard of hearing. And, if so, why don't they take turns speaking to Him one at a time; instead of everyone screaming at the same time? My knees buckle. I drop down and fall on my back.

"Here, Estie, drink some water," Daddy says as he hands me a cup of water. I take a couple of swallows.

"Okay, I'm fine," I say.

"Rev. Key has generously agreed to let us sleep here under the tent. Some of his workers are sleeping here too," Daddy says.

I look around and see Mary and JJ asleep on the ground at the front row. They hadn't moved one little iota. Someone has spread a thick, homemade quilt over their bodies.

I join Mary and JJ on the ground. I sleep under the quilt, in between them, with my head at their feet. On the ground with sawdust and wood shavings, I can see through an opening in the flap of the tent, the black sky sprinkled with stars. I wonder if this is what it felt like to sleep in a stable like Mary, Joseph and baby Jesus. Then I wonder if I can still quote the story of Jesus' birth as it is written in the Book of Luke. I recite the familiar words in my mind. This makes me miss Matt, Mark, and Luke, and all the happy and sad times we had at the "Lord's Mission" in Pilot Mountain, North Carolina. Our family has never been together again. These thoughts grip my brain and crush my heart. I store them away in the depth of my mind and again pull out happy thoughts of my Grandma. I visualize her cooking in her clean kitchen, stirring cocoa in a pan on the red hot burner of her stove. She is making circles with her wooden spoon, as quick as she can, to keep the cocoa from sticking to the pan as it slowly boils into thick bubbles. The aroma and taste of sweet chocolate flows in my nose, and spreads over my taste buds; it releases warm memories and causes my heart to explode with longing and anticipation. I can't wait to be with my Grandma again. To feel her warm arms and hear her soft voice saying, "Estie, you and I are just two peas in a pod. Come here, honey, let me give you a big hug."

Every good and perfect gift is from above,
coming down from the Heavenly Father.
James 1:17 NIV

Chapter 31
Lunch in a Merita Bread Bag

A jolly gentleman, who laughs loud and smiles happily, stops to give us a ride. He is from Camden, South Carolina, and is a minister at the First Baptist Church on Highway One. Rev. Stockton and Daddy become fast buddies as they share with each other favorite Bible scriptures, the parables, the Beatitudes, and the Ten Commandments, post and pre – millennium, and Jesus riding on a great white horse. My Daddy, I am sure, can quote the entire Bible and he has met his match.

We have dinner at his house. His wife,

Jean, is friendly, attractive and wears no make up. She wears a starched blue cotton dress with a white starched apron tied around her waist. She is a fantastic cook. We fill up on mashed potatoes, green beans, corn-on-the-cob, pickled beets and meatloaf. And for the first time ever, I eat yeast rolls. I love them more than anything else in her grand spread of delicious food. They are piping hot; and like the corn, the bread drips with butter. Mrs. Stockton offers me homemade peach jam and apple butter to smear on the rolls.

When we are 'bout to bust a gut, Mrs. Stockton allows Mary and JJ to rest on her couch in the living room in front of her black and white television. I help her in the kitchen, clear the table and dry the dishes as she washes them in her double sink. The dishes are matching plates, bowls, and saucers with pink roses on them. I don't remember seeing a set of matching dishes, no cracks or chips and my hands shake more than usual as I dry them with a white linen towel.

"Why the shaky hands?" Mrs. Stockton asks kindly.

"I don't want to drop and break any of these beautiful dishes," I say. And I notice my hands seem to tremble even more after she calls attention to it.

"Essie, they are only dishes. If they break, so what? I don't want them to break, but if one does, it won't be terrible. You don't have to worry about that," Mrs. Stockton says.

"My name is Estie and it is spelled E-S-T-I-E, not Essie. Why can't you and everyone else get that straight?" I ask. I use my meanest, toughest voice, and then, I give Mrs. Stockton my dirtiest look. I glare at her through squinted eyes and I curl up the left side of my lip, and try to distort my face as Lucino taught me. She called it her "mean dirty look."

Mrs. Stockton's mouth drops open and then she covers it with her hand. She stretches her green eyes wide in disbelief and they grow another inch. She is as shocked as all-get-out. It is obvious she is appalled by the sassy tone of my voice, and apparently she has never seen a "mean dirty look."

"Excuse me," she says faintly, and she drops her dishcloth and shakes the soapsuds off her slender hands. For the life of me, I think she is preparing to smack me in my mouth. "I love you anyway," she says in a low whisper with a smile on her lips and tears welling up in her eyes. She quietly leaves the kitchen. Now, I am the one who is surprised. I didn't realize that my nasty attitude would faze her in the slightest. I feel guilty for being snappy and sassy. I don't understand what makes me be disrespectful. Tears well up in my eyes. To distract my mind and my guilty heart, I venture to the living room and sit on the floor, in front of the small television set, which is a box on four legs with rabbit ears sticking out of the top. JJ is asleep and Mary is well on her way, so, I watch the television.

The television is so fascinating with its black and white pictures and the sound of voices. I watch a Maytag washing machine, which is said to be so dependable and long lasting that the Maytag service men don't have any work to do. Then it's *Bonanza*, good-looking cowboys, who can ride horses without their shirt-tails coming out of their tight blue jeans, and without their cowboy hats falling off their heads. They pull their pistols out of their holsters and twirl them around their index finger several times, aim with one eye and hit the target the first time, every time. And the youngest cowboy, Little Joe Cartwright, is the cutest of all. He looks through the box and smiles only at me, I smile back into his eyes.

Mrs. Stockton interrupts my flirting and blushing with Little Joe when she steps into the room and smiles sweetly. She informs me that Rev. Stockton and Daddy are out looking for a place for us to live, seeing about a job for Daddy and will be back soon. She turns off the television and hands me a soft feather pillow in a white pillow case that has yellow daisies embroidered on the edges. "You can sleep, if you want to. They will be back soon," she says.

I don't answer. I scrunch up the pillow and put my head on it. The lights in the room are off except for the dim glow of a bronze floor lamp beside the recliner where she is sitting, her fingers busy embroidering flowers.

"I think you will enjoy the school here. My sister is the librarian and….."

"I want to be at my Grandma's house," I interrupt, roll over, sock the pillow with my fist a couple of times, and sink my face into its softness. Tears come to my eyes and I muffle my crying in the feathers of the pillow.

Mrs. Stockton doesn't respond. Maybe she doesn't hear me clearly, or maybe she doesn't know what to say, or maybe she's still upset with me for being disrespectful. Either way, I'm glad I don't have to talk to her because all I want to do is figure out a way to get to Grandma's house. I know she is sick. Daddy prays for her every time he talks to God, which is more often than he talks to us. I yearn to see Grandma, the other pea in the pod, before she dies and goes to heaven.

Later the preacher, Rev. Stockton drives Daddy and all of us just up the street to the Camden Tourist Court, where he has made arrangements for us to stay. The tourist court is a row of several small buildings. Each of these buildings has a tiny kitchen and bedroom together in one area and a bathroom that has a shower.

Mrs. Stockton enrolls JJ (surely he is too young), Mary and me in yet another school, where I don't know anyone, and no one can pronounce my name. The school is in walking distance of the Tourist Court. I have lost complete interest in school. I don't want to meet any new teacher or make any friends, only to have to leave them. I miss Mrs. Woodell, and she is bound to miss me too. I only want her as a teacher. I hanker to see Lucino and skip rope with her.

Rev. Stockton allows Daddy to preach on Sunday night to a packed house and he praises God for all his blessings. He says, among other things, that his children have only worn out sandals on their feet. He sticks up his foot and says, "Just look at my own shoes, which are stuffed with cardboard to cover holes in the soles. Yes, the only thing between my feet and the pavement is a flimsy piece of cardboard, yet, I know my loving God will provide all our needs.

The next day, Mrs. Stockton ushers Mary and JJ into the back seat of her black 1954 Bel Air Chevrolet. I hop into the front seat and she drives us to Belk's Department Store. I step around the store in awe, gawk at the beautiful clothes on statues of women, who look more alive than the shriveled-up old shoe salesman with gray hair, wrinkled face, and wire-rim glasses. He chews the end of an unlit cigar. He measures our feet on a wooden slide that looks like a teacher's ruler. We leave the store, all three of us in brand new socks and black and white tie-up oxford shoes.

Outside, in front of Belk's, is a person dressed like a big yelow peanut. He hands out small white paper sacks of salty, shelled peanuts. The aroma of the fresh roasted peanuts is like no other and pervades the brisk air. My belly growls. I eat every single peanut in my sack. They are delicious and so much better than the raw peanuts from Grandpa's garden.

New shoes, Wow! New shoes. My nine year old feet have never before been placed in new shoes. What a day to remember! Shoes, purchased from a shoe store for me, put a bounce in my steps. They are brand new shoes measured for my feet only, not previously owned worn out shoes from the Salvation

Army. They are not hand-me-down shoes that are either too small or too large. Surely the crunchy mouth-watering peanuts are what rich people, who live in brick houses with picket fences, eat every day. Life is wonderful! Brand new shoes on my feet and a mouth full of warm, salty peanuts – what more could a girl want? Only to be with Grandma.

I don't understand why we stay around this town, when we are only one state away from Grandma's. Why do we attend school here when my Grandma is sick and we should hitchhike toward North Carolina?

The first day, the teacher can't pronounce my name. She asks if Essie is a nickname for Estelle. All the kids giggle. I snarl and give her my "mean dirty look" (which I am getting down to perfection). The second day, kids shun me at lunch because my lunch, an orange, is in a clear Merita bread bag and not in a tin lunchbox, like theirs. They laugh because I stick a pencil in my orange to make a hole in it, to suck the juice out. On the third day, it's my hair.

"Your hair is so straight, Assie Essie." "It looks like a bowl was put upside down on your head and your hair whacked off." (How can they know that is exactly what Daddy does when he gives us a haircut?) "It's too short.

You can't even wear it in a ponytail," and "I don't like you, or your ratty hair, or your ratty clothes. You wore that dress yesterday." On and on they jeer. All I can see is their mouths, wide open, chewing food and laughing at the same time.

I've had enough of it. I throw my orange in the direction of all of them; they duck and it misses. My orange slams into the wall, inches above a prissy girl's head, with enough force to burst the orange wide open. The fruit slides down the mint green wall, leaving traces of orange pulp, then it smacks the floor. The prissy girl hurriedly jumps from her chair and begins to run off toward the teacher's table. "I'm telling teacher on…" Before she can finish her threat, would you believe, her shiny Mary Jane shoes slide on the juicy remains of the orange, she loses her balance, slips and falls. Her head, with all its curly ringlets, strikes the corner of her chair and causes it to drop over backwards. Then there is all kinds of commotion – cries and screams. The top of Miss Priss' head crashes into the green cinder block wall at about the same spot my orange landed only seconds before. Now the prissy girl has not only chunks of orange caught in her curly ringlets, but also blood oozes from her head and splatters in her eye.

For my part of the upheaval, the teacher administers three solid licks across my bottom with her wooden "Fly-Back" paddle. Three hard licks ain't half bad, considering a clump of Miss Priss' curly ringlets have to be cut off, and her head shaved on top, (leaving a circular bald spot about the size of my orange) because she has to have the gash in her head sewed up.

This is my last day at Camden Elementary School. Thank heavens!

I am not at the school long enough to even learn Miss Priss' name; but I bet she won't be forgetting me, or that my name is Estie any time soon!

Honor your father...
Exodus 20:12a NIV

Chapter 32
There's a Party Goin' On

Mary and I join hands, circle JJ and jump up and down on the bed. With each jump, he bounces up and flops down in the middle of the bed like a limber ragdoll. JJ squeals with happy laughter. "Do it again. Do it again," JJ begs. He is having the time of his life, as Mary and I sing,

> *"Ring around the roses,*
> *pockets full of posies,*
> *ashes, ashes, we all fall down."*

We fall all over JJ and each other. We

laugh hard and loud. The sound of the high-pitched squeaks of the bed springs - metal scraping against metal - and JJ's ear-splitting squeals, cause Mary and me to scream and laugh even louder. Mary and I tickle JJ on his neck and under his arms and sing,

"John Joe, John Joe, whatcha' gonna' do…e…o?
John Joe, John Joe, where ya' gonna' go…e…o?
He's going down the road to see a little girl…e…o."

We jump and roll on the bed. We sing and laugh like crazy. We press our lips on each other's bellies, blowing hard, and creating long drawn out fart sounds. We do somersaults and toss about on the squeaky, springy bed. We giggle and laugh uncontrollably. Laughing tears spill from our eyes. Playful, heartfelt happiness is a rarity for us.

BOOM! BANG! Sounds like a loud bomb goes off. I wonder who shot who. The loud explosive commotion instantly sobers us up. We gasp and hold our breath; we stare at one another with wide frightened eyes. We lie on the mattress, still as fallen snow. I realize the wooden slats under the bed springs and mattress have dropped and crashed to the concrete floor. We are okay and none of us are shot or injured. In unison, as if on clue, we burst out laughing all over again. We clown around some more and have a blast.

The sound of knuckles hit the wooden door, knocking and knocking. Uh, oh! I'm in deep do-do! Someone must have complained about the noise coming from our room. We are pop-eyed and again scared half to death. Twice in only a matter of minutes, fear clutches the breath out of my mouth, nose, and lungs. Fear ties the arteries to my pounding heart in tight painful knots. Automatically my mouth opens in search of a fingernail to bite, but my hands are trembling, and my teeth chattering rapidly, making it impossible for one to catch up with the other. "Let's be very quiet. We can play the quiet game. Okay? Chinese school is now in session. No more talking, no more laughing. If you dare to show your teeth, you'll be punished for a week," I whisper.

I want to protect them, to hide them from the danger lurking on the other side of the door. There is nowhere to run, no place to hide, not even a bed to crawl under since it collapsed on the floor. We slowly move off the mattress and I spontaneously grab each of them by a hand. I lead them to the bathroom, the furthest place from the impatient knocks on the door. There is no lock on the bathroom door, but I close it, turn off the light and the three of us step into the shower stall, which has no curtain. I sit on the floor of the shower with my back up against the wall and keep my eyes glued to the bathroom doorknob. Mary and JJ scoot up close to me, with their heads buried on my stretched out legs. They cross their arms over the top of their heads.

The firm knocks on the front door increases to loud bangs. I hear Mary whisper, praying. I try to pray too, but fearful thoughts dash through my brain, only to be chased away by other, scarier and more terrorizing thoughts. Frightening thoughts render me powerless and paralyzed. The real life drama plays out before my eyes, like a vivid scene on television.

More banging on the door.

Could it be busy Mr. Myers, the manager of the Tourist Court, who rakes leaves, cleans gutters, and burns trash around back? If he is not doing odd jobs, he can usually be found with a paintbrush in his hand.

"Okay in there?" I realize Mr. Myers yells to us. "Open the door or I can use my key to open it. I'm not going to hurt you. So come on, open the door. Kids, the police are here now," Mr. Myers says.

"Hey in there, everything okay? I'm Officer Royals and I only want to see Abraham Culler. Mr. Myers will open the door so he can check out everything in there to see if anything is broken," the officer says in a deep voice.

We stay quiet for a long time, and we hear nothing out of Mr. Myers or the policeman. We wait and hope they will go away.

The bathroom door slowly opens wide and I quickly shut my eyes tight. "Jesus, please help us. Keep us safe," I whisper.

I squeeze one eye completely closed and barely peep through the eyelashes of my other eye. Aunt Janet's head pokes around the door. "Estie, Mary, JJ, for heaven's sake, why are you in the shower?" she asks.

"Aunt Janet! Whatcha' doing here?" I ask. I am surprised and thrilled to see her. I am so thankful it is her and not a cop pointing a gun at me.

She picks JJ up and holds him on her hip. "Come here big boy. Mary, you and Estie get out of the shower. For heaven's sake, why are you in there anyway?" she asks.

"We're hidin'. Whatcha doing in South Carolina?" I ask.

"We've come up here to get you kids and Abraham. We've come to take you to your Grandma's house. Where's your Daddy?" she asks.

Mary and I hop to our feet and out of the shower. "To Grandma's?" we squeal in unison.

"Come on out," she says. Aunt Janet moves aside and opens the door. Mary and I leave the bathroom. Aunt Janet follows close on our heels with JJ still wrapped to her hip.

The one small room, which is a bedroom and kitchen combined, is full of people. Uncle Warren in talking to a police officer in uniform and Preacher Stockton is standing beside the open front door. Through the open doorway, I see my cousins, Eddie and Kenny, playing in the u-shaped driveway in front of the tourist court. Mr. Myers has just completed putting the bed back together. My cousin, Olivia, and Mary, who are about the same age, begin talking and laughing. Olivia's older sister, Patti who is about five years older than me, sits on the now up-right bed and straddles JJ over her knees, holds both of his hands and plays and sings:

"Trot a little horsy, trot a little mule,
trot a little JJ to Sunday School.
Don't let him fall. Don't let him fall."

She holds JJ and slings him backward between her spread knees. "He falls any old way," she exclaims. When she finishes JJ's mouth is wide with laughter.

"Looks like there's a party goin' on in

here. Everyone's here but Daddy, but he'll be back soon, won't he?" I wonder if they are here to tell us Daddy has been shot because I had heard those loud bangs. Or did he get run over by a transfer truck out on Highway One and are his brains spattered all over the road? No, that can't happen to my Daddy, because he has no brains. Daddy is loco. Loco. Crazy. No brains.

"Estie! We're going to a celebration. I guess it could be called a party of sorts," Aunt Janet says.

"Well, someone forgot to tell me. Is it a surprise party? 'Cause I am surprised to see everyone!" I say.

"Yes and it is also a come-as-you-are party," she says.

"I sure don't have any party clothes to wear. It would have to be a come-as-you-are party; since my pink silky dress is all worn out and long gone," I say.

"I don't have any party clothes to wear either," Aunt Janet says.

"You know that song sung on Billy Graham's Old Fashioned Gospel Hour on the radio? You know the one that George Beverly Shea always sings? The name is, 'Just as I Am, I Come.' That would be a good song for a come-as-you-are party," I say.

"Sure would," she says.

We laugh and enjoy our playful banter.

"It could be a surprise party, a-come-as-you-are party; or, since it's February, how 'bout a Valentine Party? Or a Communist party?" I ask.

Aunt Janet's smile fades and her face shows concern.

"Yep, a surprise, come-as-you-are, Valentine's Day Communist party," I say.

"What's a Communist party?" she asks.

"My Mama used to go to Communist parties. And, if we have a Communist party, maybe she will surprise us and come to it, even if she is dead," I say.

"Estie, I think you need to rest. I've never heard such silly talk. Have a Communist party? Are you feeling okay?" she asks.

"Yeah, I'm fine. Just fine," I say and smile at Aunt Janet. I enjoy talking with her and having her full attention. I don't want the special time with her to end. Maybe it upsets her for me to mention my Mama. Maybe she knows my Mama is dead and she doesn't want to talk about it to me. Or maybe she doesn't want to have a Communist party. If what my Daddy says is true, Communist parties can be violent and dangerous, especially if John Edgar Hoover knows about it.

I try again, "Well, what's this party for? What's everyone here to celebrate?" I want to ask her a lot of questions about the things my Daddy has told me and to learn what I can about my Mama. I want her to tell me about Grandma. I plan to beg her to take me to Greensboro. I have to see my Grandma. There are things I want to tell Aunt Janet and questions I want to ask her. I'm afraid of upsetting her; after all, she is Daddy's sister. No matter what my opinions are of the mean monster I call Daddy, he is still her brother. I am sure she and the rest of my uncles and aunts and Grandpa and Grandma love him dearly, as I love my brothers and sister.

So, I tell her nothing. I ask her nothing. My lips are sealed – top and bottom, stuck together, like dry cement. Cement forms layers upon layers of solid concrete, and builds a protective wall around my heart, my soul, around me. Silence rules. It is safe.

Some things I tell nobody – but God.

Let him kiss me with the kisses of his mouth—
for your love is more delightful than wine.
Song of Solomon 1:1 NIV

Chapter 33
Your Heart -- My Home

Between the palms of two large, rough, calloused hands, rests Estie's soft pale hand. Floyd's tired, brown, seventy-six year old eyes tenderly adore her familiar face. He smiles lovingly at her broad nose and the few wrinkles around her eyes. She nods and dozes off and on. He yearns to feel again the indescribable, magnetic pull of the powerful, electrical charge experienced when their eyes connect. Flames of her brilliant, fiery hot eyes can warm and liquefy, not only his eyes; but, also melts his whole body. The sensational feeling and the thrill of floating in the damp mist of her crystal clear, blue eyes causes him to lose all concepts of time, space, and self. The very core of his being bubbles with emotional excitement, and his deep love is communicated with eager and honest eyes. Her eyes are the entrance, the gateway, the wide open door, to her pure heart.

Floyd reads to her. He reads from the Psalms. Mindful of her well-being, his eyes know when to express the naked truth of his heart, in hues of sharper and brighter colors, than the mere words of his limited vocabulary could ever begin to express.

"Oh, Estie," he whispers with a catch in his soft voice. "Estie, your pure heart is home to my soul. Your heart is my resting place. Your kind ample heart is a soft, warm bed welcoming me, embracing, surrounding and supporting my fragile, old bones. Your nurturing heart, Estie, supplies the necessities, and the nourishment to sustain, maintain, and to keep my spirit in healthy existence. I have permanent reservations with priority seating at the generous kitchen table of your heart which remains open twenty-four hours a day – three hundred sixty five days a year.

"You know, intuitively, which spices and seasonings to mix in, stir up, and serve to my wilting spirit. You serve with joy, huge portions of encouragement. You fill my plate with piles of confidence and heaping spoon loads of hope. Always, there is plenty of inspiration. Your forever flowing spigot of love, not only quenches the dusty dry thirst of my parched soul; it also, cleans, refreshes, and cools my spirit inside out." He pauses, clears his throat and places her hand gently on his knee, which is covered with the gray pants of his Sunday suit.

He slides both his thick index fingers behind the lenses of his thin wire-rimmed bi-focals, rubbing away long streams of warm tears. His fingers are not able to absorb the tears rolling down his plump, fleshy cheeks. He removes a handkerchief from the inside chest pocket of his suit jacket and he takes off his glasses and wipes them clean and then dries his wet eyes, face and runny nose. Even though his tears are still tumbling, he puts his glasses back on, folds his handkerchief and returns it to his pocket.

Slowly lifting his beloved's frail hand to his lips, he lightly kisses each finger. He, ever so softly, kisses the back of her hand and then he gently turns the palm of her cupped hand to his damp cheek and holds it there. He gazes intently upon her face and closely observes her labored breathing. "I love you Estie. I love our nearly forty years of marriage and all thirteen of our children. Thank you for your love. For your heart," he whispers.

Floyd is sure he sees her lips turn up slightly in a smile and he wonders if she is still asleep. Is she dreaming, and consequently the sweet smile lingers on her pale lips? Or, the thought occurs to him, is she listening to my every word and only pretending to sleep, playing opossum? Yep, that would be something Estie would do. Trick me, just for the fun of it.

So, he continues to meditate on her face. When he is certain she is resting and sound asleep, he notices his own breathing and realizes, as he often has over the years, that he and Estie are breathing in silent unison. Simultaneously inhaling and exhaling; harmonizing exactly, in complete agreement.

Her lips are separated only a tad, allowing her warm breath to spill out into the room. He smiles. Standing, with only a bit of discomfort registering on his face, he stretches his six-foot stout body. A sudden, quick pinch, only a little pinch (minor, nothing at all really) but it causes him to ponder anew the severity of her declining health…kidney failure and heart dropsy.

"My dear Estie," Floyd sighs, and bends his broad, stooped shoulders over Estie's bed.

He parts his lips directly above her mouth. He feels her breath. He draws in a deep breath of her exhaled air. And again, he inhales the warm air blowing from her lips. With their lips close, but never touching, he sucks into his being every ounce of the warm air passing through her lips. Her spirit, the breath of her life, is strengthening, reassuring and restoring confidence to his spirit.

Estie opens one blue eye, looking at him and slightly tightens her fingers on his hand. "I can hear you, you know?" she says softly with an inkling of a shy smile.

"So you can. Is that one eye open an attempt to wink? My dear, Estie, are you flirting with me?" he chuckles.

She opens her other eye. "I love you and yes I admit it. I am flirting with you," Estie says, with a ring of delight in her drowsy voice. "You know I love it when you tell me what is in your heart," she says.

Their eyes meet. Connect. Their eyes, blues and browns, hold each other tight, locked together and loving each other. Euphoria. Peace. All is well.

And Estie's heavy eyelids again surrender to deep sleep, as her chest slowly rises and falls.

Floyd lingers longer than he had

planned to visit. To break away from the tug of Estie's heart gripping his own heart imposes a task of physical and spiritual strength. The challenge of walking out the door, leaving her all alone, breaks his heart. Until this hospital stay, they had never slept apart. With the birth of the babies, they still slept side by side, even if one or two of the children crawled in bed with them.

Not trusting his mental capacity to recall every detail of her face, the face he has adored for so long, his eyes slowly and continuously sweep over every inch of her lovely face – from ear to ear, from her glowing white hair pinned on top of her head to her chin. The clicking of the button on the lens of his mind's eye snaps and permanently frames her radiant beauty in his memory, "Estie, your heart is my resting place. It is your heart that produces the beat of mine. I hope and pray my weaknesses have not been too heavy for your strengths. Your gentle, yet strong arms lift me to my feet every time I trip and fall down. I pray my desires and selfishness have not been too greedy, and have not taken advantage of your generosity. Forgive me if my tiredness has been a drain on your energy. Often, I keep so much of me buried deep inside. Thank you for respecting my silence, and for listening when I ramble on and on – well, like I am rambling on and on now. We both know we are opposites in lots of ways, but what I lack, you give me abundantly. And we stand, one and the same, united on important issues of life, love, family, and faith.

"I love you. Thank you for giving to me your pure heart – my home, my resting place." Floyd steps back and slips into his navy overcoat, longing to stay but knowing he must leave; he stoops and draws one more warm breath from Estie's lips.

"Thank you, now, sleep easy," he whispers.

Leaving the sterile hospital room, Floyd picks up his navy hat and carries it in his hand, until he steps out of the L. Richardson Hospital door into the North Carolina cold winter night. He then places his hat on his head, and pulls a warm glove from the depths of each side pocket in the overcoat. A few steps from the hospital's door is the bus stop. According to the sign listing the bus schedule, the next bus is the last one of the day going to his home on Old Winston Road.

Floyd, huddled against the brick wall of the hospital building, watches the bus pulling into the designated parking space and from the beams of the headlights he sees fine snow blowing. He and others, all bundled up, begin moving toward the bus. Again, Floyd feels a little pinch in his chest, and cold flakes of snow sprinkling on his face. His left arm grows hot and heavy. The pinch is no longer a little pinch. It is excruciating pain. Needle-nose pliers are squeezing his heart. He is nauseated, and under his hat, sweat is pouring off his face, dripping from the tip of his nose, and flowing down his back and forming puddles in the back of his suit pants. He knows his feet are not moving. He hears the voices of other waiting passengers talking and laughing, enjoying the fresh fallen snow. "My chest hurts. The bus musta' decided to park on my chest," he moans. No one hears.

Floyd is unable to move. His body feels heavy and his head feels dizzy. The hard frozen ground is mush under his feet, which are two large sponges under two legs of wet noodles. He tries to lift the two sponges and his noodle legs collapse.

The dignified, soft-spoken, Christian gentleman, a husband, father, brother, uncle, cousin, thirty-six times a grandfather, a farmer and neighbor, and a carpenter, who wears several hats, and fulfills the numerous responsibilities of his life, is alone all by himself fumbling on the cold ground. His hat is not on his balding head, but lying in the slush. Black smoke and soot of the foul smelling diesel fuel is pumping out of the exhaust pipe and blowing directly into his clean shaven face. Only minutes before, Floyd enjoyed the comfort, pleasure and strength in the closeness of his wife's lips.

**My Daddy's parents Floyd and Estie Culler -
Grandpa and Grandma**

Floyd takes a deep breath, and calls to her, his voice not even audible: "Estie," he breathes. "Your heart, your sweet, sweet heart is my resting place. Your heart, my home, Estie," Floyd whispers exhaling his last breath.

My Grandpa, Floyd David Culler, died February 9, 1958.

Do not let your hearts be troubled. I am going to prepare a place for you.
John 14:1, 2 NIV

Chapter 34
I Talk to Grandpa

Uncle Warren and Aunt Janet have driven into Camden, South Carolina, with a caravan from Florida. Their boys, Kenny and Eddie, are with them. They stop in Camden, South Carolina, to give their brother, Abe, and his three kids a ride to Greensboro to celebrate Grandpa's life, because he is dead.

Aunt Janet explains, "We are going to Greensboro to celebrate your Grandpa's, our Papa's life. I thought Abe would be here to share this information with you, but since he is not here at the moment, I will do my best. I'm sure he will return soon. Estie, you know your Grandma has been very sick and at the point of death. She's been in the L. Richardson Hospital back home in Greensboro. She is doing okay. Well, Papa rode the city bus to town to visit her and as he left the hospital, he had a heart attack and died."

It doesn't make much sense to me. Why celebrate his life now? Now that he has no life. He is dead; gone. I am so sad Grandpa is dead. His children, grandchildren and friends will miss him and his gentle ways. But, my Grandma! What will she do without Grandpa? She loves us, each and every one. But, no one can love anyone, as much as Grandma loves Grandpa. I remember her telling me once, "Papa (that's what she calls him) is the love of my life. My sweetheart. He will always be with me. All my children are grown and gone. But, Papa remains." Grandma's blue eyes dance with joy and complete happiness when they are in the presence of each other, whether they swing on the front porch, drink coffee together at the kitchen table, or hold hands in church.

Oh, my wonderful Grandma. Whatever will she do without Grandpa? I have never known a person who died. I am sorry it has to be Grandpa. I wonder when Grandpa and I talked last and what it was about. Mostly, I remember helping him pick vegetables from his garden, squash, cucumbers, and watermelons. He taught me to listen to the sound of his finger thump on the watermelon rind to determine if it's ripe and to listen to the chirps of birds and to recognize their different sounds. He loved homemade lemonade, and Grandma always had a pitcher full, with hunks of lemons floating in it, cooling in the refrigerator.

I am so sad our family waits until Grandpa dies to celebrate his life. If we had celebrated his life while he was still alive, I would already be back at Grandma's.

Going back to Grandma's has been my whole heart's desire ever since Daddy walked away with us and we slept that first scary night in the woods three years ago. I feel guilty, and torn in two halves, because the truth be known, I am happy. The joy of going home, the happiness of being with my Grandma again is greater than the sadness of Grandpa's death. I feel selfish for thinking of my happiness when Grandma has been so sick and then, to top it all off, Grandpa dies.

When Daddy returns to the Tourist Court, we all pile into a 1954 Plymouth station wagon which belongs to Aunt Janet and Uncle Warren.

To make conversation, Aunt Janet asks,

"Where did you kids get the new shoes?"

"Mrs. Stockton took us to Belk's and bought them for us. She is the wife of Preacher Stockton, who is the preacher at the Baptist church down the road," Mary says, which was true, but was not the wisest thing to say.

"I bought the children their shoes yesterday, when I got paid for working over at the Canada Dry Bottling Company," Daddy says. He pinches her arm so hard it leaves a bruise. "Mary has picked up an imagination, we haven't been here long enough to attend church," Daddy says.

We enter through the back door and Grandma and others meet us in the kitchen. Everyone hugs each other and cries some. Grandma, in a wheelchair, looks small and weak. The wheelchair surprises me. Her hair is fixed up in a bun – same as always. It is so disappointing to see the whites of her eyes are red and swollen; obviously from crying. She is grief stricken. Grandma has been released from the hospital to tend to the funeral arrangements for Grandpa.

Grandma's house is full. Church folks visit and deliver food: cakes, pies, ham biscuits, green beans, potato salad, plastic forks and plates. That's just what church folks do when there has been a death of a church member. Family members are in the kitchen and dining room; they eat the food the church folks have brought.

Grandma finds peace and strength from everyone, but she is also terribly sad. Everyone knows she has been in the hospital and sick, the sudden death of Grandpa is going to make it harder for Grandma to recuperate.

I wander off. Grandpa is in a box, a casket in the living room. No one is in the room with him – only me. Soft white, silky material is under him and his head rests on a white pillow. He has on his brown suit, white shirt, brown tie, and his rimless eyeglasses; his hands are folded on his chest.

I stand and stare, mouth wide open and look at my dead Grandpa. He was a man who thought much and spoke little. I watch my Grandpa lying there quiet, his lips are closed with a smile and his eyes are shut. I began to speak softly to him. Well, it's just me talking and Grandpa listening, as usual. I think he can hear me. "What you grinning about? You happy? Why are you wearing your eyeglasses with your eyes closed? Are you resting well? Grandpa, I never knew we would never have another Nehi drink together. I already miss you. I am in a state of confusion most of the time. My world is constantly being shaken up – an earthquake. It rocks, reels, shatters and destroys the slightest possibility of any hope for a home – a place to belong. Nothing is routine, or the least bit stable in my life.

"Grandpa, guess what? I've hitchhiked. Yeah, I've thumbed across America. Daddy took Mary, JJ and me, when I was young, now I'm ten years old. Of course, Mary and JJ were a lot younger than me. We've been in thirteen states since I saw you last. Daddy took it upon himself to educate me. He made me memorize the correct spelling of the states and the capital city of each state. I've learned a lot, but we don't rest too much, because we haven't been in any one place long enough to know we've been there. Mary, JJ and I have been with Daddy and he drifts from "pillar to post" with no place to call home – always in constant motion. We travel, roam and ramble, from city to city and state to state.

"You know, Grandpa, I've wasted three years. During that time, I could have shared lots of Nehis with you. We may have gotten to know each other better. You know my roots aren't planted deep. I am shattered and scattered about in pieces from here to California and back. You've taught me that seeds need to be planted properly so their roots can grow deep and healthy. Well, my roots are barely in the ground, getting scorched by heat, and trampled by life itself.

"And even though I haven't been in school too much, I am in the fourth grade, and I'm a good reader. Daddy forever yanks me out of school only to thumb on some more. It's hard to believe I've been without an address for three years, without a bed, and without my Mama and Grandma, and lots of times without food.

"You won't believe me, but I'll tell you anyway; however, I won't worry Grandma with the details. I've slept in the woods and in the windy desert. I have slept in empty boxcars, in train depots, and on kudzu growing on the banks beside the railroad tracks; but I've never ridden a train. I've slept in bus stations, gagging on cigarette smoke, back seats of cars, and in the sleepers of tractor-trailer trucks. The train depots and bus stations are good hangouts; warm, dry, have bathrooms, water fountains and benches to nap on; the authorities assume we are waiting for a bus. If we lollygag around all day and half the night, they become suspicious and order us to buy a ticket or leave. When we don't buy a ticket, they shoo us out like flies in a B-rated restaurant." Did Grandpa's lips smile a little wider? I think so.

"Mostly we hitchhike and ride in transfer trailer trucks, those big rigs with eighteen wheels. Trucks pick us up more often than cars. Truckers are awesome because they carry us a long distance, often for hundreds of miles, or even days. Sometimes they will hook us up with another trucker at a truck stop who will take us further. They always have some snacks to eat and they don't mind sharing. Mary, JJ, and I crawl up to and curl up in the sleepers behind the front seat. The static from the truck's radio, the hum of the truck's eighteen wheels, and Daddy chattering with the driver soon lulls us to sleep. I feel at home in a transfer truck," I say.

Chairs scrub the dining room floor. "Grandpa, everyone has come to celebrate your life. I hear 'em moving in this direction. I'll be back and talk with you some more. Okay?" I leave the room as a group of Uncles and Aunts file in and walk by his casket. They cry a lot, sit around in the folding chairs which Lambeth's Funeral Home has brought and set up in the living room and hall.

I reach Grandma's and Grandpa's room, where I had slept either in bed with them or on a cot in the corner under the window, when I was staying with Grandma, before we were kidnapped by Daddy. Grandma is in her room. It is only the two of us.

"Estie, dear Estie, I love you. More than ever, I need an enormous hug. Give me a hug and a kiss," she whispers, sounding both sad and sweet.

I find it awkward to give her a good hug because she's in a wheelchair. "Oh, Grandma, I love you and miss you so much. Why are you in a wheelchair? Can't you walk?" I ask.

"Oh sure Estie, I can walk. I am only slightly weak and the hospital wouldn't let me leave without a wheelchair and the doctor says I have to use it. I've got a cane over there behind the door and I can use it when I am strong enough to be out of this wheelchair. Enough about me. Estie, I've missed you, Mary and JJ so much. I've worried about you and prayed for you. I am so thankful you are back here with me."

"Oh, Grandma, I am too. I don't want to ever leave you. I love you and I want to take care of you until you're all better. Please let me stay. Please. I will not ever leave you again. Please, can I live with you forever?" I cry.

"Estie, we're two peas in a pod and I always want you to be here. Ssh, ssh, little Estie, please don't cry." Grandma pulls me to sit on her lap, and I throw both my arms around her neck and rest my head on her chest. I cry some more. Grandma cries too.

**Last Photo of Estie Irene Culler and her Daddy,
three older brothers, younger sister,
and younger brother taken together**

"We, two peas in a pod, will always be together – because a golden ribbon ties our hearts together forever," she promises.

*And we know that in all things God works
for the good of those who love him and
have been called according to his purpose.*
Romans 8:28 KJV

Chapter 35
John Edgar Hoover and the FBI Take Daddy Away

No longer is Grandpa laid out in the long, rectangular metal box in Grandma's living room. Yesterday the casket with Grandpa still in it, joined three of his thirteen children deep in the cold February ground at Guilford Memorial Park Cemetery. The first to go in the ground was Uncle Egbert, who I never met; however, all my life I've heard about him and his being a hero in the United States Army during World War II. He died in Italy in 1944 and was awarded the Purple Heart for his bravery. He was only nineteen years old.

That same year, one of Grandpa's daughters, Aunt Irene, also died a hero's death; giving up her life for the life of her son, Roland, my cousin. At thirty-three years old, she took her last painful breath before she ever had an opportunity to hold her only child. Shortly thereafter, Roland was adopted by his mother's oldest brother, Norman, and his wife. By the time Roland was around twelve, his adopted parents (who had no other children) had both died. Uncle Norman had a heart attack in 1957, at the age of forty-nine. Yesterday, Grandpa joined his son, my Uncle Norman, in the ground also.

Last night Grandma explained all this to me. Telling me with sad blue eyes, why and when three of their children had died, and now, "Papa" sees them in Heaven.

"Oh, what a wonderful time 'Papa' and those children are having in Heaven. They are resting in the arms of Jesus," she sighed with a sad, yet happy smile. "I look forward to going to my home on high too," she said, before falling to sleep.

Now Grandma's house is silent.

The day after Grandpa's funeral, my uncles and aunts from Florida are all out visiting with uncles and aunts from Greensboro. My

Aunt Nancy has taken Grandma to the doctor's office for a follow-up visit and our Daddy is in the house somewhere. Mary, JJ and I are on the living room floor (where Grandpa was in a box only yesterday). We try to teach JJ the rules to "Candyland." We insist he has to play right and follow the rules. He cannot place his pawn on red every time, just because it's his favorite color; he must wait his turn; he can only draw one card at a time. He doesn't like the strict rules and prefers to stick yellow legs in the body of a "Cootie." Mary and I finish up "Candyland" and decide to play "Cootie" and to let JJ play "Cootie" any old way he wants to.

Abruptly, the front doorbell rings and JJ jumps up and runs to the door and opens it. At the door is a stout man in uniform; he looks down at JJ. "Is Abraham Culler here?" he asks.

Simultaneously, I leap to my feet and run to the door. "Who are you? What do you want?" I ask.

"Hi there little lady," he says, all friendly like. I feel nervous. Something strange is happening. "I'm looking for Abraham Culler. Is he here?" he asks.

I am shaking and my heart is racing. "You're John Edgar Hoover, aren't you? I'd know you anywhere. Well, you're looking in the wrong place. Abe Culler doesn't live here.

He and his children have left. Gone to China or Cuba on a secret mission and you'll never find them. So you better find some other girl to rake on, Mr. Hoover! Abe Culler will never let you harm his oldest daughter," I spout off hurriedly.

Mr. Hoover screws his face up all weird, scratches his head, and looks at the papers in his hand. Then he glares at me like I'm "loco." I start to slam the door in his face, run and hide. I squeeze my eyes shut, as tight as I can. "Lord, please let me disappear into nothing. Into nothing – at all. Please! Amen."

At the same time, little JJ calls "Daddy, Daddy." Disappointed, I realize I'm still here. God didn't answer my prayer. I didn't vanish into thin air. I didn't grow wings like a bird and fly away. I slowly open my eyes and John Edgar Hoover still stares at me, like I'm a complete idiot. I put my hands on the door knob; ready myself to slam the door in his ugly, screwed up face. Then I notice the flashing red lights. Two police cars (that have "Sheriff" painted on the doors) are parked at Grandma's. One is at the front sidewalk on Old Winston Road and the other is pulled over on Grandma's grass on Spring Garden Street.

"Daddy. Mr. Hoover is at the door. Daddy, he wants to see you but Estie won't let him in the house. Daddy......." JJ calls out.

"The FBI is everywhere," I holler. "Mary, get JJ and hide somewhere!" I know I am fixin' to faint. I cup my hands over my mouth and nose and take deep breaths. I can't faint, because if I do Mr. Hoover will kidnap and rake me. He will tie up my feet and put my hands in the steel handcuffs, which he holds in his hand and spins on his finger, in circles in front of my face.

In other parts of the house, doors bang and slam. Then like a speeding round bullet, Daddy, without shoes or shirt, flies pass JJ and me and throws open the screen door; which clobbers John Edgar Hoover square in his face. Mr. Hoover – surprised, stunned and a little dazed, now looks goofier than ever. Mr. Hoover stands there like a looney-tune; his eyes roll in circles.

Daddy sails off the porch, lands way out in Grandma's front yard and continues to run. Daddy flies. The Deputy Sheriff standing next to the police car comes to life and chases after Daddy. Daddy runs faster than I've ever seen his stubby legs move.

Finally, I slam the front door. JJ and Mary squat on the floor behind the arm of the couch. They scream and cry and are scared to death.

"Okay, okay. Enough crying. Mr. Hoover has joined the race to catch Daddy." I hug them both tight. "We're safe. The FBI is gone. So let's calm back down," I say. As I straighten myself up, I take each of their hands. "No need to hide, they are gone. Surely Grandma will be back soon. I hope she remembers to get Oreo cookies while she's out," I say and pull both of 'em to their feet. JJ clings to my legs and Mary's arms circle my waist. "Okay, ya'll, I can't move an inch with you both all clamped to me like baby pigs to their mama. 'Oink, oink, oink,'" I say. I purposely drop to the floor and bring the baby pigs with me. We roll on the rug; I tickle them, root around them and grunt like a hog. They soon forget their fears and are as happy as pigs rolling in the mud.

"Okay," I say. "How's about we play 'Cootie'......here, help me put all the 'Cootie' pieces back on the board in the holes they belong in."

Soon JJ sticks pieces on the body of a "Cootie," in all the holes, but none in the correct holes. He jabs eyes in the leg holes, antennas in the eye holes, and legs on the head where the antennas are supposed to be. He has fun; Mary and I take turns and roll the dice and play a game of "Cootie" the right way.

"Let's don't worry Grandma about Daddy, Mr. Hoover and the FBI," I say. "She's been sick and has gone to see her doctor. Okay?"

"Okay, I 'bout forgot it," Mary says.

I entertain JJ and Mary for awhile and keep their minds on happy thoughts. We play "Cootie," laugh and cut-up. Grandma enters the living room; as if, she's been sitting in the kitchen waiting for us. "Don't you children want an Oreo cookie and some milk or would you rather have grape Kool-Aid?" she asks.

"Thank you, dear Jesus, for allowing me to live with my Grandma," I pray every night before I go to sleep and the first thing, before my eyes slide open every morning. Mary lives with Aunt Teresa and Uncle Curt in Jamestown and JJ lives with Aunt Sarah and Uncle Jack in Greensboro.

Grandma now has two twin beds in her room and one is my very own bed with clean sheets, blankets and a fluffy feather pillow. No one sleeps with me. I've never slept by myself; but Grandma is in her bed, across the room from me. Our beds are separated only by the vanity with an attached mirror. On it is a lamp that serves as our nightlight.

I miss Grandpa, but I don't miss the

loud and long thunderous snores he used to let roll. Grandma snores softly most nights. I want to hear Grandma snore, because I worry if I wake up and can't hear her. Sometimes, I hear Grandma crying and blowing her nose quietly. I also hear when she talks in whispers to "Papa."

While in bed Mary and JJ have always been attached to either side of me. Whether in the sleeping compartment of a transfer truck, on a Greyhound bus or on the bench in the bus station, in the back seat of a car, in an empty train boxcar (going nowhere), or on the cold ground, the hard ground or the wet ground, or on any pallet, cot or bed, the three of us stick closer than ticks attached to a hound dog. Sleeping space, like everything else, including the food we eat, the water we drink and the clothes we wear, has always been first fought over, and then shared. Nothing has ever been available – just for the taking – without considering how it can be divided and divvied up three ways.

Often, one or the other of us "wet the bed" or whatever sleeping spot we happen to occupy for the night. And the truth be known, we, all three, have "wet the bed" on the same night – more than once. Well, whenever, whoever wets the bed, we keep it to ourselves.

We don't fuss or complain. We don't want any of us to have to take a lickin' with Daddy's belt.

We never wet the bed at Grandma's.

*For I am convinced that neither death nor life,
neither angels nor demons, neither the present nor the
future… nor anything else in all creation, will be able
to separate us from the love of God that is in Christ
Jesus our Lord.*
Romans 8:37-39 NIV

Chapter 36
The Separation of Two Peas in a Pod

Swinging by my hands or by my legs from any
of the strong branches, or only sitting with my
back propped up against the top limb, with my
legs dangling over the sides, is proof that my
favorite tree – the crepe myrtle – has grown
by leaps and bounds while we were thumbing
across the United States. I, too, am stronger, if
not much taller, and when I am brave I can do
silly swings and floppy flips from the flowering

branches; which is something neither Mary, who is seven, nor five year old JJ can do!

Mary and I have eyes the color of our Mama's, and JJ's are the same as Daddy's. It has been so long, more than three years, since we've seen Mama; I hardly remember how she looks, except for her eyes. Mama's sad brown eyes droop like a basset hound's, and Daddy has Grandma's sky blues. Grandma's eyes used to twinkle when she laughed. Grandma is short, like me. She always reassures me that "big surprises come in small packages," and that "it doesn't matter how short you are on the outside. It is how tall you stand on the inside that is important." She's pretty for a grandma and we do neat things together. Grandma and I are best friends.

I sometimes get so bored playing with Mary and JJ in the sand pile. I am to watch them, because there are a lot of cars and transfer trucks that zoom by Grandma's house. JJ likes to stand at the edge of the busy road, pump his arm up and down over his head, and try to get the truck drivers to blow their air horns at him. It's a trick I wish I had never taught him. Now he wants to do it all the time. Grandma is too old and sick to play with us outside. She used to be so much fun, but lately she has been getting sicker and sicker. She doesn't laugh as much anymore.

When boredom strikes, I like to climb my tree and perch on the highest branch to sit and think. I wonder if my Mama is dead. I close my eyes real tight and with all my might, I try to remember her. I think, as long as I can visualize her in my mind, she is still out there somewhere, and she will come back; but, if I lose the memory of how she looks, she will for sure be dead and never return.

Since I will never forget her eyes, I believe she is in heaven and her eyes are peeping from behind that white cotton cloud. Her eyes sparkle with sunshine 'cause she is proud of me for being able to climb so high. The height of the crepe myrtle gives me a clear view of the Carolina blue heavens above. Now, her dark eyes slant down at the corners – droopy and weepy.

My brain power stretches and calls upon every nth of memory I can fathom, I can't visualize how Mama looks – only her eyes.

With Grandma sick, Mama dead, and Daddy locked up in a mental hospital again, what's going to happen to Mary and JJ? It's summer and soon school will start. I don't know what they will do or where they will live. I know my Grandma will keep me forever, but what will happen to JJ and Mary? I love them so much.

I really am something special to Grandma, because of all her thirty-six grandchildren; I am Estie, her name-sake. With dozens of grandchildren, she can't do much at Christmas and birthdays for all of us, but she always does for me.

Mary yells, "Come on down, big britches, Grandma wants to talk to us." I think Grandma must be sicker; I all but jump out of the tree. I pick up JJ from the sand pile, grab Mary's hand and start to run to the porch. I stop, run back to the crepe myrtle tree, and pick a cone-shaped, pink flower for Grandma. I hope to make her feel better. I place the flower in Mary's hand and we hurry off again, my heart races too fast and my legs not fast enough.

Grandma sits in her rocker on the front porch and she looks very sad. I think she's been crying. Oh no, now I am the one who is sick. My hands shake and my heart pounds. She takes JJ and puts him on her lap and hugs Mary close to her side and never takes her eyes off of me. She sniffs and says, "You three will always be together," and then very softly, "but not with me. I am too old and we can't live together any longer. In a little while, around ten o'clock, Miss Riggs, a social worker, will come and take you to your new home. It's a Children's Home; it's not too far away. I will visit you, and you can still come to see me." Grandma talks on, but I stop hearing. There are words about horses.....swimming pool.... friends....love....fun.... I don't know how long she talks, but I notice Mary and JJ are not with us. Grandma holds me on her lap and we cry.

"Grandma, where are Mary and JJ?" I ask.

She continues to rock. "They've gone in to gather up their things and you have to do the same thing."

"Grandma, you don't mean me, too. I am your little Estie, and I won't leave you now or ever." I reach down and pick up the flower Mary dropped. "Please Grandma, let me stay," I beg. I hand her the crepe myrtle blossom.

Grandma looks straight in my eyes, and I am sure she sees deep within me. She speaks with difficulty, "Oh, Estie, this may not be right. It may not be for the best. But, it must be. Please be brave for Mary and JJ, and please be brave for me. You know, we have always been two peas in a pod, you and me. You know I love you, JJ and Mary. I want this to be for your good, and all I can do is pray that it will be. Please, Estie make the best of it for me. Always remember, I am Estie too, so where you go, you take me with you," she says in a low husky voice.

Before I can plead with her anymore, I hear a car door shut, and a classy lady with long, black hair and a wide smile, walks to the porch. I want to smack her. Doesn't she know there is nothing to smile about? There is stirring around in the house as our things are quickly placed in brown A & P grocery bags. We hug and kiss; we are ushered to the lady's black car. Neither Mary, JJ, nor I will sit in the front with the smiling lady. We get into the back seat, where Mary and JJ plant themselves closely on either side of me. The car backs out of the driveway. I get on my knees and turn to look out of the rear window. I wave good-bye to Grandma, while she holds the remains of the pink crepe myrtle blossom. She appears smaller and smaller in the distance. I don't like being closed up in the car. As my Grandma disappears from my sight, I wonder: Who will buy me peaches, because I like them? Who will take me to the Guilford Dairy Bar for ice-cream? Who will help take care of Grandma with me gone? Who will be the pea in the pod? Then out of sight – she is gone. I scream loud, "Take me back, take me back to my Grandma's." Then I cry, "Take me back. I want Grandma. Grandma and me are two peas stuck tight in a pod and, it hurts me so much to be pulled away from her. Take me to my Grandma. We are two peas in a pod."

I scream over and over again and kick my feet against the empty front seat. I scream and cry, "I want Grandma. Take me back."

"Your Grandmother has sent a gift for each of you," Miss Riggs says, as she gives each of us a gift wrapped in white paper.

I gaze at my gift, tied with a gold ribbon. Tears blur my vision and drop on the gift.

THE END

He has made everything beautiful in its time.
He has also set eternity in the hearts of men;
yet they cannot fathom what God has done from
beginning to end.

Ecclesiastes 3:11 NIV

Epilogue
Where I Call Home

The day of separating two peas in a pod left a tremendous scar on top of large and small scars. Grandma, in all her wisdom, knew what was right and she did it. Her prayers were answered. She did boo coos of wonderful things for me, but one thing she did that was for my utmost good was to make the necessary arrangements for me to grow up at Mills Home, a Baptist Children's Home in Thomasville, North Carolina. There I graduated from

Thomasville Senior High School. Mills Home is where I grew, not only physically, but also intellectually, emotionally, and spiritually. It is where I learned unconditional love, no "ands," "ifs," or "buts" about it; where I developed friends, who some forty years later, are still family. It is where I call home.

Would I trade my Mills Home days? Not for all the moms and dads in the world. Would I trade it for my Grandma? That's a tougher question. Admitting it, I feel unfaithful to her memory, but I wouldn't trade Mills Home, not even for my loving Grandma, my pea in a pod. On the other hand, if it hadn't been for my Grandma, I wouldn't have had the opportunity to live at Mills Home.

I hope to tell you all about *My Mills Home Days*!

ABOUT THE AUTHOR

Estie Culler was born in Clara Cox Housing Projects in High Point, North Carolina. She was placed, by Order of the Juvenile Court of Guilford County, in the custody of Mills Home Baptist Orphanage in Thomasville, NC, at age ten. She graduated from Thomasville Senior High School, and attended High Point University.

Estie began work in the Guilford County Clerk of Superior Court office as the switchboard operator. During her career, she was promoted from a Deputy Clerk to an Assistant Clerk; in 1990 she campaigned for and was elected the Clerk of Superior Court in Guilford County, one of the largest counties in North Carolina. She is the only person, without a law degree, to be elected Clerk of Superior Court in Guilford County.

As Clerk of Superior Court, Estie served as Judge of Probate, and presided over Incompetency Hearings, Adoption Procedures, and Judicial Hospitalization Procedures, was responsible for records of the Juvenile, District, and Superior Courts, and supervisor of 115 employees. After serving thirty years, she decided not to seek re-election and retired as Clerk of Superior Court in December, 1998.

Estie Culler Bennington

Estie has been active in her community, city, and state. She has served on the North Carolina Governor's Advocacy Council for Children and Youth, Board of Directors of High Point Mental Health Association, Secretary of Mills Home Alumni Council, Secretary of the Administrative Board and Lay Delegate of Covenant United Methodist Church, and an Alpha Omega Service Award recipient for Beta Sigma Phi International Sorority. She has worked on Building Teams for a Methodist children's school in Cortasar, Mexico.

Her essays have been published in the Apogee and Lamplighter Literary Journals of High Point

University and the Greensboro News and Record.

Estie and her husband, Dr. Richard Bennington, make their home in High Point, North Carolina.

They have three children.

These days her pride and joy are her four granddaughters: Halli, Leah, Ariana and Bailey.

CPSIA information can be obtained at www.ICGtesting.com
Printed in the USA
BVOW020205010713

324762BV00002B/17/P

9 780984 000418